HOMESTEAD

American Book Classics™
An Imprint of American Book Publishing
P.O. Box 65624
Salt Lake City, UT 84165
www.american-book.com

Printed in the United States of America on acid-free paper.

Homestead

Designed by Bo Allen, design@american-book.com
Watercolor *Homesteader Barn* by Marjorie Rose

Publisher's Note: *This publication is designed to provide accurate and authoritative information in regard to the subject matter covered. It is sold or distributed with the understanding that the publisher and author is not engaged in rendering legal, accounting, or other professional service. If legal advice or other expert assistance is required, the services of a competent professional person in a consultation capacity should be sought.*

Library of Congress Cataloging-in-Publication Data is available upon request.

ISBN 1-58982-069-x

MacClanahan, Homestead

Special Sales

These books are available at special discounts for bulk purchases. Special editions, including personalized covers, excerpts of existing books, and corporate imprints, can be created in large quantities for special needs. For more information e-mail orders@american-book.com or call 1-800-296-1248.

HOMESTEAD

George MacClanahan

Dedication

This book is dedicated to Mac and Elsie, who had the courage to try, in the face of impossible odds, and didn't know the meaning of failure.

Preface

In twenty-five years there will be no one alive with firsthand knowledge of the Great Depression of the 1930s. They say there will never be another depression of that magnitude, because the investment practices that caused it have been limited or restricted by Congress to prevent its ever happening again. I hope that is so but I have my doubts, and it therefore becomes important, for more than just historical reasons, to have as much knowledge as possible of how that depression came to be, and how people who were alive at the time saw it, and how they were actually affected by it.

It began on Black Thursday, October 24, 1929. That was the day the stock market lost an unprecedented $5 billion of its market value in a single day and started a panic among the stock speculators and bankers whose greed had finally brought about the collapse of the nation's financial institutions. It ended at 7:53 A.M. Hawaiian Standard Time, December 7, 1941, when the Japanese War Cabinet made the same serious mistake of losing touch with its reality.

Homestead

Dreams of a better tomorrow are the expressions of hope that get us through today's realities. When enough dreams fall victim to the economic strictures of hard times, the human spirit grows weak and requires great resolve to endure. Should the world ever face another depression of severity equal to that of the 1930s, let us pray that the generation of that era will also have the will to survive such desperate times.

THE HOMESTEAD   3/4 Complete - One Room to Go   California 1932

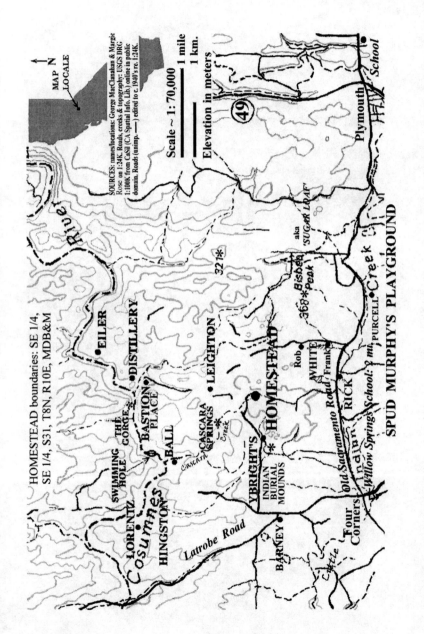

MAP N
LOCALE

SOURCES: names/locations: George MacClanahan & Marjie Rose on 1:24K. Roads, creeks & topography: USGS DRG 1:100K from CaSIL (CA Spatial Info. Lib.) online in public domain. Roads (unimp. ——) edited to c. 1940's re. 1:24K.

Scale ~ 1:70,000

1 mile
1 km.

Elevation in meters

HOMESTEAD boundaries: SE 1/4, SE 1/4, S31, T8N, R10E, MDB&M

River

•EILER

•DISTILLERY

SWIMMING HOLE

THE GORGE

LORENTZ

Cosumnes

HINGSTON

•BASTION PLACE

•BALL

•CASCARA SPRINGS

Cascara Creek

YBRIGHT'S

INDIAN BURIAL MOUNDS

•LEIGHTON

32*

• HOMESTEAD

Rob•

WHITE•

Frank•

RICK

Indian

Old Sacramento Road

Willow Springs School: 2 mi.

Four Corners

Cattle

PURCELL Creek Cr.

SPUD MURPHY'S PLAYGROUND

Bisbee
368* Peak

aka 'SUGAR LOAF'

49

Plymouth

School

•BARNEY

Latrobe Road

10

One

Spud Murphy made his appearance into this world with every indication that a charmed existence lay ahead along the trajectory of his life. Perhaps an omen of his portended good fortune might have been found in the unbridled energy, indefatigable curiosity and outstanding good health that were his heritage from the moment of his birth. By the time he was three, Elsie would say of him but for his unending questions, he was the easiest child to raise that she had ever seen. Never sick, happy beyond reason, always on the go, he had a loving and a lovable disposition and was the brightest star in her firmament.

Until the stock market crash came along on October 24, 1929— with its attendant disruptions of the world economy— and put a considerable crimp in dreams of never-ending prosperity, he spent an exceedingly blessed and happy childhood in a comfortable house with its spacious back yard, situated in a very middle-class housing development known as Colonial Heights, located on the southern fringe of Sacramento. Beyond the paved streets and the well-tended lawns, for as far as a small boy could conceptualize, stretched acres and acres of vineyards and strawberry fields in opulent productivity. In the back yard of the house on San Francisco Boulevard was a marvel of a swing set that had been custom made by Spud Murphy's father. The rest of the yard's occupancy was given over to a hutch full of rabbits and a very large, friendly Airedale that answered to the name of Skipper.

Skipper was everybody's friend. Even the rabbits liked him, but as dictated by the innate nature of the relationship of dogs to their masters, he was also the champion of all those who lived within the house, and the nemesis of any strangers who may have borne them malice. One night soon after the stock market crash some pitiful coward threw ground meat over the fence into the back yard. Skipper ate it and died. The meat had been mixed with strychnine.

Spud Murphy was heartbroken. The person who did such a cruel thing must have hated dogs very much (or been awfully angry with the world, and himself). Skipper, who loved and trusted people and knew nothing of stock markets or the multitude of other factors that contribute to people's frustrations, died a terribly painful death. To Spud Murphy, Skipper's death left upon him the first indelible impression contributing to the understanding that nature could deny the pleasure of happiness and fellowship in spite of all the well-intentioned efforts of mortals to secure them for the common good. Skipper's death was also the precursor of other ugly events that seemed to underline the despair of *The Depression*. In Mac and Elsie's minds, it came to symbolize the dreadful waste of so many of the things that represented established human values; the uprooting of society from its traditional norms, and the heralding of a monumental collapse of the human spirit that would continue for a decade.

One

Also enlivening that spacious and friendly backyard were the many children who played there, largely the neighborhood playmates of Spud Murphy's sister and his cousin, five and four years older than he, respectively, who held their make-believe tea parties on the neatly mowed and trimmed green grass. And there were toys, lots of them, some store-bought, but many that were handmade with a great deal of love and dedication by the resourceful and artistic Mac and Elsie.

The house itself was like any other, except that upon stepping into the living room one received the distinct impression of entering a shrine of sorts. Centered in an alcove opening off the living room in a manner reminiscent of a sacristy was a small table at altar height, its appliquéd runner centered on the polished wood with geometric perfection. Enshrined upon the starched white linen was a Philco table model radio that the family gathered around on Friday evenings to hear the magic sounds of Mac's weekly radio program that aired on KFBK radio, the valley's most prestigious station. The radio program was a source of fulfillment to Mac and perhaps even a greater one to the rest of the family. Listening to it was a crucial weekly ritual, one of those rare things that lend substance to your life, accenting and elevating your existence, making you somehow just ever so slightly more than you would have been without it. Not to brag about, of course, just to feel. It stood quite apart from simply being another means of supplementing the family's income and financial independence, useful though it was in complimenting the income from Mac's *regular* job as a machinist for the Southern Pacific Railroad. Mac's radio program provided a distinction beyond the reach of others less gifted with artistic talent. Spud Murphy was quite aware of this distinction, although it never occurred to him to make capital of it. (If it had, Elsie would have gently chided him about his boorishness, so he would understand that such self-glorification was in poor taste.)

By the end of 1923, a short year after its nationwide debut, radio's influence was to some degree evident in nearly every segment of the American population. Radio was a novelty; and people stood in awe of its wonders. The programs themselves, at least by the standards of those times, were often quite notable, too, as measured by the number of letters generated from the radio audience. A lot of people wrote to the newspaper, which had a special section in which you could express your appreciation of your favorite programs. Or one could call in by telephone to request a particular song to be played by the orchestra. Either way, they would say your name over the air and for an instant the whole world could hear it. In those few seconds you shared the aura of celebrity that was associated with that particular radio personality. So it was with Mac's program; a lot of loyal fans wrote in or called, saying good things about the program, and asking for different songs to be played. Spud Murphy always hoped that one of the requested songs would be "Cowboy Jack." It was the first song Mac had taught him to sing.

Cowboy Jack

Lyrics by Lesley Nelson

He was just a lonely cowboy
With a heart so brave and true,
And he learned to love a maiden
With eyes of heavenly blue.

They learned to love each other
And had planned their wedding day,
When a quarrel came between them
And Jack, he rode away.

One

He joined a band of cowboys,
And tried to forget her name.
But out on the lonely prairie
She waits for him the same.

One night when work was finished,
Just at the close of day,
Someone said "Sing a song, Jack,
'Twill drive those cares away."

When Jack began his singing,
His mind, it wandered back
For he sang of a maiden
Who waited for her Jack.

Jack left the camp next morning
Breathing his sweetheart's name.
He said, "I'll ask forgiveness
For I know that I'm to blame."

But when he reached the prairie
He found a new-made mound..
His friends they sadly told him
They'd laid his loved one down.

They said as she was dying
She breathed her sweetheart's name
And asked them with her last breath
To tell Jack when he came:

"Your sweetheart waits for you, Jack,
Your sweetheart waits for you.
Out on the lonely prairie
Where skies are always blue."

Spud Murphy would always sing along with the radio when they played "Cowboy Jack". If his older brother Jack happened to be listening to the broadcast, too, and felt inclined to say "Shut up, moron," Spud Murphy, with a big wide grin on his face, would sing out the lyrics at the top of his voice.

Mac's radio moniker was Yankee Mac. His musical associates were known as the Sierra Ranch Hands. Original members of the ensemble were Ariel "Slim" Hinds, who played the fiddle, mandolin, and banjo: "Uncle Reg" Mason, mandolin, banjo and ukulele: and Doug "Scotty" Brown, guitar, mandolin and harmonica. Mac sang and played the guitar, banjo, and harmonica. As the orchestra matured and the demand for dance bands grew, Sally Bennett joined the group, playing both the piano and the piano accordion, as did Nat Nottage on bass. As need dictated from time to time, other musicians and instruments were added for particular engagements. In practice sessions, which were held right in the family home, Mac sometimes let Spud Murphy play the drums and sing. Elsie, a pianist par excellence, while not a part of the usual performing group, did most of the musical arranging and all the mothering, and took care that the orchestra was always well fed.

It was a time in America of great popularity for cowboy music and country entertainment in general, but Mac and the Sierra Ranch Hands were not limited to that genre. They were frequently engaged to provide music for club entertainment and for social events. Sometimes the broadcasts emanated from the river boat "Delta Queen" on its run between the capital city and San Francisco, where Mac and the Ranch Hands were the favored entertainment for then-Governor *'Sunny Jim'* Rolph's frequent excursions to "The City By The Golden Gate," complete with official retinue.

In the early twenties, various arrangements existed between broadcasters and their featured radio personalities, regarding the payment for services. In the very beginning, the Ranch Hands played simply for the enjoyment of it and the opportunity to increase their audience and gain notoriety. As the Ranch Hands' popularity grew and their marketability increased accordingly, KFBK paid them to perform as a means of enlarging its own listener base. The Ranch Hands then expanded their repertoire to include a half-hour weekly radio drama. This serial program was known by the title of *The Crevicers.* It followed the adventures of a group of prospectors in gold rush times. Elsie, under Mac's general direction, became the show's playwright. Like the music program, it was well received by the radio audience.

Along about 1932, in the changing economic climate dictated by the progress of the Depression, the management policy adopted by KFBK required that the producers of radio programs find their own sponsors. To Spud Murphy's eternal disheartenment, the Ranch Hands decided that the rewards for such efforts would not be sufficient for the effort entailed, so they got out of radio. Nevertheless, they continued to make music together for their own enjoyment and continued to be solicited for dances and other social engagements.

In the middle of the 'roaring' twenties, a scant two years after Spud Murphy's birth, when the people of America had not the slightest notion of the economic blight that lay ahead, Mac found another outlet for his creative energy in the design and manufacture of airplanes, which he sandwiched in between his musical career and machinist's trade. In partnership with Roy Olson, he rented a manufacturing site adjacent to the taxiway at Mather Field. They were a little too optimistic for the times, considering that every underutilized mechanic in the country— inspired by the excitement of the developing aviation age— had the same idea, but Roy and Mac were undeterred by the competition, and they formed the M & O Engineering Company and built themselves an airplane.

To get their aerodynamic hand in, their initial undertaking was a scaled-down version of the first airplane used to carry the U.S. mail on a scheduled service between Washington, D.C. and New York City. The year was 1928, the tenth anniversary of that first flight. The small replica made its debut, engineless, in a parade down Sacramento's "J" Street, commemorating the inauguration of airmail service. In the weeks that followed, Mac fitted it with a two-stroke Indian motorcycle engine. Eleven-year-old Jack then flew it the length of the runway at Mather Field, escorted by a car at each wing tip with ropes tethered to the wings for safety. When Elsie learned of that escapade, she put her foot down so vehemently that Spud Murphy despaired of ever piloting anything, for which he never forgave Jack, or his mother or father either. Later, Mac built a half-scale racing auto, precursor of the midget racing autos that became so popular on the quarter-mile tracks of the 1930s, and used the motorcycle engine to power that. Elsie, not really mollified, bowed to the combined pleas of her eldest son and her husband and let Jack drive it in the Labor Day parade. Spud Murphy seethed with jealousy but he kept his own council rather than risk losing forever his own hoped-for moment of glory behind the wheel.

Meanwhile, on the aviation front, since neither Mac nor Roy had ever flown an airplane, they hired a test pilot. There is evidently no end of trusting fools in this world. As the engineering work drew to an end and the plane approached a state of hoped-for airworthiness, it was determined on one warm and auspicious afternoon that the time had come for a test flight, to take place the following morning. The test pilot for hire was consulted and all the skeptics and other interested parties plus some hangar bums gathered in attendance at the field at the appointed time to see how the plane would perform in its initial flight. To the amazement of everyone present excepting Mac, it was a huge success! It actually flew and after its short flight, returned to earth undamaged!

The test pilot was beside himself with amazement and wonder and joy. So were Roy Olson and everyone else who had witnessed the incredibly easy takeoff, flight, and landing. Unrestrained exuberance ruled the day. Again, except for Mac. His attention was focused on a microscopic inspection of wings, struts, airframe, empennage, controls and other such things and he found some hairline cracks that indicated a potential failure in the landing gear. He admonished the pilot not to fly the airplane until he'd had a chance to redesign the landing gear.

The next day being a workday, Mac was at the railroad shops at work and the pilot, overly enthusiastic, and wanting to demonstrate the aircraft to another flyer, ignored Mac's instructions and took the plane up. On landing, the gear collapsed, and with it went the aspirations, as well as all the assets, of the M & O Engineering Company.

From Spud Murphy's house you could walk down San Francisco Boulevard with its palm-lined median a couple of blocks in the direction of Stockton Boulevard to a barber shop. In its window a jar of peppermint candy sticks was a silent reminder to sit quietly and not scream your head off while you were getting your haircut. Spud Murphy's grandmother was always the one to take him to the barbershop when it was hair-cutting time.

There is something innately dangerous about barbers. There is hardly a four-year-old boy alive that will not tell you that the cutting of hair produces great pain to those poor children who are the barber's victims. They know it because their older brothers tell them so. And it is the barber in particular who bears the responsibility. A mother or a grandmother can cut a boy's hair with never a trace of physical suffering on his part. No, it is the barber himself who causes the pain and therefore cannot be trusted. And as far as candy is concerned, the whole jar full could not have made Spud Murphy more trusting of barbers. However, even the prospect of death in the barber's chair was preferable to having a confrontation with Grandma about the situation. Spud Murphy spent most of his pre-adolescence never knowing what a delight peppermint candy was.

A block beyond the barber shop was Stockton Boulevard and the street car tracks, where Spud Murphy often accompanied Grandma on a Saturday morning to ride the street car downtown to Capitol Park, there to stroll beneath the majestic trees that filled the grounds around the somber gray-white marble of the State Capitol. Grandma was acquainted with every officer who patrolled the park. She was the archetypical Prussian hausfrau with a posture so rigid she looked more like a general than the gentle little lady that she was. The florid-faced Irish cops addressed her as though she was royalty and they were her serfs. It was Mum this, and Mum that, and Mum so-and-so, while they bent forward from the waist with their hats held behind their backs. And on spectacular spring mornings, Grandma held court on the spacious walkways that wound across the shamrock-green lawns and through the groves of magnificent trees, calling her courtiers by their names and titles— officer so-and-so, sergeant such-and-such— as if they were her personal liege and she their gracious sovereign.

On one beautifully sunshiny day while Grandma was exchanging pleasantries with one of her vassals, Spud Murphy saw a boy somewhat older than he perched on the heavy chain that looped from pillar to pillar along the sidewalk's edge. Monkey see, monkey do. Spud Murphy, however, not yet versed in the laws of physics, hadn't reckoned with the fact that you had either to keep your center of gravity below the chain or else keep most of your weight on your feet and your feet in firm contact with the ground. And so the inevitable happened. From his perch on the chain he flipped over backward and cracked his skull on the edge of the concrete sidewalk. Grandma, despite her limitations with regard to height as previously noted, but with countenance so stern and uncompromising and spine so stiff and unbending that she appeared twice her actual height, held him at arm's length and assessed the damage to his noggin. As the policeman blotted at Spud Murphy's scalp with his white linen handkerchief, Spud Murphy gave forth with a tentative sob or two at the sight of the bright red blood, whereupon Grandma impaled him with her gaze and said in a very emphatic voice and with appropriate inflection, "MY little MAN does NOT cry!"

Spud Murphy was three months past his fourth birthday when the stock market crashed. He didn't really give it much thought, though, inasmuch as he was deeply preoccupied at that time with an attack that had just been launched against his village by the Onondaga people, whose animosity had been aroused through the skullduggery of a Delaware medicine man and a renegade French coureur de bois. Being the principal chief of a major Mohawk tribe had its own responsibilities, which often preempted things of lesser significance, such as keeping one's eye on the shenanigans of Wall Street. By the time he had resolved the threat of the recalcitrant Onondagas by engaging their chief in mortal hand-to-hand combat, it was time for dinner. After dinner he lay hidden behind the sofa in the living room studying the knot section of the latest issue of "Boy's Life & Youth's Companion," which he had just pilfered from the private cache of his brother Jack.

If he had not been so absorbed in the intricacies of how to tie a sheet bend as diagramed in a section of Boy's Life known as 'The Bosun's Locker', he might have been alerted to a note of concern in his parents' voices while they discussed certain news of recent days. It was not the stock market that was central to their fears. The difficulties on Wall Street were of little concern to Mac and Elsie. They owned no stocks. That relatively narrow aspect of the turmoil over what was happening in America was not of great significance to them. What was significant was the probability, widely rumored in the S.P. shops that the labor force would be drastically cut back due to a lack of freight being consigned to the railroad for delivery across the nation. There was talk of widespread cutbacks in the various trades the railroads employed to support its operations, and the machinist trade was one of them. To make matters worse, the loss of Mac's job was not the most alarming of the prospects for the family's future.

It was a few months prior, during the summer of 1929, that E.J. had been diagnosed as having rheumatic fever. Even before that, she had just slowly begun to fade away. From the day she was born she was never what you could call robust. She was always the first to fall victim to one sickness or another. Grandma was heard to say on one occasion after watching her dawdle over her meal as she was prone to do, "Lordy, girl, eat your food. You haven't meat enough on your body to make a good soup bone." Which was how she happened to get a second alias in addition to being known as E.J.

In 1927, she and Jack and cousin Katherine, along with a lot of the neighborhood kids, came down with scarlet fever, and from that time on, her health seemed to go from bad to worse as she became more and more frail. The irony of the scarlet fever epidemic, if you could call it an epidemic, was that Spud Murphy didn't even show any symptoms of illness at all until the day that old Dr. Foster decided to take a closer look at the palms of his hands and found them peeling— at the time an indication that the disease was in its final stages and signaling the onset of the recovery phase. Dr. Foster said, "Well! For heaven's sake!"

as though he was offended that he had been cheated out of the opportunity of delivering Spud Murphy from the ravages of the disease.

Spud Murphy never was one to get sick very much. If you watched him for a while, you would probably get the idea that the reason for his good health was that he was just too busy and didn't have time for illness. There were too many other important things he had to do. E.J., on the other hand, drifted from one illness to the next, and by late fall of 1929 the doctor made it clear to Mac and Elsie that her survival, if it could be hoped for at all, depended on her being in the children's hospital at Colfax, which bore the somewhat enigmatic name of Sunmount Preventorium. E.J. said later that she found out it was called a Preventorium because by keeping the children there it prevented them from disrupting the lives of their parents and other family members. By that time it was evident to Dr. Foster that E.J. had a very serious case of rheumatic fever.

It should be noted that all this happened ten or twelve years before the availability of those medicines that became an effective means of treatment for rheumatic fever. In 1929 the advent of antibiotics as a means of treating streptococcal infection of the sort that accompanies both scarlet fever and rheumatic fever was still at least ten years off. Lacking any other way of fighting the infection, isolation in a sterile and restful environment was the common treatment considered to be most effective in combating the disease. Rheumatic fever generally attacked children to a greater extent than adults and, too often in the case of children, the results were fatal. In E.J.'s case it was presumed that there was no question that the issue was one of life or death, and the most probable outcome was not life, much beyond childhood.

About the same time as the occurrence of the scarlet fever epidemic, and strictly unrelated to it, Mac found out from Guy

Leighton, one of his co-workers at the Southern Pacific Railroad shops, that there was a quarter-quarter section of government land in Amador County, in the foothills of the Sierra Nevada, that was open for filing under the Homestead Act of 1862. It had been claimed two or three times previously, but those claims had all been relinquished when the claimants, one after another, failed to find sufficient water on the property.

Mr. Leighton had previously purchased an adjoining 160 acres, and in the time since Mac's coming to California had allowed him and his family the frequent use of a cabin on Mr. Leighton's property. Spud Murphy was always happy on the occasion of a weekend stay at the cabin. With Mac he delighted in exploring the surrounding trails while absorbing the woods lore that Mac had brought with him from his earlier years as a young man in the pine forests of Michigan's southern peninsula. By the age of four, Spud Murphy had been taught to distinguish among the tracks of the many animals that were native to the Sierra foothills, and had learned, from Mac's telling, the secrets of trapping them. One of the places Mac and Spud Murphy frequented was a long-deserted homestead on the nearby Cosumnes River known as the Bastion place, after the name of its original homesteader.

An old weathered frame house, long abandoned and in sad disrepair, remained standing between some crab apple and cherry plum trees. The house was located against the rising slope at the foot of a hillside that had contributed to the formation of the defile through which the river passed at that locality. It sat along the edge of a large meadow that opened to the river below. You couldn't help but puzzle over the homestead's history. Spud Murphy wondered what possible events could have persuaded its owner to forsake the peace and tranquility that surrounded its sheltering walls in exchange for a life in the turmoil of some *civilized* place. Spud Murphy always imagined he heard the weathered boards calling out for the children whose voices must once have echoed across the meadow below. Elsie would have been the one to teach him to nourish such poetic aspects of his nature.

At that particular place the valley of the Cosumnes narrowed, and at a bend where the river threaded between steep opposing slopes, the erosion of ages had created what must have been the world's greatest swimming hole. From the Bastion place to Leighton's cabin was a short, one-mile walk and Spud Murphy would have been quick to note that in the old Essex it was an even easier mile ride.

One hot summer day, a month or so short of Spud Murphy's third birthday, the whole family was picnicking at the swimming hole. Elsie and E.J. were a bit upstream from a place where the river entered the narrow gorge, shading themselves under a big cottonwood and watching Jack dive off a rock ledge into the deepest part of a hole that had been formed by the scouring of the river over a span of thousands of years. Mac was perched on a nearby rock, giving Jack advice about keeping his legs straight while diving and other such oft-repeated admonishments that are intended to make great athletes out of young boys. Spud Murphy was perched on the same rock, next to Mac, learning the art of swimming instruction.

But becoming an instructor wasn't all that was on his mind. He was chafing under the circumstances of his father's attention being focused so intensely on his older brother. Never one to be upstaged, especially in Mac's eyes, he suddenly remedied the situation by hollering, "Watch me, Daddy!" and leaping belly-first into the swift flowing waters of the Cosumnes River. The thought paramount in both Mac's and Elsie's minds at that instant was "I wonder if he can swim?" Elsie jumped up and would have leapt in after him if she had been anywhere close enough to do any good. Mac, however, close by, paused just a second for Spud Murphy to surface and with that instant's appraisal, waved Jack off from an attempted rescue and settled back on his perch to watch Spud Murphy splutter and flail his way to a safe landing on the sandy beach below Mac's rock perch. It is recorded in Elsie's diary that Spud Murphy's swimming lessons started that afternoon, and other lessons about situational appraisals, the judgmental capabilities of the very young, and probability assessments, followed immediately.

Mac, possessed of an adventurous nature, and the necessary self-confidence to go with it, was attracted to the notion of homesteading. As to the question of the availability of water, he was convinced that his own water-witching power was second to none, as was also the case regarding his possession of every other kind of power.

When Dr. Foster announced his prognosis of E.J.'s future, or probable lack of one, Mac and Elsie did not hesitate. They immediately set out to make whatever life was left for her as celebrated and fulfilling as it could be. It seemed to them that the free land of the homestead was the perfect solution, truly a godsend. Knowing they did not have the financial resources necessary to keep her in hospital care for an extended period of time, and in any case not disposed to that sort of solution, they filed a claim on the government land with the intention of building a home on it. They reasoned that they could care for their small, frail child far better than any institution could, and the country surroundings of the foothills would furnish the elements— including clean air to breathe and a quiet and peaceful environment— that were a large part of what the sanitarium had to offer. In the meantime, in response to the current crisis, they followed the doctor's advice and had E.J. admitted to Sunmount, in spite of the cost, until they could build a house on the homestead. A lot of explaining and persuading went on, together with grief-laden wailing and sobbing, when

One

Mac and Elsie prepared to leave E.J. there in the hands of the nurses. E.J. was desolate at the thought of being left at the sanitarium. She was sure she was being abandoned forever, in spite of all of Elsie's reassurances to the contrary. Never before having been separated from the family, she felt alone and forsaken. The pain of separation was almost unbearable. It was even worse for Mac and Elsie, who knew what the consequences of any other course of action would be. The unhappy little nine-year-old cried herself to sleep nightly for the entire duration of the interminable fifteen months that she was a patient of the sanitarium.

It was the second week of November, 1929, when E.J. entered Sunmount. The Depression was about three weeks old and had not even begun to earn that title. It had yet to levy one ten-thousandth of the toll it would exact in the long, bleak years that lay ahead. Mac was still working five and a half days a week for the railroad, earning seventy cents an hour, which came to about thirty-one dollars for a forty-four-hour week. As little as that may seem to be now, and while not what one would call a handsome amount even for those times, it was enough, if one was frugal with one's purchases, to provide a fair level of existence for a family of six. But except for that weekly paycheck and the income from whatever entertainment opportunities that came their way, Mac and Elsie didn't have a nickel in their pockets. Any intelligent person with the ability to add and subtract could have easily seen that the odds against success were overwhelming, considering their financial condition, the travel distance from home to job, and the serious nature of E.J.'s illness. The odds were surely heavily stacked against providing the kind of nursing environment needed to be of use in E.J.'s situation. A person would have to conclude that Mac and Elsie were recklessly improvident to even consider such foolishness. It was Grandma who said that if dreams come true at times, it is only because they are paid for with someone's sweat and blisters.

As much as he wanted to, it was out of the question for Mac to move up to the homestead to start construction. Every cent of the money he earned from his job at the S.P. Railroad and the money that was his share of the proceeds from the radio show were needed to pay for the rent and the grocery bills and for E.J.'s care at Sunmount. It was up to Elsie to provide the initial homestead labor while Mac continued to earn a living. Jack was a sturdy, growing boy of twelve and would have been a good choice to go with Elsie, but he was in seventh grade and needed to be in school. There was also the matter of Grandma's care to consider. She wasn't well and she couldn't stay alone. She and Jack could look after each other's needs during the times when Mac was working, either at the S.P. or at the homestead.

As matters worked out, it was Spud Murphy who went with Elsie to the homestead to become her helper, doing what he could that was in keeping with his rather small size and limited experience. Of secondary consideration, perhaps, Elsie took him with her simply to be a companion, a soul of kindred nature with whom to communicate. Finally, and perhaps most importantly, what else could you do with him? You certainly couldn't leave him with Grandma. His nonstop four-year-old curiosity would drive her to distraction by the end of their first week together.

On Sunday morning, the day after E.J. had been sent into martyrdom at Sunmount, Mac drove Elsie and Spud Murphy the forty miles that separated the house on San Francisco Boulevard from the homestead. The old Essex was loaded with their bedrolls and groceries and other tools and supplies, all of which they unloaded at Guy Leighton's cabin, about a mile, as the crow flies, north of the site where they planned to build their new home. The cabin became their base of operations, and while Elsie was settling their things into it, Mac got a Swede saw out of the pile of tools, handing it to Spud Murphy. He took a double-bitted ax, a pick-mattock, and a six-foot track bar, and hoisted them to his own shoulder, setting off purposefully across the meadow that lay to the south of the cabin, with Spud Murphy trotting resolutely behind. They followed a trail that led down the gentle slope of the meadow for two or three hundred feet to a dry creek bed and then rose slightly for another hundred feet to meet the brush line on the opposite slope. There the trail disappeared into the thickets of manzanita and toyon and chaparral that blanketed the slopes and ridges around them, unfolding in all directions to the distant horizons, and isolating the meadow from all of civilization.

In the beginning there wasn't even a passable road into the homestead. An old county stage road, mostly overgrown with heavy brush, angled across the property from southwest to northeast. Mac surmised that the trail from which this road had grown had been part of a main north-south thoroughfare of the Miwok Indians, predating the gold rush period, because occasionally along its track a rare obsidian arrowhead or knife or other tool would be scuffed up in the efforts aimed at improving the road's surface for vehicular travel or as likely dislodged by deer moving along the trail. The trail ran from the river that wound through the hills a mile to the north, to eventually find its way onto the oak lands that lay to the west and south. Another road that branched off this main road at the north edge of the property followed a more easterly direction before turning south into the homestead proper. The latter road was of more recent construction and was important to Mac's immediate purpose because it connected the homestead to the Leighton property and that property to the Bastion place on the southeast bank of the river. It was the reopening of this road, overgrown along its south half with thick brush and occasional blue oak and digger pine stands, to which Mac turned his attention. Later, the old stage road, after it was cleared of brush and boulders and made passable for vehicular travel, would give easier access to the county road network and ultimately to the state highway. That important transportation link ran from east to west, connecting the mining communities of the Sierra foothills with the great central valley. Before work on the homestead itself could start, both roads needed to be at least passable.

Mac was not a big man, standing perhaps five foot nine, but he exuded stamina and power from years spent outdoors during his youth in New Hampshire and later in Michigan. Hours of practicing for tumbling acts on the vaudeville stage in the high school and trade school years in Chicago had developed a musculature that gave him a catlike agility and balance. Before his interests focused so narrowly on the homestead, he worked out regularly on bars and tumbling mats and was justly proud of his strength and physical dexterity.

Spud Murphy loved to watch Mac work, to see the muscles in his biceps and forearms knot and bulge as he worked the heavy track bar in under the manzanita crowns and broke them loose from the hundred smaller roots anchoring them to the soil. Manzanita tends to brittleness, and a supreme effort with a proper fulcrum will generally cause the root crown to separate from the earth-bound roots with explosive force. And then with the sweat swept away with a sun-darkened forearm it was time to settle onto one's haunches and roll a cigarette with squinted eyes while mapping out the strategy that would separate the next crown from its nest in mother earth. Spud Murphy looked at his own bony arms and wondered if he would ever grow any muscles. "It's hopeless," he thought.

That evening as Mac prepared to return to the city, the setting sun cast the shadows of the tall digger pines that surrounded the cabin far down the meadow, their twisted, strangely bent shapes adding their own mysticism to that which emanated from the softly lit ridges reflecting the sun's last light over the darkening valleys. On the opposite side of the meadow was the evidence of their first day's work: sixty or seventy feet of road bed cleared wide enough for one-way car travel, the crowns of the manzanita and toyon bushes pried out of the rocky earth with the track bar, their roots broken or cut below the surface to free them. Out in the meadow, away from the dense thicket in a place where burning would not represent a fire hazard to the whole county, was a huge pile of slash.

As Elsie cleared the table and washed the dishes from their evening meal and did that subtle rearranging of household artifacts that womenfolk are prone to, Mac went out on the porch. He stood at the foot of the stairs gazing across the meadow at the results of their first day's work. As a mind will do at the end of such a laborious day, his imagination drifted into lonely contemplation of the struggle that lay before them. Mac scarcely acknowledged Spud Murphy at all, who had followed him out on the porch, and now sidled up alongside him to sit with his short legs dangling over the porch's edge in his own best effort at solemn contemplation Without seeming to ever transfer his attention to the small boy at his side, Mac began to speak in the manner of a superintendent entrusting great responsibilities to an assistant.

"Now, son, I want you to pay close attention to what I am going to tell you. You are going to have to be the MAN here, because I am going back to take care of your grandmother and Jack and work at my job at the S.P. I'm leaving you in charge and I want you to see to it that your mother is taken care of properly, just as though I were here." At this point he turned his attention directly to Spud Murphy and noted, not without some puzzlement and more than a little amusement, the broad, infectious smile and sparkling eyes that were his youngest son's response to the solemn charge that had just been laid upon him.

There was a popular expression of the times regarding a child's interactions with the elders of its social group that would probably make little sense to young parents of today: "Children should be seen and not heard." Spud Murphy was sure that idea must have originated with his grandmother. Fortunately, not all adults subscribed to it, even in those times. Elsie did not. But Mac did and so it was a rule of the house, in a manner of speaking. In Mac's opinion, communication could only have meaning when there was a specific need for it, a meaning that could be ascribed to the demands of the immediate circumstances. Particularly in the company of other adults, casual conversation with a child had no place in his scheme of things. Maybe that was because of his own stern upbringing among speech-thrifty New Englanders.

Elsie, on the other hand, viewed communication as both an art form and a search for truth. No question was of so difficult or sensitive a nature as to be undeserving of an honest attempt at a truthful answer

Later, Elsie and Spud Murphy stood where the Essex had been parked in front of the cabin, waving good-bye to Mac as the old car lumbered up the road and out of sight. That night, getting ready for bed, Spud Murphy said, "Mama, do you like to work?" Elsie paused in hanging up the trousers she had just shaken free of twigs, berries and leaves. She stood looking at him, a somber, pensive, caring look softening her face as she considered her response. It was a look he had grown accustomed to and that he recognized as confirming the intimacy that existed between them. "Well, dear, I can't honestly say that I like *all* work. I try to like it, though, because it generally has to be done anyway, and hating it just makes it harder. There are some kinds of work that I truly like, though, and those are the kinds for which there is a special reward when you're finished."

"Like having E.J. come home?" She paused a long time before answering, and cleared her throat before she finally did. "Yes, dear. Like having your sister home with those who love her, and not off in some cold, strange, place without her family."

Spud Murphy said, "I hate work. I want E.J. to come home, but I don't like getting scratched and having to drag all those branches to the pile. We already have a house. Why can't E.J. come to that house?" Elsie smiled a gentle, knowing smile at him and said, "All right, dear. We can talk about it in the morning. I'm sure you'll feel better when you've had a good night's sleep. It's time now to go to bed and say your prayers."

After the 'Keep Daddy safe and keep Grandma safe' and so on for Mama and E. J. and Jack and Katherine and Aunt Mary and Aunt Isabelle and Ariel and a special 'Please take good care of Skipper for me,' he waited a moment until Elsie's attention was elsewhere and when he thought it was, he murmured "And please, God, if it's all right you can leave the toyon and chaparral but just make the manzanita go away."

Leighton's cabin was of rather rudimentary construction, but it was, in the sense of its being a haven from the troubles and ills of the world, a 'millionaire's mansion', as the song goes. Its setting, on the edge of the meadow in a grove of oaks and pines, gave it an atmosphere of seclusion that beckoned the passing wanderer to come and sit for a time in the shade of its long, roofed porch. It was a lazy afternoon sort of a place, one where time stands motionless, and the intense quiet has a palpable materiality.

A hundred and fifty feet away, at the head of the meadow where the mostly dry creek bed had its beginnings, was a natural spring that fed out of a crevice in the bedrock. The water in that spring was the purest, coldest, best-tasting water in the world. In some previous time a former owner had improved on nature's work by turning it into a well of sorts with a basin sculpted out of the bedrock to hold perhaps two hundred gallons of water. A small enclosure had been erected for it, with slate steps down to the water and a door to keep small animals from getting inside and drowning. It wasn't big enough to stand up in, but you could crouch down inside and reach in to fill a can that served as a drinking cup or fill a water bucket or what-have-you. It was dark and cool inside which made it a place where rattlesnakes would sometimes find their way on hot summer days. You had to be careful then. One time Mac wasn't paying attention when he reached in to scoop up a cupful of water for someone to drink. A snake struck right across the top of his forearm, spewing two tracks of yellow venom from his wrist to his elbow like they were a calling card. Mac had pretty good reflexes and got his arm out of the way in a hurry.

The springhouse served another good purpose in the summer time. Put a watermelon right in the water, where it would float with just a little of it breaking the surface, and if you left it in there overnight, it would be nearly ice cold when you retrieved it the next afternoon and cut it open. In the creek bed below the well was a watering trough for all the birds and animals to drink at. The trough was kept full by a continuously flowing pipe that carried the overflow away from the spring. Tracks of deer, raccoon, bob cat, skunk, fox, coyote, squirrel, jack rabbit, cottontail and many bird species abounded in the wet soil around the trough, attesting to its popularity. The spring was one of the many things that contributed to making Leighton's cabin a mansion. There were others.

Even on the hottest day, when the shadows began to lengthen in late afternoon, a cooling breeze would come up the long slope from the river a mile to the north, and it would spill out onto the meadow, cooling the oncoming night so that sleep came easily to those in the cabin or on its porch. Coveys of quail came with the darkness, running through the dry grass on their way to water at the spring, hens admonishing their chicks with the strange staccato quail call that warns of nearby danger. In the morning, if Spud Murphy could stay still long enough, a doe with a fawn or two or even a buck with its showy antlers might be seen standing motionless at the edge of the meadow, waiting to cross at a safe moment.

Sleepless, Elsie lay in bed listening to the steady breathing of Spud Murphy and thinking of the daughter she had left at Sunmount. E.J. was her second born, her only daughter, two and one-half years younger than Jack. She had come into the world after Mac came back from the war, where he had served with the A.E.F. in France as a member of the 318th Engineer Battalion. Leaving her young daughter in the sanitarium was the hardest thing that Elsie had ever done, but she trusted Mac to build the house with all the haste that he could manage, and she prayed that it would be in time. She told herself that under her own care, E.J. would have the best possible chance of surviving the illness that had beset her. In the meantime Elsie would do everything within her power to hurry the construction of the home by helping Mac in every way that she possibly could.

Elsie herself had been brought up in a world beleaguered by adversity and trauma and so she was well equipped, both in spirit and skill, to cope with primitive conditions. Her mother, Ida Battell, was a trained nurse. Early in her career at Hahnemann Hospital in Milwaukee she was attracted to the mission of the newly created American Red Cross, reformed by Clara Barton in the aftermath of the Johnstown Flood of 1889 to minister to the needs of victims of civil disasters as well as those of military adventurism, for which it was originally founded. Ida was compelled in 1893, by the first of several disastrous hurricanes that struck the Carolina Coast in that decade, to join her mentor there, where she worked in the relief effort that the Red Cross undertook on behalf of the distressed victims.

The same storm that brought Elsie's mother to South Carolina caught the SS City of Savannah off the coast of the Carolinas and blew her onto the reef at Hunting Island. John Macdonald was a passenger on the Savannah, bound to New Orleans from the city of Boston. John, a Scottish émigré and also a trained nurse, was on leave from the marine hospital at New Orleans. He and other survivors were taken off the sinking ship by the crew of another vessel and set ashore at Savannah, Georgia. Like Elsie's mother, John Macdonald also elected to stay at Hilton Head Island to help Clara Barton with the relief effort, although it may have been more than humanitarian considerations that impelled him to stay, since John and Ida were married less than a year later, on November 23, 1893.

Elsie was their second child, born in January 1898. After leaving Hilton Head Island in 1900 the family moved to Milwaukee where they lived until 1911, at which time John bought a twenty-acre farm site in central Michigan near the rural community of St. Helen. Elsie's older brother Duncan stayed in Milwaukee to attend high school. Her father was on the road representing R. L. Polk Company, a Chicago publisher that produced the preponderance of mid-west city directories in those years. Her mother was a medical circuit rider of sorts, delivering health care to the community's residents. It was left to thirteen-year-old Elsie to care for her three younger sisters, the housework and the farm. Later when Mac, drawn to the north woods by their wilderness appeal, after growing up partly in rural New Hampshire and later on the streets of Chicago, contracted with Elsie's father to build a house, Elsie worked side-by-side with Mac and through that association she developed the knowledge and skills and physical capability that later enabled her to carry more than her share of the work of developing the homestead. From this employer-employee relationship in Michigan Mac and Elsie developed the bonds that led to their eventual marriage. She was a hard-working, skilled, inspired and industrious partner.

At about nine thirty of the second day of road construction, (the morning of the day after Mac left), Spud Murphy was ready to give up the homestead idea and head back to the city. The truth was, he had been ready to head back to the city by mid-afternoon of the day he got there, but he didn't think it would be such a good idea for Mac to know that. By ten o'clock he couldn't stand it any longer and so he sent up a trial balloon in the form of a plaintively voiced assertion that he didn't really care as much about country life as he thought he would. It was about then that he got, from Elsie, the beginnings of a gentle education on the subjects of responsibility and work ethic and family unity. In the face of Elsie's beliefs on those subjects and in response to the convincing presentation of her views, Spud Murphy set aside his reservations for the moment, albeit not permanently, and decided against striking out on his own for the city. Due to the convincing manner with which his mother stated her views, and in deference to her long abiding patience and, perhaps as well, her skill in fixing dinner, it was an easy choice.

Two

Although Spud Murphy never thought he would live to see the last of the manzanita, it had only taken a matter of a few weeks to get the road cleared and smoothed so it was drivable into the homestead. When it was, Mac came up from the city on a Friday evening towing a borrowed trailer loaded with lumber and other building materials. Spud Murphy heaved a sigh of relief over the fact that he didn't have to pile any more brush, at least for a while, and immediately found himself outfitted with a claw hammer and a crowbar, facing a big pile of used lumber and getting instructions on how to pull out and straighten the nails from boards that Mac had scrounged or bought at ten or fifteen cents on the dollar.

The worst of that job was the straightening. A lot of them were square nails, rusted through, some of them probably already in their second use, and they easily broke when you tried to straighten them. And then you had to put them in different cans, one for each size. Mac explained it to him.

"Twenty pennies all in one can, sixteen pennies in another, just like that. Twelves and eights all the same way, all in their own separate cans." Spud Murphy looked down into the can and then turned his head up to look quizzically into his father's face. He decided his father was serious, as he most usually was, but decided against asking the question that was uppermost in his mind. If he were to ask, he suspected the answer would be something along the line of: "Now why don't you use your head and see if you can't answer that yourself, son. Did God give you brains? Maybe you should try using them once in a while." And so Spud Murphy used his brains as his father had bid, and the next time he was alone with his mother he asked her, "Mama, why do they call the nails pennies?" She, of course, told him that the word 'penny' when it was used in that way wasn't being used as the name of a thing, it was really a measure of size in terms of weight— and thus were opened all sorts of possibilities for later discussions ranging from matters of carpentry (20d common vs. 20d box nails) to parts of speech (noun vs. adjective). And then there were roofing nails and small little shingle nails and occasionally a staple or two or a huge spike, all to be straightened and saved and talked about. Elsie, in her most cheerful, positive voice said, "Waste not, want not," so as to inspire her balky helper, and Spud Murphy said querulously "But Mama, I don't *want* 'em in the first place."

So it went on, an endless, hypnotically exhausting ritual. After pulling each of the sunken nails and straightening them and putting them in the right can for their size, Spud Murphy stacked each piece of lumber with other pieces of the same size. Then he pulled another two-by-four out of the inexhaustible pile and went through the whole process again.

One Friday evening in early spring, about the time Elsie and Spud Murphy were looking forward to moving from Leighton's cabin to the homestead, Mac came up for his weekend work of house building, bringing with him the bad news. Rumors at the S.P. had it that the railroad would soon be cutting back its work schedule in the shops to a two-day week. He had brought Jack with him, as he often did these last few weeks, to help out in deepening the well and building the roof for the two rooms of the house whose walls were framed, since Aunt Mary had volunteered to stay with Grandma. By that time the house consisted of two partially roofed rooms and there were no materials on hand to finish them. And of course no money in the bank, either, and no source from which to borrow. That night, instead of going back to Leighton's, they all rolled their bedrolls out on the ground under a huge valley oak where the front yard would someday be and went to sleep watching Orion in his endless pursuit of the Pleiades.

The next morning Spud Murphy woke up just at daybreak with not a soul other than himself anywhere in sight. Worse, the Essex was gone as well, which meant that they had intended to sneak off and leave him on purpose, probably to go down to the river to swim or maybe go to Plymouth. He was hopping mad and an hour later when he heard the sound of the Essex working up the slope to the house site on the other side of the ridge, he sulked off into a thicket of toyon and manzanita and hid. When the old car came huffing over the ridge he was startled to see the amount of lumber stacked up on the trailer. Thinking of all the labor required to load up that much lumber, he decided not to complain too much about being left behind. Without even bothering to look for Spud Murphy or call his name or anything, Mac and Elsie and Jack got to work loosening the tie-down ropes and pulling two-by-fours and one-inch boards off the trailer and stacking them. After a bit, so as not to appear too interested, he sauntered out of the brush and, addressing the only one he dared, said to Jack, "Well, I suppose you thought I needed more nails to straighten." Mac said, "Cut the smart talk. Get up on the load and start throwing boards off."

After a while Spud Murphy could stand it no longer and said, "Well, I wish I knew where you went to get this lumber."

Mac eyed him speculatively for a moment and then turned his back on him and went on unloading the trailer. Spud Murphy knew then that the subject was closed and he had best not pursue it further. Later when he was alone with Elsie, he asked her, "Mama, where did you go this morning?"

Her answer was, "Spud Murphy, if that were something that you should know, your father would have told you." Mac and Jack brought two more loads of lumber that afternoon, while Elsie and Spud Murphy stayed at the homestead and pulled nails and stacked the precious boards that would become their home. On Sunday morning after breakfast, Elsie packed a picnic lunch and they all got in the Essex and drove to Sunmount to visit E.J.

With the fresh supply of used lumber, the house took shape in a hurry, at least two rooms of it did, those being the kitchen and a bedroom. When the tar paper roofing material was all tarred and nailed down on the roof of those two rooms, Mac got busy inside on shelves and tables and benches and such and it wasn't long after the big cast-iron range was moved into its place that Elsie and Spud Murphy were moved out of Leighton's cabin and onto the homestead. The rumored two-day work week at the railroad shops came into being about the same time, and the consequence of that was that Mac had more time to work on the homestead but less money to do it with. He still had to be in the city for his radio program and rehearsals and other musical engagements, which interfered with his weekend work but at the same time took on more meaning now that he had less income from the S.P.

Spud Murphy set off in the afternoon for the Barney ranch, an empty half-gallon cider jug swinging from his left hand. His right arm he kept unencumbered in case some dangerous animal or wild Indian or highwayman accosted him and he had to defend himself with the bullets that he carried in his pocket in the guise of round pebbles, throwing them at the blue jays and cottontails and jack rabbits in which form the enemy was apt to be disguised. The cider jug was the approved container for the milk he brought home from the Barneys on alternating days. It had a nifty little round glass handle cast onto the neck that you could crook your finger through as a way of carrying it. Spud Murphy was taken by the efficiency of such a thing and marveled at the skill of the glass-jug maker. Sometimes when no jug was available you had to take a two-quart wide-mouth mason jar to get the milk, which was a lot more cumbersome and you had to hold it with two hands.

He came down the slight grade to the old Ybright place, envisioning it as the stagecoach stop and himself the driver, lucky enough to have avoided the prowling Indians that infested the territory hereabouts while the cavalry was preoccupied with the defense of the gold miners in the Dakota Badlands. He sat dreaming on the porch, seeing in his mind's eye the stableman as he changed the team, shouldering Old Bill and the others into place abreast the wagon tongue. He could hear the drone of voices from inside the house as his passengers took on the midday meal that Ybright's injun squaw had prepared for them.

When he got to Barneys', Mrs. Barney told him that Waldo was down at the barn milking so he hurried to the barn, not wanting to miss watching the combined miracle of nature and science that resulted in his having fresh, rich milk to pour over his corn meal mush in the morning. Squeezing a cow's teats by hand to get the milk out was an understandable thing, a feat that he had performed himself after some patient coaching by Waldo, but getting the same results by hooking up the milking machine with its tubes and suction cups seemed nothing less than a miracle and he was much in awe of miracles of that sort. As often happens with newfangled devices, however, the milking machine left something to be desired, because it wasn't able to completely empty the cow's udder, and you had to strip the last out by hand or the cow would eventually go dry and wouldn't give milk again until she had another calf. All this he knew, 'cause Waldo told him so. Spud Murphy found a one-legged milking stool and perched on it as close to the cow's udder as was possible, watching in a veritable trance the pulsing surge of the tubing and the suction cups as the milk was extracted from the big Holstein's udder.

As miraculous as the milking machine was, the cream separator was even more so. When you turned the crank, the stainless steel bowl holding the milk spun at a high rate of speed and by some magical circumstance this somehow made the cream rise up to the top of the milk and come out of a spout that was for that purpose. Waldo tried to explain that process to him, like he had explained the wizardry of vacuum in the case of the milking machine, but Spud Murphy just seemed to bog down when it came to the concept of specific gravity.

To Spud Murphy, Barneys represented the larger world that included places like New York, Chicago, and San Francisco. Not that he had ever been to any of those places or even knew very much about them. But he quickly learned at an early age the usefulness of attentive listening to the conversations of grownups and hours spent pouring over the Sears Roebuck catalog. From those sources he assimilated a general knowledge of a wide variety of subjects, including those concerned with exotic-sounding cities in far away places. Like Chicago, New York, and San Francisco.

For one thing, Barneys had a telephone. A few houses like Barneys that were lucky enough to be located along the county road were connected to the telephone line. The phone had a crank on it so you could ring, say, two short cranks and a long one, and the person you wanted to talk to would know that was their signal. They would pick up their receiver and hold it to their ear and you could have a conversation. Spud Murphy often wondered how the words got by each other in the copper wire if both people kept on talking at the same time. His worrying about the matter finally brought him to the conclusion that there was probably some way of holding your mouth that made your words stay on one side or the other of the wire. Probably like the right side for automobile travel on the county road. It was called talking out of the corner of your mouth, and gangsters often talked that way. There was little doubt but that his world-wise older brother Jack put that idea in his head to start with. As a result, Spud Murphy practiced talking that way sometimes when he was alone, just in case the chance ever came along to talk to someone on a telephone.

For another, Barneys had running water, right in their kitchen. After Spud Murphy had become aware of that, he went outside the house and began nosing around and after he had sauntered around outside for a while he noticed a big redwood stave barrel up on a tower above the eaves with a couple of pipes leading out from under the eaves and running up to it. Above the roof of the tank was a windmill. It wasn't long before he became an authority on windmills.

Then there was the fact that of the cars the Barneys owned, not a single one had to be hand-cranked or parked on top of a hill to start by coasting. They all had little buttons on the floorboards next to the gas pedal that you could push with your foot to start the engine. In that respect they were very different from the cars Spud Murphy's family owned at various times. Even the farm tractor that Waldo or Mr. Barney would give him a ride on from time to time had a self-starter.

And finally, most wonderful of all, there was the engine-driven Delco-Remy 32-volt electric generator that provided electric lights for the house and barn and a light at the entrance of the driveway itself where nobody was, as if advertising in prodigal fashion to the universe itself the prosperity of the owner of the house who owned such an incredible device. You didn't even have to blow the light out when you were done using it or trim the wick or clean the soot out of the chimney. There was a switch to shut it off and the bulb was sealed so you couldn't even get a cleaning rag inside it at all.

As Spud Murphy arrived home it was nearly a half hour since the sun had slipped over the horizon and quickly turning dark. Elsie had lit a kerosene lantern and together they went to the well with the milk. Like Leighton's spring, the well was a multipurpose facility, serving as both a water supply and a cool room. Being bigger than the spring at Leighton's, it accommodated more perishables and was easier to move around in without stumbling over a rattlesnake. The only trouble with it lay in the fact that a very little amount of water managed to trickle through the seams in the bedrock into which it was dug. Mac said it just had to be dug deeper, but there were so many things that had to be done all at the same time it would just have to wait. In the meantime, to supplement the well water on laundry days and for dishes and for general cleaning up and bathing, Mac would carry a fifty gallon galvanized barrel tied onto the running board of the Essex that he filled at Leighton's spring. At the homestead he siphoned it into a wood stave barrel with a wire mesh top and that had to last for the whole week or until he came back the next week from the city and so on. Spud Murphy, watching him, waited until Mac had left for the city and then spent a half hour examining the siphon hose, trying to make water come out of it until Elsie, wondering at the quiet, found him blowing bubbles into the water barrel and explained the mysteries of a siphon to him.

Two

Some days after the mysterious acquisition of the three trailer loads of lumber, and after moving onto the homestead, Spud Murphy went on the milk run and stayed longer at Barneys than he should have because he was listening to Waldo and Mr. Barney talk about spring cattle drives to the forest-grazing leases in the 'Sierras' of years past. Mr. Barney finally realized the time and said to Spud Murphy, "You'd better scat, young'un. Your mama's going to be wondering where you are. It'll be pitch dark afore you get home." As Spud Murphy was going out through the gate to cross the county road to the pasture on the other side, Waldo called after him, "If you see Old Bill over there, go ahead and climb on him. He'll take you home." Old Bill was one of two plow horses that the Barneys had used in past years for farm work before they modernized and bought a tractor. These two old steady hands were retired now and spent their days between the warm sunshine of the pasture and the cool shade of a small grove of live oaks and some scattered blue oaks. Wallace was a heavy-chested dark bay, but Bill was white as snow, looking like a knight's charger when he trotted up and planted himself in front of you, waiting for his apple core or whatever treat you happened to have. Both horses stood over sixteen hands, huge in relation to a five-year-old boy.

Neither horse was in sight, nor came when he whistled, so Spud Murphy crossed the pasture and climbed through the three-wire fence on the other side, following the road for a half mile until the abandoned Ybright house loomed before him like a foreboding derelict in the darkening gloom, and there he left the road and cut up into a wooded draw on a direct line to the homestead, thinking to save some time in getting home. Night had set in rapidly and it was dark, the moon not yet up.

Spud Murphy was not what you would call comfortable in the dark at night. He had a fanciful imagination and he was well versed in the fables and legends of the wayward spirits and vagrant ghosts that haunt the moors and other dark, forbidding places seldom inhabited by mortals.

As he committed himself to the trail through the woods following the creek, he began to have a sense of uneasiness and felt that something was moving abreast of him but off to his right in the thicker, shadowy darkness of the dense woods and brush on that side. Several times he stopped and stood perfectly still, facing back on the trail over which he had just come, to confront his fears— his skin crawling at the suggestion of what real danger might be somewhere hidden from his sight, waiting for its opportunity to strike— and found nothing. Finally, out of the dark, salvation came to him in the form of his mother striding down the trail to meet him. The flickering flame of her lantern's wick was a beacon in the dark, radiating its promise of safe haven.

That night Spud Murphy woke from a sound sleep to the most terrifying screams he could ever have imagined. The screams were those of a terrified woman in despair and for a moment he thought it was Elsie. She was crouching by the window looking out over the windowsill as though she was hiding from something outside. Spud Murphy slid out of bed and crawled over to the floor beside her and whispered "Mama?" And she answered him with a whispered "*Hush!*" and put her arm around his shoulders, as though to shield him from some danger.

The moon had come up by that time and it was bright enough to see clearly all the way to the large quartz outcrop that was located squarely at the apex of the ridge, a hundred and fifty feet from the bedroom window at the back of the house. The outcrop rose fifteen feet above the ground at its base, and having spent a number of hours sitting up there as Chief Running Wolf on a mission to reconnoiter the strength and numbers of the pale-face settlers in the valley below, Spud Murphy knew the value of that location as a lookout point. But childhood fantasies were no part of this night's events and his fearful eyes traced the outline of the outcrop and the ridge in detail and found nothing. Nor were there any more screams from the demoniacal banshee that he well knew to be hiding up there behind the outcrop.

Elsie volunteered no information on what sort of creature she thought might have been capable of emitting such terrifying screams. Keeping Spud Murphy close at her side she went to the kitchen and got the most effective weapon she had, which was a bread knife with about a nine-inch blade. She told Spud Murphy to get back in bed and then she lay beside him, one arm encircling him and the other clutching the bread knife against her chest.

Morning came and Spud Murphy woke to the sounds of Elsie fixing breakfast in the kitchen. After breakfast she wrote a note to Mac and they walked to Four Corners to mail it in the outgoing mailbox that was there for that purpose, knowing that the mail truck driver would pick it up on his trip from Plymouth to the city. Then they walked the half mile back to Barneys and Elsie told Mr. Barney about the terrible screaming that they had heard the night before.

Mr. Barney listened to Elsie, and when she was done with her story, he said "Yes, missus, there's a big mountain lion that has moved into that country back there. It's got a couple of our calves, for sure, and more fawns, probably, than you can imagine. I told the county trapper myself, and he'll be making some sets back there soon. I seen its tracks around the kills, and it's a big one, probably a female, and with all the killing she's doing, feeding a couple of cubs. I'd keep the young'un," nodding at Spud Murphy, "pretty close to home. No need taking chances." Spud Murphy missed the significance of this last remark, mainly because his mind was already leaping ahead, making the change from a principal chief of the Cheyenne to the persona of Jim Bridger, greatest of all the mountain men who ever lived, who could fight a mountain lion barehanded. Ghosts? What kind of sissy stuff was that? Mountain lions! You bet! Now, that is a whole different story. Wait till Jack hears about that!

As Elsie stood to leave and called Spud Murphy, Mr. Barney went into the house and came out with a lever-action Winchester carbine in 30/30 caliber. Handing it to Elsie he asked, "Can you shoot one of these, missus? I know how bad one of those dang cats can scare a body, screaming like that. And because of the boy." Elsie took the rifle with an appreciative smile. "I can handle it, Elmer. And I thank you kindly."

The mountain lion came back again that night and then again on the following night. And while they heard its blood-chilling screams on those occasions, they never caught sight of it, even though Elsie sat all night by the open window with the barrel of the 30/30 resting on the sill and her eyes searching the darkness. Each morning there were fresh tracks along the crest of the ridge and down to within a few yards of the bedroom window, where the soil was soft and damp from the autumn rain.

In response to Elsie's note, Mac came straight home after the Friday night radio show, bringing with him the Model 56 Winchester .22 that had been Jack's birthday gift on his tenth birthday. It wasn't as powerful as Mr. Barney's 30/30 but Elsie was a dead shot and the bolt-action Winchester was a very accurate rifle. With hollow point bullets, it adequately fulfilled the defensive needs of the homestead's occupants. The conclusion of the mountain lion episode came when Spud Murphy, waiting up for Mac long after his normal bedtime, heard the sounds of the Essex approaching and ran to open the gate where the road entered the homestead. In what seemed to Mac like just a few seconds, Spud Murphy rendered a nonstop accounting of what might otherwise have been a ten- or twenty-minute discourse on the mountain lion episode, leaving out not one single incident in an excited retelling of the events of the last three days. It was one time that Mac willingly allowed the 'children should be seen and not heard rule' to be violated with impunity. He was actually laughing about it later as he told Elsie of Spud Murphy's wide-eyed excitement in recounting the story. Of course, the seriousness of the matter did not escape either Mac or Elsie, and there was a lot of relief felt when the county trapper was successful in his efforts to destroy the animal. Unfortunately, as Mr. Barney suspected, the mountain lion was a female and it was necessary for the trapper to destroy her two cubs as well. When Spud Murphy learned of that by innocently overhearing a conversation between Mac and Elsie, he became very troubled. For some days it stayed with him and several times he was on the verge of talking to Elsie about it, but in the end he knew no good could come from sharing his sadness with her. She must have known, anyway, because she was even more considerate of his feelings than usual, and that would speak much in terms of her understanding and compassion.

It wasn't long after the lion incident that Mac returned to the homestead from one of his weekly sojourns to the city with a female German shepherd. Her name was Queen and she was probably ten years old, according to Mac, all knowing in such matters, who closely examined her teeth before making that determination. Queenie, as she soon came to be called, had a crippled right forepaw with only two toes and a dewclaw. She may have been born that way, but more likely, said Mac, she had been caught in somebody's trap and had sacrificed the other toes in escaping the steel jaws. Her crippled foot was no impediment to getting around, however. She rarely even limped on it.

Although in reality intended as a family dog, Queenie immediately attached herself to Spud Murphy, following every step he took. She waited patiently on the back porch until he came out on whatever mission Elsie had dispatched him or that he had devised of his own accord and each time the screen door slammed behind him and he bounced down the stairs, Queenie would bound off the porch behind him, ready for whatever adventure was at hand. Spud Murphy couldn't wait until he could show off his dog to Mr. Barney. The first time he went to Barneys for milk after Mac brought her home, Queenie was with him.

Just past the Ybright place on the way to Barneys was a wooded knoll to the south of the road and the beginning of a trail that took one beyond the knoll to a place that was supposed to be an Indian burial ground. Sure enough, there were a couple of mounds there, and Jack, who had an interest in such things, had found a number of flint arrowheads while digging around in those mounds. Spud Murphy, having acquired a reverence for things sacred to native culture, always avoided approaching the burial site, certain that he could hear the deceased ancestors of the modern Miwok populace ready to bring vengeance down on one who would desecrate such a hallowed place. Following the main road west beyond the knoll, one came to a lane that ran a half mile straight to the county road, and at the foot of the lane as you approached it was a gate that opened to a small ranch on the south side of the road where sheep and goats were pastured.

When Spud Murphy passed this place with Queenie, he noticed that she became very excited and couldn't be induced to take her attention away from the sheep. When they arrived at Barneys, Mr. Barney looked at Queenie and began to question Spud Murphy about the dog, who was now lying at Spud Murphy's feet. The gist of what Mr. Barney had to say was that sometimes German shepherds were not too friendly to other animals and Spud Murphy should be very mindful of not letting Queenie get to chasing the cattle and sheep.

In the course of the next few months Queenie, while still inclined to become aroused at the sight or smell of the sheep, showed no signs of hostility and the urgency of Mr. Barney's message began to fade. It was approaching early spring and Spud Murphy moved his steel-framed cot out of the house and into the coolness of the spring night on the back porch. Queenie slept on an old folded blanket on the porch beside his bed.

The night came when he woke to find Queenie gone and although he intended to stay awake and watch for her return he fell asleep and in the morning she was back on her blanket. Her nocturnal wandering, at first only occasional, soon became a habit and word began to come back through Mr. Barney or Waldo or Frank White of her being sighted by themselves and other neighbors, running with a pack of dogs at different ranches in that part of the county. And then one morning as he was bending down to tie his shoes, she stuck her nose in his face and he noticed bloodstains on her muzzle.

Spud Murphy was working at the lumber pile, pulling and straightening nails and stacking boards when he heard the sound of a car engine echoing softly from the flat below the house. Queenie was lying with her head raised and turned toward the road where it wound up from below through the white oaks clustered in the draw. She came and stood beside Spud Murphy as Mr. Barney parked his pickup and stepped down off the running board. His eyes met Spud Murphy's just for a second and the warning he had given the boy was written sadly in the expression that crossed his creased and weathered face.

Elsie came out on the back porch and stood watching him approach. He said, "Just a word with you, missus," and they went into the kitchen together. Spud Murphy felt the knot build in his chest and his throat tighten. It crossed his mind to call the dog and run to the brush line and hide, but he knew that would do no good. Instead he slowly walked to the quartz outcrop at the crest of the ridge and climbed to the top. He sat there with the dog looking up at him from between his knees and gazed at a far-off horizon that to him was invisible through a mask of tears.

Queenie lay on the back porch, tied with a length of hemp rope to Spud Murphy's cot until Mac came home on the weekend. She never fought the rope or pulled at it or tried to chew it. She just lay there, her sad eyes following Spud Murphy as he pulled and straightened nails and went about his other chores, her head resting on her fore-paws. It was as if she knew what lay ahead from having been there before, but that this time there would be no reprieve.

They walked up to "the rock," as they had come to call the quartz outcrop now, and sat there in silence, until Spud Murphy said, "Daddy, can't we just take her back and give her to somebody?"

"There's no one to give her to, son. The man who gave her to me found her starving in the alley behind his house. People can't afford to feed their families, let alone a stray dog. If we don't do anything, she's going to be shot by the next rancher or sheepherder that sees her.

"We take her someplace else in the country, same things going to happen. Abandon her in the city and she'll starve to death or get run over or poisoned, like Skipper. If you care about her, son, we'll put her down here, where we can bury her on the hillside under a big pine tree and you will at least know that she's not hurting."

So Queenie was "put down," as Mac had suggested, far enough away so Spud Murphy couldn't hear the sound of the rifle shot, while Elsie held him on her lap and rocked him and dried his tears, and afterward Mac and Spud Murphy dug a deep grave so the coyotes would not dig up her bones and they piled rocks on it to mark it so they could always find it in the years to come.

Three

When his school let out for the summer of 1930, Jack joined the pioneers at the homestead. With Mac's two-day workweeks he was spending almost half his time at the homestead, and he also recruited Ariel Hinds to that cause. Ariel was the fiddle-player for the Sierra Ranch Hands as well as being an apprentice machinist at the S.P. shops. Each apprentice was assigned a six-month stint with each of four different journeyman machinists, and Ariel was apprenticed to Mac at the time of the cutback. A strong bond had developed between Mac and the younger Ariel, who, like Mac, had never known his own father. Ariel rated highly with Mac for his fiddle playing and his talent as a developing machinist, and as Mac would say, just for the general 'cut of his jib.'

You would have thought that with all that help to speed up the construction work, Spud Murphy would have been overjoyed, but that wasn't exactly the case. In the first place, three or four nail pounders all driving nails meant that it became impossible for him to straighten nails as fast as they could drive them. It finally got to the point where they ran completely out of used nails and Mac had to buy new ones on credit at the hardware store. Spud Murphy was quite astonished to find that nails actually started their lives so straight and shiny and symmetrical and he felt more than a little put upon that nobody had ever told him that, instead of making him spend so many hours banging his hands up and smashing his fingers trying to straighten all those used ones. Of course, as Mac dryly put it when Spud Murphy grumbled about the shoddy treatment he was getting, he didn't notice Spud Murphy's name on anything having to do with payment on the charge account.

The second thing that riled him even more was that just when the nail supply department got taken over by project management and Spud Murphy had visions of semi-retirement, he found that getting rid of the nail detail only meant he had to start a new career hauling two-by-fours and one-by furring strips and cross bracing and other such lumber items and supplies to the sawyers and hammerers.

When he wasn't doing that he was supposed to keep all the cutoffs stacked out of the way for splitting into kindling for the kitchen stove. If he took a minute to rest, and Jack saw him, there would be a yell of "Hey, Gunga Din! Bring me another two-by-four." If Mac was out of sight Spud Murphy would find the shortest cutoff in the waste pile and throw it at His Highness, otherwise he would drop the two-by-four on the ground just out of Jack's reach.

The general method of house construction, then as now, was to build a floor frame consisting of beams and joists supported by posts whose ends rested on rock piers or bricks or concrete blocks if there were any to be had, and cover it with one-inch thick flooring. On that platform, frame walls of two-by-four studs and plates were built and stood up and fastened in place for the exterior walls and the partitions. In the case of the homestead, horizontal furring strips of one-by-six lumber were then nailed to the exterior sides of these framed stud walls on eight-inch centers. Tarpaper was used over the furring strips to wrap the building's exterior walls as a moisture barrier. Hand-split cedar shakes were then nailed to the furring strips over the tarpaper. All of that followed pretty normal construction practice, but the part that had its own unique character, reflecting the Depression- era economics in vogue at the time, was the treatment applied to the inside wall surfaces.

The KFBK radio station, where Mac's weekly radio program originated, was owned by the Sacramento Bee newspaper publishing company. One of the processes in printing a daily newspaper using 1930s technology was the creation of something called a "flong," or a "mat", for each page of the newspaper. The process was complicated enough to cause one to wonder how a newspaper ever managed to meet its deadlines.

The first step in the printing process was the operation of the "linotype" to produce continuous strips of typeface known as "slugs." The slugs were then arranged in a "type-form" to compose the newsprint on a particular page of the newspaper. The flong, as used by the Bee of that era, was a sheet of very stiff, dense, pasteboard about one-sixteenth-inch thick and of the same overall dimensions as a sheet of newsprint. A mechanical press forced the flong against the type-form, making the flong an intaglio (negative) facsimile of the type-form. With the impression of the typeface on it, the flong was then used as the face of a mold, into which molten type metal was poured to produce a curved, type metal sheet called a "stereotype". The stereotype, installed on the huge rotary presses and coated with ink, was what printed the newspaper.

Flongs, complete with all of yesterday's news legibly printed on the reverse of the side used as a mold, being of no further use to the publishing company (or anyone else, either) after their one-time use to cast the stereotype, were available to Mac at no cost through his association with KFBK. The flongs became the wall covering for all the interior walls of the homestead. With the reverse side facing out and the proper page orientation and sequencing of pages maintained, the flongs were clearly readable, even from a distance of fifteen or twenty feet across the room. Nailed securely to the studs with roofing nails, their stiff, unyielding composition provided, in one simple application, a unique decor, amazingly effective insulation, privacy, and a never-ending source of contemplative reading, including some very incisive opinions from time to time about the progress of the Depression, along with an ongoing panorama of "life in America," all of which was available from almost every perspective within the house.

It would be several years before Spud Murphy could appreciate the wry humor inherent in the contrast of life lived in "hard times", to the unique and uplifting experience of growing up inside the pages of a newspaper and looking out, so to speak. There is no gainsaying the fact that it made life a whole lot more educational and probably somewhat warmer than growing up in a packing box in a hobo jungle alongside a railroad track, or in a 'Hooverville' on the backwaters of some slough, as was the lot of some who were of Spud Murphy's age and circumstance.

And finally, by far the most difficult thing he had to contend with, which resulted from the increased population of the homestead, was that after a year of being the only one to share his mother's life on a daily basis, he now found he had competition for her favor from the rest of the family. With everyone vying for her attention, there were too few times when he could engage her in the exclusive manner he had come to enjoy during the year of their relative isolation.

It was a fact, however, that with many hands sawing and pounding, the house building took on a stronger semblance of purpose. Up to that time Spud Murphy never thought of it as

Three

having an endpoint. It was just something he did after breakfast until it was time for lunch, and then after lunch he did it some more until it was time for supper, unless it was a day to get milk from Barneys, in which case he was able to quit house building in mid-afternoon. Spud Murphy looked forward to milk days, not just for being free of the work on the house but because of all the neat things he learned about ranching and cattle drives of bygone years from his visits with Waldo and Mr. Barney. The milk run also gave him opportunity to build a closer relationship with Old Bill.

Bill was going on twenty-six or twenty-seven years, in Mr. Barney's reckoning. Bill and Wallace had always been a team from the time they were three-year-olds. Their retirement was made possible by the acquisition of a shiny new green John Deere model D tractor.

Bill was no pony. He was so big Spud Murphy, even with a downhill run, couldn't jump high enough to hook his elbows over Old Bill's withers to shinny up on his back. Bill's back was swayed by age and he would have had every right to balk at carrying some half-baked, pint-sized, going- on-five-year-old city-bred kid around just for the purpose of playing cowboy, but he never did. Instead he followed Spud Murphy into the fenced yard of the Ybright ranch and stood dutifully and patiently along-side the front porch rail of the old house while Spud Murphy climbed up on the rail and made a wild leap for Old Bill's back. After feeling Spud Murphy settle on his back, Bill would take a long look back and, in answer to a nudge from Spud Murphy's bare toe, move off in the direction of the yard gate.

The gate through the fence that surrounded the house and was meant to keep the livestock away from it was one of those gates that used a chain with an iron weight fastened to it with bailing wire to make it close automatically after you went through and let go of it. One end of the chain was fastened to the gate and the other end to a post set in the ground. When the gate opened, the chain straightened out, raising the weight. Bill would walk up against the gate and stand there, with his chest against the wooden gate frame, waiting for it to be opened. Spud Murphy would get scrunched around as far forward as he could on Bill's neck and push the gate open with his foot, holding it open with his foot as horse and rider passed through. It wasn't as hard as it sounds, although it did take a little bit of scrabbling around, due to Bill's being so long from one end to the other and Spud Murphy's legs being so short.

One day, as Old Bill and Spud Murphy went through the routine of getting out through the yard gate, in preparation for riding fence and checking for strays in the breaks along the upper reaches of Cascara Creek, a tag end of the bailing wire that fastened the chain to the gate got caught in the turned-up cuff of Spud Murphy's overalls. Bill, not quite understanding the meaning of the sliding weight on his back, walked right out from under Spud Murphy, who had let go of Bill's mane, that being the only handhold available, in the interest of getting a little more range with his foot for the back-end part of the gate-holding-open operation.

When Spud Murphy came to the end of Bill he got lowered by gravity to a not-too-gentle landing on the ground. Bill stopped dead in his tracks when that happened, bending his head back to see Spud Murphy lying on the ground. Spud Murphy wondered for a long time afterward how it could be that a dumb animal could make a person feel so embarrassed by the way it stared like that.

It wasn't long before Mac, not one to give up easily, came home with another dog, this time a mixed breed 'ranch dog' that with today's need for pedigrees would probably come close to being called an Australian sheepdog or a somewhat too large, flop-eared border collie, in coloring and looks at least. The man who had previously owned him told Mac the dog was about a year old. He had very quiet and polite manners but was not shy and he had serious eyes that looked directly at you as though he was trying to read your mind. Spud Murphy, still carrying the sadness that came from Queenie's unfortunate demise, held out his hand and the dog came to him and sat down in front of him. Spud Murphy leaned down and petted him and anybody who was interested in animal psychology could have seen in that instant there had occurred the formation and solidification of a "boy-dog" bond between them.

In Spud Murphy's mind there were only certain names that you could give to a dog of the looks and mannerisms possessed by this dog and those would be maybe Shep or Pard or Prince or maybe Hiderack, all dog names he had learned from stories he read in *Boy's Life & 'Youths Companion.* Shep and Pard and Prince were ranch dogs in stories about Montana and Arizona cattle ranches and Hiderack, Spud Murphy's personal choice for a namesake, was the hero dog from a series of stories about Sergeant Renfro of the North-West Mounted Police, soon to have a name change to Royal Canadian Mounted Police. From somewhere near the pinnacle of happiness at the notion of having his very own edition of a Shep or a Pard or a Hiderack, Spud Murphy plunged to the pit of despair as he heard his father's voice say, "I thought we'd just call him Abdul. Abdul Abulbul Amir. That ought to be a good name for a dog". so it came to pass that the would-be Shep or Pard or Hiderack became known as Abdul, and Spud Murphy would spend the next ten years explaining to his peers how he came to own a dog with the strange name of Abdul.

Abdul Abulbul Amir

Percy French, 1877

Oh! The sons of the prophet are valiant and bold
and quite unaccustomed to fear,
but the bravest by far in the ranks of the shah
was Abdul Abulbul Amir.

If you wanted a man to encourage the van,
or harass the foe from the rear,
storm fort or redoubt, you had only to shout
for Abdul Abulbul Amir

Now the heroes were plenty and well known to fame
in the troops that were led by the Czar
and the bravest of all was a man by the name
of Ivan Skavinsky Skavar.

One day this bold Russian, he shouldered his gun,
and with his most truculent sneer
was looking for fun when he happened to run
into Abdul Abulbul Amir.

"Young man," quoth Abdul, " has life grown so dull
that you wish now to end your career?
Vile infidel know, you have trod on the toe
of Abdul Abulbul Amir.

"So take your last look at fair sunshine and brook
and send your regrets to the Czar.
By this I imply you are going to die,
Mister Ivan Skavinsky Skavar."

Then this bold Mameluke drew his trusty skibouk,
singing : "Allah! Il Allah! Al-lah!"

Three

And with murderous intent he ferociously went
for Ivan Skavinsky Skavar.

They parried and thrust, they sidestepped and cussed,
and of blood they had spilled quite a lot;
the philologist blokes, who seldom crack jokes,
say that hash was first made on that spot.

They fought all that night in the pale moonlight.
The din, it was heard from afar.
Huge multitudes came, so great was the fame,
of Abdul and Ivan Skavar.

As Abdul's long knife was extracting the life,
in fact, he was shouting "Huzzah!"
when he felt himself struck by that wily Calmuck,
Count Ivan Skavinsky Skavar.

The Sultan drove by in his red-breasted fly,
Expecting the victor to cheer.
But he only drew nigh just to hear the last sigh,
of Abdul Abulbul Amir.

There's a tomb rises up where the Blue Danube flows
and graven in characters clear,
is, "Stranger, when passing, please pray for the soul
of Abdul Abulbul Amir."

And a Muscovite Maiden her lone vigil keeps
'neath the light of the cold northern star.
The name that she murmurs in vain as she weeps,
is Ivan Skavinsky Skavar.

And so for Spud Murphy, neither Shep nor Hiderack ever came into distinction as a real dog, but Abdul, immortalized in song and quite real in spite of the mythic nature of his namesake, assumed all the courage of that fabled warrior and offered his allegiance without reservation to his young new master.

When the three main rooms of the house— meaning the kitchen, bedroom and living room— were framed and roofed with roll roofing, Mac turned his attention to the matter of siding for the outside walls, which at last telling consisted of some flimsy tarpaper fastened with roofing nails over the horizontal furring strips. It didn't take very much of a gale to rip the tarpaper into shreds and send pieces of it sailing across the homestead.

The siding that eventually protected the tarpaper and in fact made a house of what otherwise looked to Spud Murphy like a large, nondescript chicken coop consisted of cedar shakes, primarily because Mac didn't have to buy them from a lumber-yard. They came free from the forested slopes of the Sierra Nevada Mountains, close by the foothills wherein the homestead lay nestled. Free, that is, if you didn't count the cost in terms of the sweat and blisters that was the price of their harvest.

The U.S. Forest Service was born in 1905 after a long gestation period that began in 1881. By the 1930s, forest resource management practices had reached a level of sophistication that included forest thinning to encourage more vigorous growth of younger trees and thus enable a sustained yield of merchantable timber. Since penetration of sunlight to the forest floor was necessary for accelerated growth of the young seedlings, much of the thinning involved the removal of forest monarchs, particularly the cedars with their dense branch structure and thick foliage. These trees were often prime material, as in the case of yellow cedar, for split shakes and cedar fence posts. By issuance of a special permit from the Forest Service, a rancher who held a grazing permit could harvest fence posts or shakes from these fallen giants within the needs of his grazing permit, and at no cost. The forest ranger identified those of the felled trees or windfalls that a certain permit holder could use and that was all that was needed to satisfy the legalities of acquiring the necessary timber rights for shake or fence post production.

The White ranch was about the same distance to the southeast of the homestead as was Barneys' to the west. Frank and Rob White ran their cattle on about 640 acres of their own property plus another 640 acres or so that they leased from the Garibaldi Ranch, which included the Bastion place. Additionally, they had a permit for summer grazing on a large tract of land in the El Dorado National Forest Reserve at Leek Springs, off the state highway that led to Silver Lake. It was due to the neighborliness of the Whites that Mac was able to set up a shake camp on the Leek Springs' permit and produce the shakes with which to side the exterior walls of the homestead.

Making shakes was a pretty simple operation as far as theory was concerned. Having picked out a well-seasoned cedar of four-to five-foot butt diameter that had been felled in the thinning operation, and after stripping the bark, the idea was to cut the trunk into sections that were as long as the length of the shake you wanted to make, which in Mac's aesthetic and structural considerations happened to be two feet. These cylindrical sections were then split into rectangular bolts that measured eight-by-eight-by-twenty-four inches. The shakes, three-eighths to one-half inches thick, eight inches wide and twenty-four inches long were rived (split) from these bolts using a froe and a wooden maul. The froe was a riving tool having a heavy blade set at right angles to a wooden handle. To start the split the froe was driven into the bolt with the wooden maul hitting the blunt back edge of the blade. Twisting the froe in the split would complete the split and the finished shake would pop off the bolt like it was spring loaded.

The tedious and time-consuming part of making shakes lay with sawing the trunk into two-foot sections, which was extremely labor intensive. It was normally a two-man operation using a two-man saw and taking a couple of hours or more per cut. Considering the work that still had to be done on the homestead, there was no one that Mac could call on for help. The solution was to obtain an engine-powered drag saw with a six-foot blade, sufficiently long to cut through a five-foot log. Scraping up the funds to buy the saw blade, he turned to his mechanical skills and engineering wisdom and within a short time had manufactured a reciprocating saw mechanism powered by the engine of a well-used 1925 Star Motor Car as manufactured by Durant Motors Company. The Star had a reliable four-cylinder L-head engine that furnished the necessary power to cut through a sixty-inch cedar log in under an hour. Mac bought this gem from his ex-partner and co-conspirator of airplane manufacturing days, Roy Olson. Since that ill-conceived venture, Roy had become a used car salesman.

With a somewhat intermittent supply of shakes dependent on when Mac had the time to drive the sixty miles to Leek Spring and operate his drag saw, there followed an equally intermittent application of them to the furring strips that girded the house. The shake material arrived from the slopes of the high Sierra in the form of bolts, and it became Spud Murphy's job to convert the bolts into shakes that Elsie, Ariel or Jack applied to the furring strips. After snapping a chalk line to provide a straight and level alignment for each course, the shakes were nailed to the furring strips with four or five three-penny shingle nails per shake.

A person applying shakes would fill his mouth with nails to free his hands for driving them. According to Jack, the reason for Spud Murphy not being on the shake-nailing detail was because he couldn't hold enough nails for more than one shake at a time, the reason being that his mouth was going so much of the time he'd either swallow them or they'd fall out on the ground.

With Mac being such a major player in the events that went with the development of the homestead and because he's apt to continue that way for most of the story, it's probably time to take a closer look at this amazing fellow and find out how he got to be so resourceful. To fully understand Mac, however, you must first know a little more about his mother, Spud Murphy's Grandma.

Grandma was born in 1855 in Watertown, Wisconsin. Her mother, who came from Berlin, Germany, died within a year after her birth. Her father, also from Berlin, died five years later, in 1861, when she was six years old. She was raised by her older brother William, no doubt under some very austere circumstances, although he somehow managed to put himself through law school and eventually became a judge in Watertown Township. He also made provision for his younger sister to have a musical education, and after her schooling she taught theater arts and music theory at a conservatory in Chicago. In 1893 she married Mac's father in Omaha, Nebraska. There is no further record of her husband after that ceremony. He simply disappeared without a trace. Except for having sired a son, he might never have existed.

Those who had suffered the bite of Grandma's often-acerbic tongue would probably understand if it were found that Mac's father had furtively slipped away to escape her tyranny. On the other hand, there is another line of reasoning that holds she only married him to gain an heir. Once having achieved her goal and seeing no other reason to be burdened with a husband, she somehow rid herself of him through fair means or foul. It would be far-fetched to believe that after spending most of her adult years in Boston and Chicago, she would ever have given a moment's consideration to spending the rest of her life in Tilden, Nebraska, population three hundred. Who and what her husband was, and why they parted, were matters Grandma did not share with the rest of the family.

Although Grandma was very short in stature, her posture was so erect and unbending that you knew she pressed herself to the limit to gain every inch of it. She carried her head tipped back, chin jutting forward and nose elevated as though it was an aiming device for the laser artillery that was manifest in her piercing stare. The several vertebrae of her neck must have been fused together because her head didn't swivel about as heads are prone to do, but then it seemed not to need to for purposes solely related to matters of vision. It was certain she had a full three hundred and sixty degrees of visual acuity without having to turn her head an inch. To make her overall appearance even more menacing, she wore severely elegant black hats of the kind that proper Victorian matriarchs found stylish around the turn of the century, some thirty years past. Her hats seemed always to add to her appearance of ultimate sovereignty. Having been a designer of millinery fashions at one point in her lifetime, she made the hats herself, which may have been the reason for her developing millinery talents in the first place. Grandma was the quintessential, stiff-necked, self-sufficient, autocratic, German matriarch. Spud Murphy was not only very impressed by her; he was absolutely and unconditionally of the opinion that she was the greatest. As she was, as well, of him.

Possibly because she judged herself unqualified to raise a boy without a dominant male figure in the house, whose presence she never would have tolerated on her own behalf, she sent Mac off to live with foster parents from infancy through grammar school. She waited out this stressful period of his cultural modeling by teaching at the Julliard School of Music and the Boston Conservatory. The Emerson family, to whom she gave over

Three

Mac's care and upbringing, consisted of three spinster sisters and a bachelor brother. The Emerson's were strict Presbyterian New Englanders who lived in Lebanon, New Hampshire. Mac was raised under the governing principles that children are to be seen and not heard, and that swift punishment for undisciplined behavior is the key to successful social indoctrination.

Throughout his life Mac perceived himself as being a misplaced New England Yankee. He thought like one, talked like one, and in everything and every situation he exemplified the characteristics of that breed, including a contemptuous disregard for others of lesser genius and a complete disinterest for those facets of life that are emotional in nature. He was extremely laconic, dry of wit and sharply critical of the shortcomings of others.

When Mac was thirteen, Grandma reclaimed him from his foster aunts and uncle in Lebanon and moved back to Chicago, returning to her work as a milliner, handcrafting outlandish hats for major Chicago stores. She enrolled Mac at Lane Technical High School at Sedgewick and Division Streets in Chicago. At about that time he began spending all his spare hours at the vaudeville theaters that abounded on State Street. He brought with him the ability to play the guitar, which he had acquired in Lebanon from 'Uncle' William Emerson. He was befriended and encouraged by the professionals who made the theater their life. Under their tutelage he learned the stage and worked with many of the acts that found their way to vaudeville theaters throughout the nation. Most of these were passing through Chicago on tour, and as a result of his aptitude for the theater he had several invitations to join one troupe or another as his theatrical education progressed. He turned these offers down because of Grandma's disapproval, which came not from a feeling of disparagement for the theater but from the fear of losing him.

At about this time he met Bert Hazelton, who was the proprietor of the Acme Lock Works on South State Street. Mr. Hazelton was taken by Mac's talent and industriousness. Having no family of his own, he became a sort of surrogate father to Mac, then in his teens, who turned to Mr. Hazelton perhaps more than he would have to a natural father, had he had one. It was at Hazelton's strong urging that Mac, after completing high school in 1911, enrolled at Armour Institute of Technology, a Chicago trade school. He took a trade course in electrical engineering, which he completed in 1913. Although he applied himself to his education and was also apprenticed at Hazelton's shop as a locksmith, he continued to develop his talent on the vaudeville stage, becoming a skilled musician and an impresario of theater arts.

After finishing at Armour Institute he left his mother in Chicago and moved to East Moline, where he worked for the John Deere Plow Company as a grinder foreman. He soon became bored with a single life in the city. Quitting his job, he bought a used motorcycle and moved to the outskirts of civilization near Lake St. Helen, Michigan. There he went to work for the St. Helen Development Company in various occupations while building a log cabin for his own use on company land. At various times he was a logger, a carpenter, a telephone lineman, an electrician, and a mechanic— truly a jack-of-all-trades and man Friday to the company manager. The rate of pay was seventeen and one-half cents per hour or one dollar and forty cents for an eight-hour day. To supplement his income he also ran a trap line. Muskrat pelts brought twenty cents apiece, mink one dollar. He loved the sense of living with nature but his compulsion was that of bending nature to his will, not the other way around.

Mac was born with a superior intellect. In addition to that gift, he was brought up by his New England foster aunts and uncle to be resourceful and hardworking. From his German mother he inherited a self-aggrandizing nature, an aura of invincibility, a biting wit and an appreciation for the dramatic. From somewhere, perhaps his father, he received a compact, athletic body and a handsome, vital appearance. It is understandable that Elsie, who was brought up to be discriminating about intellect and strength of character, was attracted to him. It is also understandable that to many others he was a brash, egotistic young man without much sense of responsibility or maturity but full of a sense of his own self-importance.

In St. Helen, as in most of rural America in the early 1900s, entertainment was largely a do-it-yourself proposition. There were occasional visits of a traveling circus or vaudeville troupe to the nearby town of West Branch, but the primary entertainment for young adults was that which they furnished for themselves. There were dances and skits and picnics and music, athletic contests and games, and socials at various homes or at the lake, both impromptu and planned. Mac stood out at these events. Dark-haired, handsome, athletic and skilled as an entertainer, he was in demand and at the center of whatever was happening socially, whether as a musician, square dance caller, Mr. Bones in the minstrel show, or reciter of the poetry of Robert Service. In an environment that he owned lock, stock and barrel, he could afford to disregard the inevitable consequences of his often-arrogant behavior. It was not at all surprising that his insufferable arrogance did not seem to diminish his value as the prize catch at the monthly box socials.

Elsie had grown up to be an attractive young woman: red-haired, neatly groomed, intelligent, and distinguished by the good breeding and manners which were the stock in trade of her family traditions. Her nature was by heritage willful and stubborn, but experience with her sisters had taught her the value of persuasion and negotiation. Like Mac, she was sought after by the opposite sex and had many suitors.

It was inevitable that of all the choices that were available to Mac and Elsie, they would ultimately choose each other. Perhaps that was because they were intellectual equals but more likely it was because of the sense of challenge that their volatile natures promised. The prospect of blissful harmony in this union was on a par with the anticipation of looking for buried treasure in the caldera of an active volcano. There just isn't anything quite like a good fight at times, and it is unlikely that there were any other two people in the whole state of Michigan who could have been so prepared to do battle and were so evenly matched, although not always armed with the same weapons. It didn't take much of the summer of 1916 for them to start thinking seriously about marriage.

During that summer Grandma became 'ill' and quit her work and her apartment in Chicago and moved to St. Helen to live with Mac. It is quite likely that she was influenced in making that decision by Mac's announcement of his and Elsie's marital intentions. She saw what she considered to be his unnecessary absence from her as a statement of rejection, which to some extent it probably was. As Mac matured, Grandma had become increasingly neurotic. Feeling alone in the world, she saw nothing to replace the companionship that she had always assumed would be her reward for what she felt had been a lifetime of sacrifice on his behalf.

People did not talk very much about psychological problems that existed within their families in those days. Those that one cared for were not supposed to have weird connections in their neuronal structures, particularly those who perceived themselves as the intellectual superiors of most of the rest of mankind. Grandma could definitely have used some psychiatric help, but she would have been the last person in the world to admit it, let alone seek or accept it. No one else in the family would have admitted it even to themselves, or presume to suggest it aloud if they did.Before Mac and Elsie could be married, Mac had to get his financial affairs in order. He was indebted for his building costs, the additional cost of providing for his mother, and his general prodigality, including the cost of spare parts for his motorcycle and all the guitar strings he probably had to buy in serenading Elsie, any of which, I suppose, took several hours of work to pay for at a pay rate of seventeen and a half cents per hour. Elsie was still trying to finish her high school education in Milwaukee, working as a governess and housekeeper for the Trekker family. The general plan was that she would stay in Milwaukee to work part-time as housekeeper for them and attend school part-time. After Mac had worked off his indebtedness in St. Helen, he would find a paying job with steady hours in Moline, where he had worked before for the John Deere Plow Company. When all that had happened and Mac could in good conscience ask his prospective father-in-law to entrust Elsie's life into his keeping, they would set a date and get married.

As fall wore on and cold weather set in, work petered out in St. Helen and Mac's income was reduced to what he could make from his trap line. He finally borrowed seventy-five dollars from his uncle, William Voss, the judge in Watertown, Wisconsin, and paid off most of his St. Helen debts. He then moved to Rock Island, Illinois, where he went to work this time for the Moline Plow Company, still in his old position as a grinder foreman. He received the relatively high wage of twenty dollars a week for forty-eight hours of work. In late December Elsie's father acquiesced to the marriage, and Mac and Elsie were married by a civil judge in Milwaukee on December 23, 1916.

On December 28, five days after the marriage, Elsie's mother went out at nine thirty in the evening during a blizzard to find her way on foot seven miles to the home of an expectant St. Helen woman whose time was near. She intended to spend the night at her patient's house and return home the next day. She never made it. After getting lost in the blizzard she wandered in circles until she was overcome by cold in the minus-forty-degree weather and froze to death. Her body was found the next day by another neighbor.

From the time Mac and Elsie moved into their first home in Rock Island until her death in 1933, Grandma was always a part of their household except for a time during World War I. She was dictatorial, temperamental and at times a very cantankerous old lady, opinionated and manipulative. Spud Murphy knew those things only by hearsay. At his age you are in no position to make those kinds of judgments for yourself. And you wouldn't hold it against a person even if you did, because to a small boy those are the normal traits of most all adults. The simple truth is that it was not in Grandma's power to associate with anyone and not be totally dominating in that relationship. The year 1917 must have seen some trying times for Mac and Elsie, facing the desperate task of trying to subdue their own obdurate wills each to the other while being supervised at every step of the way by Grandma. Somehow they survived, even to the extent of having a son, Spud Murphy's older brother Jack, who was born on November 11, 1917, at the Lutheran Hospital in Moline, Illinois.

On February 15, 1918, two months after Jack's birth, with America joining the war against Germany, Mac volunteered for the U.S. Army and was sent to Vancouver Barracks at Vancouver, Washington for training and assignment to the 318th Engineer Battalion. After training he was sent to France, arriving in Brest on May 18, 1918. He saw duty as a motorcycle dispatch rider and received a shrapnel wound fighting in the Vosges Mountains. He was then reassigned to duty installing and maintaining electrical generators and distribution equipment at various command centers in the Meuse, Marne and Argonne sectors. With the war over, he returned to the U.S. in 1919 and was honorably discharged from the army at Camp Grant, Illinois on June 21, 1919.

When Mac went overseas, Elsie moved to St. Helen with her new baby, staying with her sisters at the family home. Aunt Mary took care of Jack while Elsie commuted daily to West Branch, where she completed high school. When Mac was discharged he and Elsie and Jack moved back to Chicago with Grandma.

Unable to find steady work in Chicago, in desperation, they moved back to St. Helen. Mac once more found work with the St. Helen Development Company as a carpenter. The wages paid were little better than they had been before, but it was an improvement over walking the streets of Chicago. On July 18, 1920, E.J. was born at St. Helen, Michigan.

With little hope of finding a job in St. Helen that would support his family, Mac turned for help to his friend Bert Hazleton. Early in 1921 Acme Lock Company was able to secure a contract with the Cook County Sheriff's Department for the maintenance of the security systems and locks in the jail. Mr. Hazleton brought Mac down from St. Helen and put him in charge of this contract with the title of Superintendent of Prison Maintenance. Mac was deputized by the sheriff's department so he could work within the premises of the jail. The title was more exalted than the salary, but he had escaped once more from the poverty of St. Helen.

Early in 1922 the Southern Pacific Railroad, with home offices in Chicago and San Francisco, advertised nationwide for machinists for their main repair shops in Sacramento, California. The unions were attempting to get a foothold in unionizing the railroad industry and the S.P. sought to subvert the union organizing effort. by hiring employees that would remain non-union, and would, in fact, agree to cross the union picket lines, physically resisting the pro-union strikers. The S.P. provided the prospective employee with transportation to Sacramento and a .45 caliber handgun, presumably for his personal defense. If his employment continued for three months, he would then get free transportation to Sacramento for his family. Mac applied for a job and was accepted immediately. He arrived in Sacramento on August 14, 1922. Elsie, Jack, E.J. and Grandma were on the train to Sacramento immediately following the expiration of the three-month probationary period. To the best of Mac's knowledge, no one was ever shot and the union movement was forestalled until after the end of World War II.

California was paradise, a utopia, the golden land of opportunity. To Mac and Elsie it meant escape from the oppressive environment of bleak, big-city poverty and cold, gray, winters. They came to a middle-class economy that represented jobs and houses and automobiles, as contrasted with the depressed working conditions and the tiny crowded apartments and the public transportation that had been their lot in Michigan and Illinois since Mac's discharge from the army.

Four

It eventually came to pass that the man who owned the Bastion place, one Joe Garibaldi, was brought face-to-face with the fact that someone had gotten away with his ramshackle old house. Spud Murphy knew that, of course, because he went by there as often as he could, which was whenever he could get away from house building or whatever else was going on at the homestead. Early in summer, after the arrival of the three mystery trailer loads of lumber, Spud Murphy had made a special trip down to the river just to visit the old house. Where it should have been, there was nothing left but a rock-walled basement dug into the hillside. As he lay out on the rocks in the gorge where the water came cascading down the river channel— as it would have done in 1804, as Meriwether Lewis and William Clark tried to navigate the Salmon River— Spud Murphy reflected on the providence of .nature with regard to such things.

But now something else that smelled even more fishy had come to Spud Murphy's attention, such that his alter ego, Sergeant Renfro of the N.W.M.P., who had recently been posted to the Cypress Hills from Fort Saskatchewan, needed to make an investigation in order to know exactly what was going on in that part of his territory. His concern arose directly as a result of Mac's cautionary instructions to Spud Murphy about staying completely away from the gorge and the Bastion place. "You mustn't ever go down there anymore, not on any account. Not ever! Y'hear me, now, son? Have you got that straight?"

What was going on was not at all clear to Spud Murphy, but if he had been wiser to the social customs and peculiarities of the times he would have suspicioned that perhaps a still from which to produce bootleg whiskey might be about to start operations there. Because of the availability of water the bootleggers chose the Bastion place as a good site for their still, across the draw and the little creek, thick with watercress, from where the derelict basement was. They built a couple of long buildings– back under some big oak trees– that looked like warehouses in which to house their operations.

There was usually an eighteen-wheeler flatbed trailer rig parked inside one of the warehouses. A few men could be seen coming and going from inside the buildings, and several cars were scattered around. For an hour at a time when he could get away unnoticed, Spud Murphy would lay hidden in the miner's ditch that followed the contour of the hills, forty feet above the river level in the gorge, watching the activities below him. He was never able to figure out exactly what the purpose of it all was until later, when he happened onto the solution of the puzzle in a stack of flongs, made surplus to the needs of the wall-covering operation when the house construction was near completed.

Four

AMADOR MAN SHOT
BY DRY AGENTS
DURING RAID

Wounded Man Booked At
Stockton, Four Others Held
Without Charges Being Filed

Although a squad of prohibition agents operating out of the Sacramento office early today shot one man of five arrested in a raid on an alleged alcohol distillery on the Leonetti Ranch, six miles from Jackson, Amador County, Prohibition Agent L. C. Phillips had not been apprised up to noon today by his agents that they had shot the man.

Sacramento Bee, October 2, 1931

But the other mystery, the one about Joe Garibaldi and his missing house, was more easily figured out. Mac had simply appropriated it. Anybody could have known that. Heck, nobody had lived in it for years. It stood leaning all aslant from years of abandonment with gaping spaces between the weathered, gray boards. There was no doubt in Spud Murphy's mind that Mac had dismantled it, board by board, and hauled the lumber home on the trailer behind the Essex. No doubt either that when Mr. Garibaldi went down to the river to tell the bootleggers where to hide their still, he was probably startled to discover that his house was missing. Except for Prohibition and the bootleggers, he might never have found out it was gone for the next ten years.

Sometime after the start of the bootlegging activities Mr. Garibaldi and Sheriff Lucot showed up at the homestead and stood outside with Mac, pointing at the house and talking for a long time. Spud Murphy never did know for sure, nor dared to ask, what was said in that conversation or what arrangement was reached, but he had some pretty strong hunches, and none of the house ever got taken back and Mac didn't go to jail. The Depression was getting to be full blown by that time and Mr. Garibaldi might have figured that the jails were probably already too full of bootleggers and their conspirators and the better part of valor might be for him not to bring up matters like disappearing houses, especially leaning-over ones and such, lest he find himself involved in something much more serious. Ariel commented later that it looked to him like a clear case of one hand washing the other.

Summer was soon over and a lot had been done but much more remained. Some new fence had been built on the boundary of the homestead. Before that happened, though, Mac had surveyed the property lines, beginning at a rock monument that was the main reference point for all the property lines in the township. He borrowed a transit for that purpose from the state highway department through his friend Harry Bennett, whose wife Sally was the accordion player with the Sierra Ranch Hands. Harry worked for the highway department and had access to a lot of useful things. Not exactly kosher, perhaps, but so long as there was no harm done to any of the parties involved, meaning in this case the state of California, folks did what they felt they had to do to satisfy the exigencies of the Depression, whatever they may have been.

It was a good thing Mac had gone to the effort of surveying the property. It turned out that two of the neighboring ranches sharing boundaries with the homestead had in the early days built their fences to take in about five acres of adjoining meadow not belonging to them, including a small year-around spring, all at the expense of the homestead. Just in case, when that information developed, Spud Murphy started packing his six-shooter cap pistols, which had been a birthday present from Elsie, whenever he was out riding fence on Old Bill, in anticipation of a possible range war.

Jack was the main fence builder. The fence posts were made from two inch boiler flues six feet six inches long, enough to leave a fence post that stood four and a half to five feet above the ground with as much of the post buried as you could get, up to a couple of feet, which was only possible in a few places that had soft ground. Spud Murphy thought the rusty old boiler flues looked ugly. He would have much preferred the split cedar posts that were the cowboy's way. Mac told him, "When you work for a railroad you think steel. Cedar may look more 'cowboy,' but used boiler flues at three cents apiece are cheaper and faster. Not only that, they'll last longer. You want to work for cowboys, go see Frank White."

"Well, how are you supposed to fasten the wire to them? You can't drive the staple into a steel flue!"

One of the first things that Mac turned his attention to after he had accomplished the goal of roofing and siding the house was the construction of a forge. It was made of a large truck wheel mounted on pipe legs. The bed of fireclay was cast in the basin formed by the wheel rim and the hub plate. The blower was a hand-cranked fan type that Mac designed himself and manufactured on "government time" at the S. P. shops. Government time referred to time the machinists occasionally spent working on projects that were of their own inspiration and did not pertain to company business. It was a concept so universally used that it practically had the stamp of an accepted and recognized fringe benefit.

Mac's reply was without hesitation. "We'll put the flue in the forge and heat it right where we want the staple. When it's red hot, we'll tap the point of the marlinspike through the wall of the flue just enough to make a hole a little smaller than the width of a staple in the exact spot where we want the staple to be. When we staple the wire to the flue, we'll squeeze the points together enough so the staple can start into the hole and then driving it in will spread the points apart again so it can't fall out. Think that'll work?"

Of course it worked, just as Mac said it would, and while that and a thousand other things went to enlarge the image of Mac in Spud Murphy's eyes, it did nothing to establish the acceptability of steel fence posts when all the real "cowboy" ranches around had cedar fence posts. And also, of course, Spud Murphy found himself with a new job. He had to crank the blower on the forge so Mac could punch the staple holes in the flues.

Every day before breakfast, Mac spent the cool hours of the morning working on the well, with either Jack or Ariel helping him. First they broke the bedrock out with a drill bit and a single jack, following the seams that carried the trickle of water, then they hauled the broken rock up to the surface with a windlass. Once Mac tried to speed the excavation with a half-stick of dynamite, but the seeping water stopped as though it had been turned off with a faucet and for over a day they labored, thinking they had lost everything, before the seams in the serpentine once more began to yield their precious treasure. When the day grew too hot to work in the closeness at the bottom of the excavation, they went about their main projects of building fence and working on the house. Eventually the well was capable of producing three or four gallons of water an hour in August, during the hottest and driest part of the summer. With the promise of no more than that much water, Mac began working on the distribution system.

When it came to the end of summer, Jack went back to the city and his last year of grammar school. Ariel had already gone to find part-time work and take classes at the junior college. Mac scurried back and forth between the homestead and his labors to provide what little income there was to be had from his job at the S.P. and from KFBK and the orchestra's occasional engagements.

After Mac's workweek was cut back to two days, his pay at 70 cents an hour for the sixteen hours amounted to $11.20. From the radio station he received ten dollars a week above the salary costs of the Ranch Hands and if he could line up a dance for Friday or Saturday night he might earn another ten after giving the orchestra members their shares. On the other side of the ledger, rent for the house on San Francisco Boulevard which he had to keep for Grandma and Jack and where he stayed when he was in town cost twenty dollars a month, five dollars a week. Gasoline was fifteen cents a gallon and it took maybe five gallons for a round trip to the homestead. Then there were the food and clothing costs and E.J.'s board and medical expense at Sunmount and a constant need for building materials and supplies. It's not hard to see how things got pretty desperate through the fall and winter of 1930-31. They stayed that way for a couple of years after that, too. It wasn't long before you got used to being broke, and being mired in poverty didn't seem to be quite so cataclysmic.

From someone's junkyard Mac acquired a positive displacement piston pump that needed new packing leathers and which probably started out life in a fire engine in some small town in the valley. Having completed the production of enough shake bolts to finish the house as it stood, plus another bedroom and a woodshed and then some to spare, he no longer needed the drag saw, which meant he could dismantle it and modify the drive train of the Star to accommodate a flat-belt drive needed to run the pump. For a storage tank he paid twenty dollars for a confiscated five-hundred-gallon redwood vat which had been liberated from some bootlegger's erstwhile list of assets by treasury agents and which Mac put at the crest of the ridge near the base of the quartz outcrop. From that elevation there was plenty of fall for gravity to deliver water to the house and garden and barnyard with a good head of pressure. Finally, for the pipe itself he turned once more to the flue salvage department of the S.P. boiler shops.

There were no threaded couplings of the same diameter as the two-inch flues, the actual diameter of which was one-and-three-quarters inches. To join two flue sections together one had to heat three or four inches of the end of one of the flues in the forge and drive a slightly tapered swage into it to expand the end. The slightly enlarged end was then returned to the forge and reheated to cherry red, causing it to expand even further, in which condition the cold end of the next adjoining flue was quickly inserted and driven in as far as possible and when it was all allowed to cool it created a water-tight welded joint. About eight hundred feet of pipeline was initially constructed in this manner, although another thousand feet were added later in an effort to develop another well at a different location on the property. When it was all said and done and Mac started the engine on the pump, so Spud Murphy could see the water swirling into the redwood wine vat from the pipeline that came from the pump and from there by way of more pipeline to the house and on to the watering trough at the corral, he thought the whole system was every bit as miraculous as the windmill at Barneys. He knew now that it wasn't a miracle at all, it was just gravity, and that knowledge brought him a step closer to knowing about *specific gravity*, and thereby solving the mystery of the Barneys' cream separator.

From the beginning of summer there had been an increasing number of farm animals that Mac brought home from his trips to the city. Some were bought from the feed store, but a lot more were the donations of his coworkers at the S.P. shops or the radio station or even in a few cases from the neighboring ranches,

Four

mainly the Barneys. First were the chickens: a number of laying hens of different breeds— White Leghorns, Rhode Island Reds, and a Barred Plymouth Rock or two— along with a couple of roosters to keep the hens laying. As fast as coops, granaries, feeders, hutches, runs and pens were built or cobbled together, the menagerie grew accordingly. Next after the chickens, Jack's rabbits from the back-yard at San Francisco Boulevard showed up and then there was a flock of Emden geese and a big obstreperous gander, some Peking ducks and a drake named Ezekiel, a couple of dozen Broad Breasted Bronze turkey poults, two small pigs of unknown breed (Durocs were pretty common), three cats named Ike, Mike and Spike, and finally, a very obnoxious bantam rooster and three or four bantam hens. By the end of summer the barnyard looked like Old MacDonald's Farm, lacking only the cow and the sheep from what you'd expect to find around a barnyard. There was even a pair of goats that were supposed to keep the toyon suckers and other native brush cropped down around the house. It never happened. It turned out they liked to indulge their curiosity about brush and tin cans and weeds and such, but when it came right down to dinner-time, fresh stuff out of the garden was more to their liking. Elsie was in overall charge of the farm operations, including an extensive vegetable garden. Extensive, that is, considering the scarcity of water and the frequent predations of the goats, cottontails and deer. Abdul took charge of herding the goats and ducks and geese and cats to whatever corner of the barnyard he thought they belonged in, in his opinion. He just naturally took up that line of work after watching Elsie shoo them out of the garden a few times. Even so, the garden never had much of a chance until Mac built a rabbit-proof, goat-proof, and almost-deer-proof fence around it.

There had been very few trips to Sunmount over the summer because of the urgency of working on the homestead. Mac tried hard to arrange his time so he could drive Elsie to Sunmount every other week or so, but it wasn't always possible. The drive was long and tiring and the county roads that were the most direct route north to the highway that went to Colfax were rough and hard on the car. There was a lot of letter writing to do. E.J.'s letters sometimes showed her desperation but generally she tried hard to bear her cross and not dwell too much on homesickness and the constant wish to be at home with her family. The letters were a poor substitute for being together, but for some of the time, that was all there was to offer.

> Sunmount
> Colfax, Calif.
> October 1, 1930
>
> Dear Mother
>
> How are you? Im alright. Mother can you come up next sunday try to. wont you? You left your purse here. Write today and tell me if you cant come up. So Ill be expecting a letter friday or saterday and if I don't get one Ill be kind of disapointed. I couldn't go to sleep monday night try as i could I didn't go to sleep till I don't know how late. hows everybody? mother please come up. gee I wish I was home now say hello to Jack and spud murphy daddy and everybody else. what is new or isnt there anything write soon and don't forget to come up next sunday if you can tell grandma Ill write to her next week
>
> Your loving Daughter
>   your rascal Elsie Jane (alias soup bone or E.J.)

Of all things loathsome, nasty, unpleasant, and without redeeming virtue of any kind that are commonly encountered in

Four

the foothills of the Sierra Nevada, the most unwelcome are the rattlesnakes. Rattlesnakes found their way to the homestead in endless numbers. Hordes of them. Big ones, little ones, and all sizes in between. And there was something menacing about this proliferation of venomous intruders. It seemed to be concentrated specifically on the homestead, to the relative exclusion of the surrounding properties. Occasionally, snakes could be found throughout the territory that Spud Murphy roamed over either on foot or on Old Bill's back, but no place else attracted the infestation that existed on the homestead. As spring unfolded into summer, the day never passed that someone didn't yell, "Snake!" And Mac or Elsie or Jack, whoever was nearest, would take the .22 and shoot the unwelcome guest, preferably in the head. If Spud Murphy was wearing his gun belt with the cap pistol six-guns, he would make a fast draw and point a six-gun at the snake and yell, "POW! POW! POW!" while he fanned the hammer. After the snake was dead, you cut off its head with a pole ax or a hoe or a shovel and threw it in the backhouse or buried it so the dogs wouldn't find it and start chewing on it.

If you came across one while you were riding Old Bill it didn't do any good to yell, "POW!" You had to jump down off Bill's back and find some rocks to throw at it or find a limb maybe, that had fallen off a tree, and hopefully beat it to death. One way or another, no matter how you killed it, either by shooting it or beating it to death, when it was dead—GOOD and DEAD— you always took your pocket knife and cut off its rattles, so you could put them in the glass mason jar that was on the cup-shelf of the kitchen cabinet (and later on the fireplace mantel) for everyone to admire. And then you probably had to walk home unless you could find a stump or a big rock to get mounted up again on Bill's back. Old Bill would stand there all stiff legged and never take his eyes off the snake, even when it was dead. Abdul did the same, except he'd sit down to watch, keeping his distance.

Mac finally figured out that the reason for having so much rattlesnake traffic on the homestead was because there was a huge den under the base of the quartz outcrop on the ridge. He tried all sorts of things to get rid of them including pouring kerosene into the den and lighting it on fire. He might have fried a couple of them but it didn't cause a big exodus, which is what he was hoping for. He tried using the renowned gopher exterminating method where you take one end of a garden hose from the exhaust pipe of the Essex and poke the other end of it into the hole and give them a good dose of carbon monoxide. When that didn't work he shoved a couple of quarter-sticks of dynamite in the den and touched them off. Nothing seemed to bother them. They just kept coming out of that opening under the rock every morning as soon as the sun was high enough to warm things up. Of course, that was only during the spring and summer months. Rattlesnakes, like most other reptiles, hibernate in autumn and winter.

The day the snakes left Ireland, as Mac was later fond of saying, was the day he got desperate and bundled up several sticks of forty per cent dynamite with a fulminate of mercury blasting cap on the end of ten feet of safety fuse He lit the fuse after poking the dynamite bundle under the rock as far as the fuse would let him. He came strolling down off the ridge and when he got down to where Elsie and Ariel and Jack and Spud Murphy were all hiding behind trees, he yelled "FIRE IN THE HOLE!" good and loud a couple of times.

In a few minutes the earth under their feet trembled and went {{{{{{{{{{{WHUMPH}}}}}}}}}}} and all of the acorns came raining down out of the oak trees within a hundred foot radius of ground zero.

Four

For years thereafter you couldn't find a snake within a quarter mile of the rock. But that final resolution of the snake problem didn't happen until a couple of years after the house building days, when there somehow came to be a few extra dollars left over after the groceries were paid for. In the meantime the war between the homesteaders and the rattlesnakes continued unabated, something termed by Mac to be sort of a Mexican standoff. In the summer of 1930, all the spare cash in camp wouldn't have bought a roll of caps for Spud Murphy's cap pistols, let alone a half-dozen sticks of dynamite.

Sometime after Labor Day, the cattle drives started, bringing the cattle out of the mountains and back to winter range on the home ranches. The drives took from five to seven days depending on how far they had to go, right down Highway 88 to the Fiddletown cutoff or continuing down 88 to Jackson for those ranches that lay to the south. When the drives were all finished, a lot of the ranchers of the county gathered at a place called Nick's Lone Acre, off the state highway near Pine Grove on the Volcano cut-off, to celebrate having survived another year— what Ariel called a "celebration of hard times.' Somebody would donate a steer or two and there would be a pit barbecue with enough food to feed a couple of hundred people or more. The ranchers, their families and their hired hands would come and there was more than one bottle of bootleg whiskey passing back and forth among the cowboys, although the drinking part of the celebration was pretty discreet and low-key. Wherever it was that the "Roaring Twenties" were doing their roaring, it certainly wasn't there amongst these country folk.

Through the neighborliness of the Whites and the Barneys, Mac and his family were invited to the celebration, along with Mac's guitar. Mac went them one better and threw in the whole band. There was no pay involved for the Sierra Ranch Hands, but you couldn't beat a free meal when times were hard, and the publicity they got out of that happy afternoon and evening probably helped for other more remunerative occasions in the months and years ahead.

That day marked the beginning of Spud Murphy's career as a "singing cowboy." After getting through "Cowboy Jack" without missing any verses, Mac had him sing "When The Works All Done This Fall." "Pretty shrewd booking agent, that Mac," said the ever-observant Ariel.

When The Work's All Done This Fall

D.J. O'Malley

A group of jolly cowboys, discussing plans at ease.
Says one, I'll tell you something, boys, if you will listen, please.
I am an old cowpuncher and here I'm dressed in rags,
But I used to be a tough one boys, and go on great big jags.

But I have got a home, boys, a good one, you all know,
Although I have not seen it, since long, long ago.
I'm going back to Dixie, once more to see them all;
I'm going to see my mother when the work's all done this fall.

When I left my home, boys, my mother for me cried,
Begged me not to go, boys, for me she would have died;
My mother's heart is breaking, breaking for me, that's all,
And with God's help I'll see her, when the work's all done this fall

That very night this cowboy, went out to stand his guard;
The night was dark and cloudy, and storming very hard;
The cattle they got frightened, and rushed in wild stampede,
The cowboy tried to head them while riding at full speed.

While riding in the darkness, so loudly did he shout;
Trying hard to head them, and turn the herd about.

Four

His saddle horse did stumble, and on him it did fall.
Now the boy won't see his mother when the work's all done this fall.

His body was so mangled, the boys all thought him dead,
They picked him up so gently and laid him on a bed.
He opened wide his blue eyes and looking all around
He motioned to his comrades to sit near him on the ground.

Boys, send my mother my wages, the wages I have earned,
For I am sore afraid, boys, my last steer I have turned.
I'm going to a new range, I hear my Master's call,
And I'll not see my mother when the work's all done this fall.

Fred, you take my saddle, Joe, you take my bed.
Bill, you take my pistol, after I am dead;
And think of me so kindly, when you look upon them all,
For I'll not see my mother when the work's all done this fall.

They buried him at sunrise, no tombstone at his head,
Nothing but a little board, and this is what it said:
Charlie died at daybreak, he died from a fall,
And he'll not see his mother when the work's all done this fall.

Spud Murphy's take was $4.25, mostly in nickels and dimes. He gave it all to Elsie, later, saying "Here's for my keep, Mama."

Five

It was momentarily a big relief to Spud Murphy to have most everyone gone when summer was over, so he could sit back and catch up on his long-running but often interrupted readings relative to "life on the early American frontier" as detailed on the pages of "Boy's Life," and in such other books and magazines on the subject as had found their way to the homestead. Unfortunately, about the time he was ready to assume the role of a country gentleman, Mac, not being one to suffer long vacations, gave him to understand that with all the things that had been accomplished over the summer there was now a need for serious attention to maintain what had been so arduously achieved. As he so fittingly put it, this was "no time for lollygagging around." It was generally Grandma who went around saying such things, but Mac certainly had a strong tendency toward that point of view, as well.

Most critical of the chores that required constant attention were those connected with the operation and maintenance of the water system. No matter how much time the well had in which to recover after being pumped dry, the water level would only come up to a certain height depending on the state of the ground water in that general area of the country. In wet years the water was so abundant there was enough trickling into the well from the small fissures in the bedrock to completely fill the five-hundred-gallon storage tank, sometimes even twice in one twenty-four-hour period. But in the hottest, driest months of a drought year there wasn't enough water left to lick a postage stamp after all the animals had a morning drink.

That in itself was a problem, because if there wasn't water left over after the animals' needs were met, and the garden had to be short-changed, it meant little or no garden produce for home consumption, let alone any vegetables for Mac to sell at the shops. Aside from that, however, the staves of the redwood tank would shrink as they dried out and the tank would become progressively less capable of holding any water at all. It was necessary for Spud Murphy to check the condition of the tank every day and tighten the barrel hoops as necessary to stop all the leaks, in order to save what little water the well did produce, as well as protecting the tank itself from being rendered useless by shrinkage of the staves. Of immediate significance was the fact that 1930 and 1931 were drought years for the whole southwestern portion of the United States, and while the Mother Lode was not exactly the heart of that region, it was still marginally affected by the same generally dry conditions.

Mac wasn't totally blind to the sometimes-questionable dependability of small boys who have great, unfilled voids yet to be addressed in their acquisitive thirst for knowledge. He most surely would have given Elsie instructions about those matters for times when he had to be in Sacramento, but he approached Spud Murphy in such a way as to give him the general impression that responsibility for the success or failure of the entire homestead enterprise rested upon his shoulders, including the deliverance of E.J. from the desperation of Sunmount. Mac thought the water system was at the heart of the matter and should therefore be the imperative assigned to his best man (so he said), one who inspired his confidence more than any other. Spud Murphy accepted this charge with the solemn concern that such a trust should properly invoke, while at the same time scarcely able to conceal his youthful exuberance at the implications of his appointment to such an exalted office.

It was August 1930 when Mac decided that the water system should become Spud Murphy's responsibility. Optimum production of water from the well in this drought year meant pumping it dry two times a day, once in early morning and again in the evening. All the watering of stock and garden was done at those times, too, to get the maximum benefit from what little water there was, and suffer the least amount of loss to evaporation.

Spud Murphy, just recently past his fifth birthday, was painstakingly instructed in the importance of checking the oil, fuel and radiator levels before starting the Star engine that ran the pump. He then followed the ritualized procedure of opening the valve to the pipe that ran to the redwood tank, which let gravity fill the pump and the suction line above the foot valve. After setting the spark and throttle levers with great care and precision, he turned the switch on and in the manner of any well trained barn-storming pilot, looked to left and to right and yelled "Contact!" although no one was there to hear him after the first two days when Elsie tactfully quit hovering over him like a mother hen. He enjoyed yelling things like "Fire in the hole!" and "Timberrrrr!" and "Contact!" even when no one was around to hear, although he probably couldn't tell you exactly why. Most likely, he would have said just because he liked the way it sounded. For a while, before he got his six-shooter cap pistols, he went around sticking his finger out at things and hollering, "Stick 'em up!" until one day he did it to a wooden fence post and a red-headed woodpecker who had been hiding acorns in the holes on the other side of the post flew off and nearly startled the liver out of him.

He couldn't crank the engine by hand, because it had too much compression, so he tugged on the crank until the crank handle was at the top of its stroke and then he put his right foot on it and, with all the strength he had, abruptly shifted all his weight onto that foot. Mac had taught him the trick of doing that, but when he did he cautioned Spud Murphy not to ever try it with a Model T or any other magneto-equipped engine, because "it'll probably backfire and break your leg." Nine times out of ten the engine started on the first try and ran flawlessly, thanks to the subtle ministrations of Mac, the Super Mechanic. With the engine running, it was then just a matter of adjusting the spark and the throttle, shoving in the clutch and putting the transmission in gear and you were pumping water. All that was left to do was take the stick of belt dressing and hold it momentarily against the moving belt to keep the belt from slipping.

Elsie would go to the tank and just before the tank overflowed, if there was enough water to make it do that, she would wave her arms and Spud Murphy, watching from a hundred yards down the hill at the well, would turn the ignition key off to stop the engine, after which he closed the valve between the pump and the line to the tank to keep the water in the tank from running back into the well.

That fall it started raining in late November and it rained so heavily for a while that the road got muddy and Mac got stuck practically every time he tried to get any closer to the homestead than Barneys'. The Essex had big wooden spoke wheels with narrow tires and it was a heavy automobile, so it would bog right down in the mud and bury itself, especially with the chains on. To avoid getting stuck, Mac had to leave the car at the wire gate on Lorentz Road at the head of the lane and walk the rest of the way in. The few times he had to make a try at coming all the way in because he was bringing a lot of materials and supplies, it was raining and he got stuck and had to walk in anyway. Elsie and Spud Murphy, armed with shovels and a kerosene lantern— because it always happened after dark— would walk back with him and shovel mud out from around the wheels. Mac would roll around in the mud under the car, putting the chains on and swearing, and then he and Spud Murphy would push while Elsie steered and eased the clutch out. Eventually the old Essex would lurch and get unstuck, but not without a lot of cussing and shouting and yelling. More often than not Elsie would end up crying. In the ten years of the Depression that were spent living at the homestead, Mac and Elsie spent more emotion and yelled more insults and spilled more tears on automobile-related foolishness than any other single issue except for the subject of finances and the lack of them. But about the mud, it was really without explanation: the whole homestead and country nearby was all solid bedrock starting two inches below the surface anytime you wanted to plant something or put in a fence post, but if you took a car down any of the dirt roads after a good rainstorm, there wasn't a sign of rock within three feet of the surface, anywhere.

When the rains first came in earnest that winter, the little creek that ran down the draw dividing the house site from the barnyard was soon running bank full. Spud Murphy loved the rain, especially when the heavens really opened up and it poured cats and dogs, as Grandma would say. He stayed in the house and watched the little creek swell for as long as he could stand it, but eventually he had to go out and slosh around in it, even though the rain at that time was still coming down hard. Elsie was kneading bread dough as he passed behind her to the kitchen door, and she said over her shoulder, "Don't go far, dear. It's really too wet to be outside for long. Put your rain coat and rain hat on." He said, "That thar's a slicker, girl. Cowboys don't wear rain coats."

She asked, "Do cowboys go to school and learn correct grammar?" and he answered, "Nope." His rain clothes were hanging on a nail on the back porch, and he put them on as she had asked.

He played in the creek for a while, where it passed behind the woodshed, building a dam of rocks to create a waterfall. Then he found a short cut-off of a one-by-two, left over from Mac's project of building a screened-in cooler, that would pass in his microcosmic world for a raft on the Missouri River, carrying the returning Lewis and Clark and their Shoshone interpreter Sacajawea home from their expedition of discovery. He set it afloat, watching it ride up and over the crest of the dam. He followed it downstream, watching it turn and spin in the eddies and over the miniature falls and through the standing waves of tiny rapids as it progressed downstream, using a slender limb to extricate it from the shoals and ensnaring backwaters from time to time and sending it further on its journey of return to civilization.

During the summer's well-digging operation a lot of the rock and dirt that was hauled up out of the well with the windlass had gone into building a dam across the creek below the well site. Needing a pond for the ducks and geese, Elsie had prevailed on Mac to excavate even more earth from behind the dam so as to raise the dam level with the excavated material, substantially enlarging the surface area of the pond and the volume of water it impounded. When the Lewis and Clark raft floated out into the duck pond, Ezekiel the drake, leading his tribe across the pond in order to keep a safe distance between them and the giant Gulliver wearing the yellow slicker that was invading his territory gave the raft several good pecks, sending it surfing along in the direction of the pond's overflow. As the raft went over the overflow, Spud Murphy ran down to the creek below the dam to retrieve it, thinking to go back up to the woodshed and repeat the journey. He noticed Abdul sitting on the creek bank way out on the flat, looking back at Spud Murphy as though pleading with him to come along further into the meadow. Since setting the raft off down the creek, Spud Murphy hadn't given Abdul's actions much attention, aside from having an awareness that he had always been close by, as he always was when Spud Murphy left the house. With the assurance received from seeing his dog eagerly waiting for him, he let the Lewis and Clark raft continue its journey on down the wide Missouri, following it as before.

He was familiar with most of the half-mile-long meadow that was known as "the flat" and the land that bordered it, having seen most of it from Old Bill's back a number of times, as well as navigating a lot of it afoot. The exception was that portion of the valley that was defined by the drainage of the creek, now running bank full, that extended north-westward beyond the point where it passed the spring at Cascara and plunged out of sight down through a section called Grapevine Ravine and into the levels of the wider valley below. The spring itself was located in a grove of live oaks so that the creek and the trail that followed it all seemed to disappear into the subdued light inside the grove before they took their downward plunge. When he entered the grove, Spud Murphy noticed that the storm-darkened interior of it had a mysterious tone and he felt an apprehension about going on yet he was impelled to do so, having a curiosity about what lay ahead. Abdul, with tail wagging, was also urging him on. As he moved forward it crossed his mind that with all of his rambling, this was the first place in his life that he had ever gone to without first having visited it with Mac's or Elsie's or Grandma's guidance and company; and except for a dedicated dog encouraging him onward now he felt very much alone, unsure of himself and very vulnerable. Always before there was someone's hand to hold when entering unfamiliar territory. But in the end he could not turn back. He had lost all thought of the one-by-two raft carrying Lewis and Clark, which had plummeted ahead in the surging current of the flood. He was determined now to continue on no matter what the consequences.

In a few places the trail was quite precipitous and he crawled down over small cliffs and miniature escarpments. The trail made a switchback and leveled out somewhat as it approached a wider part at the bottom of the valley. Then he was out of the brush and walking in a grove of cottonwoods following a pair of wheel tracks that wound between the trees. As Mac had taught him, he marked the trail where he turned out of the brush with a dead limb pointing back along the trail to where he had emerged from the thicket. He followed the wheel tracks and they brought him eventually to a river. The river was wide and somewhat fast moving, and it was high with muddy brown water. It did not look like the same river as the Cosumnes that he had always seen running clear and sparkling through the gorge near the Bastion place. Scattered among the cottonwoods were picnic tables, looking abandoned and out-of-place in the rain. Abdul went to the edge of the muddy water and put his head down and lapped the water. Spud Murphy wondered why a dog would drink muddy water when he was already sopping wet from it raining so hard and if he really was that thirsty there was plenty of clean water in puddles in the water grass. He put it down on his list of things to remember to ask Elsie or possibly even Mac himself.

After fifteen minutes spent watching driftwood being carried downstream on the flooding river he thought he had better go home, that Elsie would be wondering what had happened to him if he didn't get back soon. He was still nervous about his unfamiliar surroundings and he wanted to tell her about the new river, as well. He turned back on his tracks, and Abdul was soon leading the way again, as he always did, as happy to be heading home as he had been to leave it. When they passed Cascara and the grove of big live oaks, Spud Murphy felt the same oppression he had felt before. After he was well up the trail from the grove he turned and looked back, half expecting to see a demonic figure of some sort, part man and part beast, perhaps, staring out of the mist at him from among the trees. But there was nothing, and he trudged home in the steady, slanting rain, sloshing up the creek at times, but remembering the mountain lion incident, and always mindful of his back trail. His thoughts were mostly on telling Elsie about the muddy new river he had found.

Elsie questioned him in close detail about the river and various landmarks he had seen and then from his description told him he had been at the Ball place and that the river he had found was actually the same river that flowed through the gorge from the Bastion place. She said it would be equally high and muddy there, with all the recent rains, but it would be much faster running, because of it's narrow confinement where it passed between the cliffs of the gorge.

They went to Sunmount at Christmas time. E.J. was not doing well and the doctor thought it would be unwise for her to make the trip to the city. The whole family, including Grandma, cousin Katherine, Aunt Mary, and Aunt Isabelle had Christmas at Sunmount. Elsie packed a couple of lug boxes with the roaster and pans and platters and bowls of turkey, dressing, mashed potatoes, cranberry sauce, brussels sprouts, green beans, Waldorf salad and candied sweet potatoes, which, along with buttered mashed potatoes, were Spud Murphy's favorites. There were pickles and olives and carrot sticks and stuffed celery and raised bread rolls with apple cider to drink. For dessert there were mincemeat and pumpkin pies.

The three girls that shared a room with E.J. had all been allowed to go home to spend the holiday with their families The empty beds and white walls and the smell of disinfectant were a reminder that this was a place of danger which cast a pall on the celebration. E.J., who at the age of ten still believed in Santa Claus, got a book and a pair of pajamas. Jack, who was a thirteen-year-old cynic and believed in nothing, got a Boy Scout official pocketknife. And Spud Murphy, who believed in everything, got a wonderful toy tractor with a dozer blade, windup motor and rubber tracks that let it climb right up and over a book or your foot or most anything else you wanted to put in front of it.

Mac asked the blessing as he did at all meal times. He didn't call it "asking the blessing." He called it "saying grace." "We thank thee for this food, Lord, and ask thy blessing upon us." Then he looked at all the food and each of them in turn and added, "It sure doesn't look to me like we're having much of a Depression around here." And at that, Elsie smiled at Spud Murphy. He beamed back at her, because they were both thinking of how much grumbling he had done when Elsie had asked him to spade and cultivate the garden and feed the turkeys and chickens and gather the eggs and help with other chores that Elsie said had brought them to this meal together, right down to weaving the pie dough strips into a lattice-work top crust on the mince-meat pie. Mac, while not usually stirred by matters involving sensitivity of the human emotions, looked keenly at his eldest son and said, "Well, I want you all to know that my boy Jack, here, made a contribution, too. He used his newspaper-delivery money to buy the cider and the olives and the sweet potatoes. We couldn't very well have Christmas dinner without those things."

After about five or six small bites E.J. could eat no more and no matter how much Elsie pleaded and persuaded, she just couldn't get any more to go down. It may have been the excitement of having all her family there, or it more likely might have been due to her long hospitalization and homesickness, but anyway, it turned out that she had been having more of that problem of not eating the longer she stayed at Sunmount and it had gotten to the point that her weight loss and the anemia that accompanied it were becoming very critical. That evening when it was time to leave, there were a lot of tears and Mac and Elsie both promised E.J. she would be home soon.

It wasn't long after that before Mac came walking home from Barneys leading a pretty-looking little Jersey cow with big brown Jersey-cow eyes that he had bought from a dairy in the valley. A man with a truck had brought her to Barneys, following Mac in the Essex. From there Mac had walked her home with a rope around her neck When she saw the barnyard with all the geese and chickens and other animals, she must have known she was home, because she quickened her pace and when she got amongst the others she lowered her head and brushed them with her nose as if she were saying hello and introducing herself to them, telling them how glad she was to be there and such. Mac said that he thought maybe her name should be Katie, and Elsie and Spud Murphy both agreed, so that was what it came to be. Spud Murphy put Katie in the corral while Elsie walked back to Barneys with Mac to get the Essex, which had a couple of bales of alfalfa tied on the luggage rack where most of their weight rested on the back bumper.

The family's fortunes must really have taken a turn for the better about then, because not long after the addition of the cow, Mac bought a 1926 Buick sedan. Like the Essex, it also had wooden spoke wheels but not quite such narrow tires. Of course, it was an especially good buy, he told Elsie, and they were lucky that their old friend Roy Olson had managed to get his hands on it in a real 'sweetheart deal.' Mac said it made sense to get it, because Elsie would need a car to haul the kids to and from school when that time came, and the Essex would be ideal for that. Anyway, he said it really wouldn't cut into their budget too much because he bought it on time payments.

On March 2, 1931 Mac and Elsie made their last trip to Sunmount, bringing E.J. home at last to the homestead after her fifteen-month exile. Fifteen months in the sanitarium hadn't done her any noticeable good, although you couldn't necessarily say it had harmed her, either. She was still the same delicate, under-weight, anemic-appearing child of fifteen months before. When Mac and Elsie went to get her, Spud Murphy was left behind alone to watch after the homestead, much to his unhappiness. He wanted to be the one to point out all the important landmarks and places of interest and to make sure she saw Old Bill and knew about the Ybright place and where Queenie was buried and about the ducks and geese in the pond and Abdul running beside the car as they came through the gate at the fence line where the road turned up the hill past the well and on to the house.

He tried to explain to Elsie the importance of E.J.'s knowing all those things and Elsie said, "I know you want to be the one to tell her about everything, but you have to understand that as much as she is your sister, she is also Daddy's daughter and you must respect his right to tell her things, too. But the important reason for your staying home is that we must do everything we can to keep her from becoming too excited and getting sicker than she already is. I need you to help me with that and I know you will." Hours later, when Mac parked the Buick in front of the house and carried the small blanket-wrapped form up the steps, Spud Murphy held the screen door open for them and as she passed him he said, "Hi, E.J." and a frail voice from within the blankets answered him back: "Hi, Spud Murphy."

Five

When school let out in early June, Jack graduated from grammar school and there was no longer a reason to keep the house on San Francisco Boulevard. He and Mac and Grandma all moved up to the homestead. For the first time in eighteen months the family was permanently together under one roof, so to speak. Well, maybe that's stretching it a mite. Mac and Elsie had their bedroom and E.J. and Katherine and Grandma slept in the living room, but Jack, Spud Murphy and Ariel, who was back again for the summer, all slept under the stars without much need for a roof.

Mac continued to spend half his time in Sacramento, but now he stayed in a boarding house on "F" Street. Ariel went back and forth to the city with Mac because of the music activities, staying with Mrs. Hinds, his mother, when he was in town. Life on the homestead settled into a routine centered on the comings and goings of Mac and Ariel. Although the Essex was there for Elsie's use, it sat idle most of the time because there just wasn't time to spend "gallivanting" or money to be spent for gas and there wasn't much need to go anywhere. Grandma would go to town with Mac on occasion to spend a day with Aunt Isabelle, who had followed her foster son from New Hampshire, first to Chicago and again when Mac moved with his family to California. Those two, together with Deaconess Clark of the city's Episcopal Cathedral, formed a kind of spiritual and behavioral advisory board to Mac, who must have seemed to them to be a totally unstable, sometimes unfathomable, but none-the-less adorable and favorite specimen of the male species.

At first, after the acquisition of Katie, Elsie had assumed responsibility for the milking. Spud Murphy offered to do it, reminding her that Waldo had taught him, but she felt the water detail was enough responsibility for a boy who was not yet six. So in the course of the summer realignment the chore of milking fell to Jack, which displeased him mightily. There was nothing novel about that, since most everything about the homestead displeased Jack mightily.

Jack was not meant to be a pioneer. He didn't resent E.J. or hold her responsible for his misfortune in having to leave the comfortable life of a suburban environment. He more or less accepted it as the inevitable. It is no easy task for a teen-age boy to establish his place among his peers, and some boys find it even more difficult than others. Jack was one of those. Up to the time when he moved permanently to the homestead, his life revolved around the associations he had developed with other boys his own age in the Colonial Heights neighborhood. Not all of those associations were considered by Mac and Elsie to be desirable. Mac had given him a Benjamin air rifle on some past birthday, and then as punishment for careless and dangerous misuse, inspired by the show-off nature of some of his companions, Mac confiscated it. And then there were other occasions when Mac felt called upon to use corporal punishment in disciplining Jack for violating the rules of the house and when he did, he carried it to extremes. The real problem arose from the willingness with which Jack accepted that sort of discipline, building resentment but at the same time assuming it was nothing less than his due. Jack was a victim of the common despair of young men whose fathers cast an overlarge shadow and expect too much from their sons.

There were those in the family or close to it who believed that Jack's difficulties with Mac originated when Mac was discharged from the army and came home to face the demanding realities of fatherhood, when what he expected to return to was the carefree existence he had known in pre-war Roscommon County. It was Aunt Mary who said Mac had no tolerance for a squalling baby who was cutting teeth and beset with colic. And she was there to see and would have known. From that point on, it just never got better. Mac doled out punishment with the back of his hand or in some cases his doubled-up fists, and he was merciless in its application. To see it so upset Spud Murphy that when his older brother was being punished in that way he would run off to hide under a manzanita or toyon bush and cry. But Jack never did cry or react to Mac's intemperate anger with the resentment one would have expected. It was just as though he bought into the premise that he didn't amount to much. A boy growing up has enough problems. He deserves more help than that. Jack was a sensitive boy who needed an understanding and sensitive father.

The truth of the matter was that Jack's problems when he was growing up had their origin in a time when Mac's own father and mother decided, for whatever reason, to go their separate ways. Grandma's arrogance and the false pride that prompted it must have indirectly made a large contribution to the unhappiness that was later visited on Jack in the course of his boyhood.

Six

Mac always had a seemingly inexhaustible list of projects planned from which to draw on, depending upon the season, weather, available funds, state of mind, and various other contingent frames of reference. There never was a time when the last nail of a project was driven or the last bolt tightened, when he didn't step back to admire his handiwork and say, with deep satisfaction, to himself or any other within hearing, "Well, *that* job's finished, and I don't mind saying that I got a pretty good *scald* on it, at that!" Spud Murphy never could figure out what scalding had to do with it, if they weren't butchering a hog, but he understood the general meaning to be that Mac was pleased with himself. Regardless of the self-admiration that went on, however, not much time was wasted before he was knee-deep in whatever project was next on his list.

After the granary and the chicken coops and runs and other farmyard structures and facilities were complete, Mac got a contract to remodel the kitchen on Mr. and Mrs. Wann's house and at about the same time he turned his attention to building a cabin for Grandma, because at her age and station in life Mac felt she deserved to have a little privacy. Because of Grandma's penchant for taking charge of everything that was within the range of her voice and vision, Elsie felt that Mac was a hundred per-cent right, even though it wasn't Grandma's privacy that Elsie had in mind when she cast her vote. So another load of lumber and materials, paid for in part by the profits earned in the Wann remodel, found its way to the homestead. The foundation and floor for Grandma's cabin began to take shape under some big valley oak trees directly across the driveway from the well.

One of the things that people can do really well when they're mired down in a depression and don't know which way to turn, is to celebrate. Especially country people. If you want to be considered one of them, you have to accommodate that inclination yourself, whenever possible. That's just the country manners you abide by although you are only a bunch of transplanted city folks. So when there got to be a lot of desperation about the economy, along with a pretty good dance floor for Grandma's cabin, even though there still weren't any walls or money to buy them with, Mac proclaimed that there was to be a house warming kind of "barn dance," except that in this case since there wasn't any barn you would have to call it a "Grandma's cabin" dance.

It was mid-summer, so it was warm under the stars. Mac and Ariel hung kerosene lamps and Coleman lanterns around on the trees to light the dance floor. Everybody who had been at Nick's Lone Acre the fall before, plus half the rest of the county, came to the celebration, no matter what kind of dance you called it. They came lugging their potluck suppers and their musical instruments, if they had any— fiddles, guitars, accordions, and banjos— whatever. The Sierra Ranch Hands got things started and then everybody else joined in. Sometime after midnight Spud Murphy fell asleep under the stairs leading up to the dance floor that just happened to also be in the vicinity of the picnic table where the beans and the potato salad were doled out in great quantities and not too far distant from the clumping boots of the square dancers that pounded almost unnoticed over his head. It was a memorable evening.

Shortly after the house-warming, Mac got another remodeling job, this one at the Orr place. That job brought in enough money to frame some walls on Grandma's cabin and buy a little siding. Mac's reputation as a carpenter was growing, and after he finished the Orr remodel, the Willow Springs P.T.A. voted to give him a contract to build a stage, a kitchen, two service entries and porch for the Willow Springs school house. The stage was a first-class, professional design with complete stage lighting, including recessed footlights and remote spots and color filters for the spots and wings and stage curtains and all the operating hardware. With the income from this project Mac was able to finish Grandma's cabin.

Just about the time the cabin was ready for occupancy, Grandma decided she wasn't going to live in any cabin all by herself, separated from the hub of family activities in that way, so she couldn't exercise her God-given right to be in charge of everything. To be honest, there were other issues involved in the decision for her to continue to occupy the living room with E.J. One was her health problem, which was becoming a serious matter. Another was the economic consideration, which always seemed to be a determining factor in the family's decision making. It developed at that time that one of the bootlegger families needed living accommodations and could afford to pay money for rent.

By this time Mac and Elsie felt there was no longer a need to hide the facts of the bootlegging operation from Spud Murphy. The rule was that you just didn't talk about it to outsiders or strangers. After all, the evidence was there for anyone with half a brain to figure out.

In the first place, there was a new telephone line that ran from Barneys down to the river and followed upriver through the gorge to the warehouse buildings at the Bastion place. Spud Murphy came across it on a hike down Cascara Creek shortly after his journey of exploration with the Lewis and Clark raft. He followed the wire up through the chaparral and past the fig trees, from where it wandered through the open field, barely hidden in the grass. From there he followed it along the fence line to the Barney house.

Consumed now with curiosity, he took another full day, a week later, to follow the wire in the other direction to a bend in the river that yielded to a long straight stretch headed by the gorge, thus confirming Elsie's statement that the two were one and the same river. The wire continued along the river to end at the still. It was at that point he noticed a second pair of wires that ran south and on another day of investigation he followed those wires out to where they ended at Frank White's house on the Old Sacramento Stage Road.

These two telephone lines each paralleled a different route that meandered along various back roads from the bootleggers' still to the county roads and from there out to the state highway, the theory being that if you got a call from Barneys that the "revenuers" were coming at you from that direction you would make your escape through Whites' property and vice versa for any revenuers that might come from the Whites' direction. The homestead occupied a very strategic position at an intersection of the two escape routes that marked the approximate midpoint of each.

Another dead give-away to the notion that certain illicit trafficking might be going on could be found in the fact that you don't often find eighteen-wheelers loaded with grain and corn and raw sugar and other materials and supplies of a highly suspect nature traveling along barely discernable back country ranch roads at two o'clock in the morning.

Because of the rural public's general disregard for law enforcement and its perception of terminal ineptness on the part of government agencies, combined with the unpopularity of the Volstead Act, and considering the contributions that bootleggers made to the local economy, most distillery operators ranked fairly high in regard to community acceptance and were well thought of and supported by the local citizenry. After all, they were just more Americans trying to make a living in lean times. To make sure of the continuation of that support, the distillery operators were very generous with locals, especially those who contributed to their security arrangements. In the case of the homestead, that generosity extended to the weekly delivery of a hundred-pound sack of either raw sugar or feed corn or barley.

And so it came to be that one of the bootlegger families, a Mr. and Mrs. Pond and their two children, Helen and Wendell, moved into Grandma's cabin near the end of the summer of 1931, just before school was about to start. Helen was a year younger than E.J., making her about ten, and Wendell was just a little older. The generous rent money, received monthly in cash in an unmarked envelope from bootlegger headquarters, went to buy more materials and bring the payments on the Buick up to date. The Ponds, including Helen and Wendell, were refined, mannerly people and caused no distress by their presence. They were, of course, "city folk" so there was a certain distance maintained between themselves and the Willow Springs community. The kids, however, were totally unconcerned about social standing or economic level and managed to get along together without discrimination or distinction (other than that which has to do with age), which still left Spud Murphy in uncontested possession of the bottom rung of the social ladder.

At the same time that the Pond family moved into Grandma's cabin, Katherine took up residence again at the homestead in preparation for the start of school, which was a quite normal thing for those times. She was part of the family, after all, the only child of a widowed mother, and would otherwise have had no one to care for her after school until Aunt Mary came home from work. And what is one more mouth to feed, anyway?

E.J.'s progress after leaving Sunmount was nearly miraculous. Along with a lot of other precautions taken before she moved to the homestead, Mac had taken a sample of the well water to the state testing lab in Sacramento. The results were a long time coming back, but when they did, they showed that a considerable amount of arsenic was present in the water. It isn't clear from what medical authority the information came, but Mac somehow determined that the arsenic had a beneficial influence on E.J.'s anemia and contributed to the improvement of her health. At any rate, Dr. Foster, his confidence once more restored in his own medical wizardry, even though he didn't buy into the arsenic theory, pronounced her fit to go to school.

Elsie commenced her school-bus-driving duties on the first day of school in the fall of 1931. All six kids, sporting shiny, scrubbed faces, loaded into the Essex with hands clutching lard pails filled with sandwiches and apples and Elsie's legendary oatmeal cookies with raisins. The Essex didn't have a self-starter, or if it had one, it just didn't work. At any rate, if there was no hill to coast down to start, the old buggy had to be cranked. That was probably the reason for Mac choosing to build the house near the top of a hill. On the fateful morning, with the transmission in second gear, Elsie released the brake and pushed in the clutch, heading down the hill from the house. With the car rolling along at a pretty good clip, she turned on the ignition switch and let the clutch out and as Spud Murphy yelled "Contact!" the motor roared into life The car lurched a couple of times like a barefoot boy who had just stepped on a sharp rock and came to a dead stop except for one of the back wheels which went rolling along past the car, down the hill through the gate and beyond, picking up speed as it rolled, until it reached the far side of the meadow, where it went bouncing and crashing up into the bushes for another fifty feet.

Elsie and Jack retrieved the errant wheel and enough of whatever other parts had fallen off to fasten it back on again. The car had to be jacked up and the wheel fastened back in place, after which the school bus was back in operation again. I don't suppose anyone who hasn't driven a nineteen-twenties automobile with wood spoke wheels could understand how such a thing could happen— or having happened, that it could be repaired so simply by a fourteen-year-old schoolboy and his unmechanical mother— but it could and was. The only consequence of their harrowing flirtation with disaster was that the Essex group was noticeably late for school, which fact Spud Murphy explained in detail in the report he later gave to Mac on the incident of the three-wheeled car. Teacher said that tardiness is not the approved way to start off a new school year, but she said that in this case the circumstances made it understandable. And, since the Essex people represented a third of the entire student body, she had little recourse but to forgive and forget, a quality very much in evidence in her nature, anyway.

Driving anywhere in the Essex was an adventure, especially with Elsie at the wheel. Not that she wasn't a good driver. She was careful to a fault, and courteous beyond reason. It was simply because in her hands mechanical things no longer worked in accordance with the rules of Newtonian physics. It was just one of the rare, inexplicable mysteries of life. Perhaps it was that facet of her being which prompted Mac to carefully teach Spud Murphy the fundamentals of the water distribution system and assign its operation to his care.

On its way to school Latrobe Road crossed an old miner's ditch that in these later times carried irrigation water to the ranches lying along its winding course until it finally terminated at an abandoned hydraulic mining site at Michigan Bar. As the road approached the canal crossing, it rose precipitously to match the elevation of the top of the concrete box culvert used to convey the water under the road. Gloriously, after crossing the culvert, the road descended just as precipitously to return to its normal elevation. The common name for such an irregularity in the road elevation was a "whoopee bump" because it offered the passengers the opportunity to yell "WHOOPEE!" if the car passed over it with any speed at all. It also tended to leave one's stomach somewhere else during the descent. It had a kind of roller coaster effect.

Day by day the kids begged Elsie to go increasingly faster over the whoopee bump, which request she timorously declined until one day, in a surprising reversal of character, she gave in to the sudden urge to satisfy her passengers and at the same time experience the ultimate thrill one time herself. The take-off was everything one could have hoped for, but the impact on landing broke the battery carrier, which was under the floor boards, disemboweling the poor Essex, which had always given such yeoman service through the family's times of greatest needs. Its momentum carried it for a distance down the road, dragging its battery by the connecting cables, and there it died. Once more Elsie and Jack stuffed things back together enough so the car got safely home, but the poor old girl had received what proved to be a terminal blow. Soon afterward Mac brought home a 1923 Studebaker Brougham (with hard fabric top and opera windows) and the Essex was relegated to Mac's list of pending projects, to be transformed someday into a stationary cutoff saw for sizing firewood to length for the kitchen stove (and for the fireplace which had yet to be built.) But reincarnation in her new life was not before the old girl had performed one more important task as a farm utility vehicle.

Frank White, the rancher to the southeast of the homestead, had a big Holstein cow with a white-face calf at her side and Frank had decided to dehorn her for some reason known only to himself. He wasn't milking her, so it's hard to say what he was going to do with her, or why he wanted to saw her horns off, but after he got one of them off she broke out of the dehorning chute and nobody could catch her. Frank offered to sell her on the hoof to Mac for five dollars if Mac could catch her, providing Mac would give him back the calf after it was weaned. She was running loose on about three hundred acres and nobody had been able to even get near her, which is why Mac could buy her so cheap. The calf could have been part of the reason she was so independent-minded. Spud Murphy and Jack finally pushed her up into a fence corner and got a rope on her. Neither of them ever saw a wilder cow than that nor a bigger one, and never expected to. They snubbed her up to the spare tire on the Essex and with Jack driving got her through several gates and down about a quarter mile of county road and home.

Jack was about fourteen then and Elsie gave him the job of milking her. Spud Murphy was milking Katie and a pretty little Guernsey Mac had bought that was called "E.J.'s heifer", because she was supposed to belong to E.J., both of them being first heifers, which the dairies used to sell cheap during the hard years of the Depression. The reason for that became obvious when the heifer started to drop her calf prematurely and the whole family spent the night in the corral delivering a dead calf by lantern light and trying to save its mother, which they did, barely. After that E.J. got tired of everyone calling her heifer E.J.'s heifer and changed her name to "Rosy."

After Spud Murphy got the milking assignment he said "If E.J. owns her, she ought to be the one to milk her." Elsie gave him her most loving smile and said, "Well, we could help her out for a little while, dear, don't you think? Just until she gets a little stronger and is able to be up and about?" Spud Murphy wondered who, outside of himself, made up the 'we' she was referring to. Besides, Rosy had teats so small you could only get one finger and a thumb on them which doesn't make milking any picnic, especially if you've got big hands for a six-year-old.

Most cows will frequently kick to knock the bucket out from between your knees and spill the milk. There is nothing malicious about it. It's just a game. Or maybe they're getting fly-bit. They don't mean any harm, but just when you get a gallon or so of milk in the bucket, Bang! Clang! and then they twist their head around in the stanchion and look at you with those big brown limpid eyes and smile. If a smile could be expressed in words, the words for that particular one would be 'Boy, what a JERK you are!'

With Patsy, however, such kicking clearly had nothing to do with games, nor was it a random reflex brought on by fly bites, the breeze, or any other act of nature. When Patsy kicked, she did so with the express intention of killing or maiming you. The way you milk a cow that won't stand still is to make sure you have a stool that is high enough to put your head up into her flank, so your head is sort of a wedge between her leg and her belly. That way, when she kicks, she kicks herself in the belly, even though it's by way of your head. If that doesn't solve the problem, you hobble the cow, and that's when, if they get too rambunctious, things can really get out of hand. What happened on this particular occasion was that when Jack got ready to start milking he neglected to make sure that the hobbles were secure. True to her disposition, old Patsy snatched her foot out and was striking out in all directions with it. Jack was clearly on the defensive, trying to save what milk he had while getting tangled up with the milking stool and then, just as everything was for a split second lined up and clear for a straight-in shot, POW! I'll bet you'll never guess where she kicked him. If you ever want to hear a fourteen-year-old boy scream and cuss in pain, that's clearly the way to do it.

There was a three-tine pitchfork leaning against the stanchion; that being the first thing that came to hand Jack swung it down on her shoulder, and then, realizing what he had a hold of, he buried it in her belly.

There was a whole lot of confusion and yelling going on, with Jack howling in pain, and Spud Murphy cheering everything on. (They always had their separate ways of seeing things, because of that eight-year age difference, even later when they grew up enough to start liking each other a little.) When Elsie heard all the commotion she came running out from the kitchen to the corral. She got the pitchfork away from Jack and out of Patsy's belly before giving Spud Murphy a couple of whacks with it for having such a good time about Jack's difficulties and thinking every thing was so funny. She also decided, in that instant, that Spud Murphy could do ALL the milking, including Patsy, from that time on. To finish getting the hobbles off Patsy they had to bulldog her, which made it a good thing that she still had at least that one horn on, to get her down on the ground, getting a rope around her hind feet so she was stretched out and couldn't kick

When Spud Murphy brought the milk in he asked Elsie why he had to do all the milking. She said, "It's not punishment. It's just a better arrangement of the work. Jack needs to get the fence work finished, and he's not as fast a milker as you are. You're not big enough to drive fence posts. This way, everybody gets to do what they're best suited to. That makes life a lot easier." Spud Murphy thought that what he was best suited to was riding around on Old Bill checking up on the neighborhood or laying out on the rocks down at the river on a warm afternoon, but he didn't bother to say so.

A few days later at milking time Mac was working on something in the granary and Spud Murphy, bucket in hand, told him what Elsie had said. Mac was rolling a cigarette and he eyed Spud Murphy over the paper full of Bull Durham saying, "Well, son, it's all got to be done. And your mother's right. That's why she's boss." Later, when Spud Murphy was finishing up on Patsy, who, because of the size of her teats turned out to be the easiest milker of the three, Mac was rolling another cigarette and he said, "You know, I'd milk sometimes, but with my hands so callused from working at the shops all day, a cow just won't let her milk down for me." Since Mac was looking off in the other direction and not at Spud Murphy, Spud Murphy cocked his head and squinted his eyes under raised eyebrows, saying nothing at all, but parroting an expression he had often seen Mac use in questioning someone's credibility. That night when he was closing up the chicken house, he went into the roost and holding the lantern up so its light shined into the blinking eyes of a white leghorn rooster, he said in his best Edward G. Robinson imitation, "Okay, sonny, let's just cut to the chase, here. Why don't you just explain to me now about all of those calluses, wise guy."

E.J. didn't bring all the harmony to the homestead that you might have thought she would, now that the novelty of having her at home was wearing off and her health was getting better. According to the billing she was getting when all the brush cutting was going on, you'd have thought she was a real angel, but at times she turned into a real little snitch. Maybe it was just part of being a girl, but it seemed to Spud Murphy that being at Sunmount had focused her mind too narrowly on manners and proper language and such. Maybe her fellow roommates were too prissy or she just read too much of Louisa May Alcott and Kate Douglas Wiggin for her own good. Elsie would on occasion correct Spud Murphy's grammar but E.J. went at it like a pedantic old schoolmarm, Emily Post and Father Edward J. Flanagan all rolled into one.

There was a day when Spud Murphy had reason to keep the geese locked up in the chicken coop, most likely because he needed to do some work in the well, and he didn't want the geese dirtying up the water while the well-house door was open. It was raining, and doing anything in the rain with animals is twice as hard as when the weather's dry. Except for turkeys— who are so dumb that they'll stand out in the rain looking up at the sky open-mouthed until they drown themselves— most animals, even those that shed water, try to find shelter during a rain storm, likely under a tree, and consequently are hard to get to go anyplace else where you might think they ought to be. Every time Spud Murphy got the geese headed toward the chicken coop, with Abdul's help, the old gander would start honking and flapping his wings in mutinous disregard and lead the whole flock back around behind Spud Murphy to head off in some new direction. Spud Murphy kept getting more and more exasperated and started pummeling the geese with rocks when they evaded him

E.J. was standing in the outhouse door, watching the show and silently enjoying Spud Murphy's frustrations while she waited for enough letup in the rain so she could run back into the house and continue with her fourth reading of Rebecca of Sunnybrook Farm. Eventually frustrated by the intransigent gander beyond any ability to think in a rational manner, Spud Murphy erupted, charging at the flock of geese and yelling a string of profanities ending with "You rotten, lousy, vermin— get in that chicken coop!" at the top of his lungs and sending a barrage of rocks at Ephraim. Well, that sent E.J. into the house a' flying, regardless of the downpour, where she made a full report of the whole sorry matter to Elsie, who she certainly hoped would have a serious discussion with Spud Murphy about his abominable use of such vile language, including taking the Lord's name in vain.

When Spud Murphy saw E.J. go flying off in the direction of the house, he knew the jig was up so he preempted the necessity of being sent for and headed in that direction himself. Elsie was again in the process of kneading bread dough, which job had become, with all the boarders, a daily necessity, while she listened to E.J.'s indictment of Spud Murphy on charges of blasphemy as well as numerous other transgressions. When E.J. was through delivering her outrage about Spud Murphy's language, Elsie, continuing to knead the dough, said thoughtfully to Spud Murphy, "Well, you know, Spud Murphy, I honestly don't think Ephraim and his family even know what those words mean, so I believe that you're either going to have to find some way of explaining it to them or else go get a can of dried corn out of the granary and see if you can't convince Ephraim to follow you to wherever it is you want him to go. Chasing geese around in the rain doesn't sound as though it would be the smartest thing to do, or much fun, either."

Spud Murphy got along well with Patsy from the start. Evidently she figured out that if she had to be milked anyway, better him than Jack. He noticed that her teats were all cracked and bleeding so before he even tried milking her he got the can of bag balm out of the granary and greased her up plenty. He tied the calf up to a gate post where Patsy could see she was all right and in no time at all Patsy was half milked out. Then he untied the calf and let him have the other side and when that was done he washed her udder good and greased her up once more with bag balm.

Patsy was an easy milker, once you got to the actual milking part of the project. Unlike Rosy, she had great big teats that you could really get a good hold of and when her bag was full you could get about a half-cup full at a time out of each teat, maybe more. With a full teat she had a range of about thirty feet. The three resident cats at the time, which Mac named Ike, Mike and Spike, in spite of the fact they were all spayed girl cats, would sit around in a quarter-circle about fifteen feet out from where the milk production was taking place. They'd patiently wait there, guarding their territory and watching every move made until one of them would suddenly get a stream of milk right in the snoot compliments of Spud Murphy's unerring accuracy. He would aim over their heads high enough to cause them to stand on their hind feet with their mouth open, flailing at the stream of milk with their front paws, as if they could catch it and hold it in mid-air.

As much as Spud Murphy made fun of those cats, they had an important job to do and that was to let it be known when a rattlesnake was around the house. They'd surround it or pen it in a corner somewhere and then they'd snarl and spit with the hair standing up on their backs until one of the family members or other homestead dwellers would hear the commotion and come out with a .22 and shoot the snake.

No matter how much was owed the cats for standing snake watch, there was one place they dared not go, and that was inside the house. Elsie always had pans of milk covered with cheesecloth spread out on a long counter that ran the length of the kitchen wall. Some of the pans had fresh milk where the cream was rising, waiting to be skimmed off for use as whipping cream or for churning butter. Others had sour milk waiting to clabber as the first step in making cheese. One day Elsie came in and found all three cats on the counter lapping up milk. Quicker then you could say "Jack Robinson," Ike came shooting out through the back porch screen door airborne and the other two were right behind her. Spud Murphy commented later that he thought for a moment it had taken to raining cats. He got out of there right away, before he had to answer a lot of dumb questions, like who in heaven's name left the darned screen door unhooked? (Which was about all the cuss words that Elsie knew, or made use of, anyway.)

Another animal that's good to have around if you're pestered by rattlesnakes is an old gander. Ganders are nasty, obnoxious creatures anyway. They'll sneak up behind you and clamp down with their bill on whatever part of your anatomy that is available and even if the injury isn't all that critical, it sure does startle the daylights out of you to have that happen. A natural enmity existed between Patsy and Ephraim. Whenever he'd get within range of her she'd drop her head like a Tijuana bull and charge him.

When an occasional rattler would make it through the cat defenses, that old gander's neck would stiffen up and stretch out until you'd think it was a lethal weapon. He would spread his wings as though he was going to launch himself like some kind of a missile with a fully operational warhead on the end of his neck where his head should be. The gander would be hissing and honking and the rattle snake rattling and between them they'd raise a pretty good ruckus until the rattler would decide to hell with it and just crawl off to some other place that was less hostile.

Getting back to Patsy, it happened that one time on a hot summer day she was doing what she liked best, which was to lay under a digger pine up by the corrals, meditatively chewing her cud as cows do, eyes half closed, a vacant look clouding her expression and her attention appearing to be fixed on absolutely nothing. As was normal, a bunch of flies was pestering her and her tail was on autopilot, doing its prescribed business of stirring up the flies every so often, sort of like the windshield wiper of a modern automobile set for a little pause between the strokes.

It could have been that Ephraim, coming on the scene unexpected as he did, misunderstood the whole situation, taking the sudden movement of Patsy's tail for the lightening strike of a timber rattler. In any case, he did what he had to do, and with a mighty *HONK* launched himself at the offending tail.

Patsy bolted up, more in the manner of "The Strawberry Roan" than the slow and cumbersome way a cow usually gets up, and when she came back to earth she was running and bucking and bawling in a fashion that would have done credit to the top bucking bull at the county fair rodeo. Ephraim couldn't do much by then but hang on, so that's what he did, sailing along on outstretched wings all the way down to the "flat," the big open meadow that was a quarter mile below the house and corrals and halfway to Leighton's cabin. They were too far away by then to see just how or why Ephraim finally managed to dismount, but later on when he made an appearance back at the barnyard Spud Murphy noticed his feathers were all stuck together with dried cow manure. When Frank White heard the story he said, "I don't doubt it none. That's just exactly the way that ole cow left the dehorning chute. One horn off and t'other still on, just a'bellerin' and a'gittin'!"

There was one more piece of unattended business that had yet to be undertaken that fall. The Homestead Act of 1862 specified that certain requirements be satisfied prior to issuance of patent. Aside from the requirement that the homesteader had to be a citizen or show his intent to become one, he or she had to build a livable house and dig a well on the homestead, fence a portion of it, live on it for five years, cultivate some unspecified part of it and then induce two citizens to sign an affidavit to the effect that all those conditions had been met. Only the five-year residency and the cultivation requirement remained between Mac and the rights of property ownership. The five-year residency was just a matter of continuing to live on the homestead for the requisite five years. Mac decided it was time to get busy on the cultivation requirement.

Cultivation amounted to more than simply plowing the land and sowing it in some kind of crop or other. Of the forty acres, there were only ten that had enough soil to grow anything other than greasewood, manzanita or toyon bushes. The rest was bedrock right up to just inches below the ground surface. The first thing that had to be done was clear the brush and the boulders off the ten acres, which existed in two separate plots of about five acres each. With as many hands as there were now to help, the clearing went fast. The girls were now the brush pilers and Spud Murphy, along with Jack,. was swinging a full-sized single-bit cruiser axe. He did notice, however, that in spite of some good-sized calluses that he was acquiring, he still had to milk the cows and, somehow, they still all managed to let down their milk.

They stacked the brush and Mac burned it, being careful not to set the countryside on fire. The bigger stumps Mac pulled out of the earth with the Buick, or blasted with dynamite. When the clearing was finished Mac took some timbers that had seen previous service as railroad ties and bridge timbers and built a stone-boat, to gather the boulders from the fields that had been cleared for planting. Spud Murphy, wondering where the team was supposed to come from to pull the stone-boat, finally concluded that it was Mac's intent to use the Buick for that purpose, as he now used it for everything else, since the Essex was retired.

You can imagine Spud Murphy's surprise when Elsie and Mac took off in the Buick after breakfast one morning and came back an hour later with Elsie driving the Buick and Mac driving Bill and Wallace hitched to a hay wagon with a spike-tooth harrow and a single-bottom moldboard plow in the wagon bed. He tried not to pay too much attention when Bill nickered at him, but he found it convenient to stand close by while Mac was hitching him to the stone-boat, to stroke Bill's nose a little and give him a couple of pats on his shoulder. To be fair, he gave Wallace the same treatment.

Spud Murphy just sort of took over as drover when the rock gathering began. At first he watched Mac roll a huge boulder on the stone-boat and as he straightened, scoop up the reins and with the gentlest touch turn the team to bring the stone-boat alongside the next boulder, which Jack was waiting to roll aboard. Spud Murphy, supposed to be throwing smaller rocks on the stone-boat with Katherine and E.J. as it went from boulder to boulder, began clucking to Bill and Wallace as he saw Mac pick up the reins, so the team was moving by the time the reins were in his hand. It wasn't long before the reins were looped over the hames and the chinstrap of Bill's headstall was in Spud Murphy's hand as they moved across the field, the girls running alongside to throw the smaller rocks in.

At lunchtime Mac said in an aside to Elsie, with Spud Murphy out of earshot, "I got a hunch that kid and that white horse met someplace before." Elsie, who had been brushing white horse hairs off Spud Murphy's jeans for months, said, "Oh, do you think so? Well, you very well may be right."

They pulled the stone-boat with its load of rocks near to the front door of the living room and with a four-part block and tackle Mac rigged to the limb of the huge oak tree that stood there they tilted the sled and rolled the boulders off into a pile as material with which to build the living room fireplace. After they had enough fireplace rocks piled up to build a couple of fireplaces, they began to fill the dozens of "coyote holes" on the property from which chromite-bearing serpentine was mined during The Great War.

Before the rains came, they broadcast barley in the plot above the house where the deepest soil was and then made a final pass with the spike-tooth harrow to cover the seed. In the other five-acre plot over the ridge down toward Whites' they planted brome, which was a native grass. In the spring there was a nice stand of barley, but where the brome was planted it was love's labor lost. The soil on that side of the ridge was just too sterile and thin. The quail all seemed to be getting fatter eating the non-germinating seeds, however.

Seven

There was no kindergarten at Willow Springs Elementary School, and even if there had been, it is unlikely that Spud Murphy would have attended. At the age of six he was already a proficient reader, enjoying books and short stories about Indian life and early pioneering settlements probing into the Hudson River Valley and the Great Lakes region, and other areas to the south along the colonial frontier. The intellectual environment he grew up in, coupled with the intensive tutoring of Elsie and Grandma, combined to provide him with a more-than-adequate foundation from which to conquer the more stringent requirements of the higher-grade levels. The competition that had developed early on between Grandma and Elsie to be his mentor, and the certainty with which Mac held to the belief that one of his own lineage must of necessity have a naturally endowed intellectual superiority, were often sources of great frustration to him. This double-edged system of keeping the pressure on him served to achieve the intended goal, although not always in a way that was wholly benign in its effect on Spud Murphy.

In any case, because he was only six years old, Teacher's wisdom prevailed, and 'for his own good' he was not allowed to skip first grade, although he was certainly qualified to do so from a purely academic standpoint. Spud Murphy joined the Class of 1938 of Willow Springs Grammar School, together with its two other members, Lola Stone and Boogee Waters, and spent his time writing endless lines of script while Lola and Boogee learned to read.

Lola lived with her grandmother, Mrs. Hinkston, whose last name was troubling to Spud Murphy because it was not the same as Lola's last name, although Lola's father was Floyd Stone, which worked out okay. Elsie explained it all to Spud Murphy and it prompted him to ask about his own maternal grandparents, who Elsie advised him were both gone to a greater glory, and his paternal grandfather, who, if not dead, was certainly among the missing. His conclusion from that was that every family should have at least one complete set of grandparents, preferably paternal, so they would all have the same last name and not be named differently as in Lola's situation.

Mrs. Hinkston's property was about a mile down-river from the Ball place, right next to Charlie Lorentz's at the end of Lorentz Road. And that was another thing. Spud Murphy didn't think the road should be named after Mr. Lorentz when his kids weren't even old enough to be in school at that particular time, like Mrs. Hinkston and Floyd Stone did. Besides, the Lorentz's hardly ever came to the P.T.A. meetings unless it was an election or something.

Spud Murphy liked Lola, even though it was kind of a hard thing to do when other kids and especially grown-ups wanted to kid you all the time about having a girl-friend and ask you when you planned on getting married and stupid things like that. It bothered Lola even more than Spud Murphy and so they acted all the way up to fifth grade as if they didn't even know each other.

Boogee was the first boy of his own approximate size, age, and inclination that Spud Murphy had ever seen from an up-close perspective. It had never really occurred to him that any such other than himself might have existed anywhere on the planet, not that he would ever have taken the time to think about it. There were none who had lived in his immediate neighborhood in Colonial Heights, and certainly none had ever come to the homestead in the eighteen months that he and Elsie had lived there. The only boys of any age he knew on a first-name basis were Wendell Pond and Jack, and they were enough older and unlike him as to be members of another species. In the seventh grade, Wendell actually wore a bow tie to school.

Thus far Spud Murphy's cultural peers had been limited to Loraine Mason, the daughter of Reg Mason, mandolin and banjo player with the Sierra Ranch Hands, and to an endless number of girls of Katherine and E.J.'s age who brought their favorite dolls to backyard tea parties or lived most of the younger portion of their lives within the antiseptic confines of Sunmount Preventorium. Until he found his own heritage among the Wyandotte, Algonquin and other such aboriginal tribes on the pages of Boy's Life' & Youth's Companion, Spud Murphy even had his own favorite doll to lug to tea parties, thanks to the extreme thoughtfulness of his older sister. It is indeed a fortunate thing that he learned to read at a very early age or he might never have found out first-hand what being a boy was about.

Boogee's real name was Norman. He had an older sister Mary and another older sister Norma, who was the same age as E.J. He also had a brother John, and another brother Willard, who bore about the same age and tolerance relationship to him that Jack bore to Spud Murphy. Willard suffered from infantile paralysis. Boogee's family lived a couple of miles east of Willow Springs

Grammar School on Highway 16, just past Wait's Station on the way to Central House, which was where the high school bus stop was located.

Spud Murphy spent the night at Boogee's house a couple of times. The first time, they passed the day wandering along the banks and through some of the not-so-shallow pools of Willow Creek, looking for turtles to turn over on their backs so they could investigate their abilities and methods of getting back on their feet again from that unusual position.. The second time he was invited to stay overnight, he wet the bed so they never invited him back again. After a few years of thinking about it, it didn't distress him all that much. Some people have been known to let something like that ruin their life. Spud Murphy actually directed most of his concern toward the turtle population of the world.

Now that some sort of order had been imposed on life by the advancing state of the homestead development, the coming back together of the family members, and the start of school, and ever mindful of Grandma's admonition that "idle hands are the devil's workshop," Mac and Elsie decided it was time for Spud Murphy to begin his musical career. With the addition of the fireplace, the living room was near enough complete to allow Elsie to acquire from some source on a temporary arrangement an upright Kimball piano, primarily so E.J. could continue the piano lessons she had been taking before she went to Sunmount, but also to allow Elsie to pursue her own musical interests. It was only a natural assumption that Spud Murphy would also embark on some sort of a musical education. When the question came up, he did make mention of his heavy schedule which included keeping the wood box full, pumping and watering, milking, feeding the livestock and providing other services on demand, but Elsie was not much impressed and after that balloon was pricked Spud Murphy didn't even bother bringing the issue up with Mac. When he was hesitant about playing the piano, he was given his choice of piano or violin. He chose the violin based solely on his newly acquired masculinity factor. All the little girls he knew took piano lessons, including Katherine and E.J., while the only violinists he knew of were Ariel, Fritz Kreisler (by reputation only) and Bob Wills of The Texas Playboys (by radio). On consideration of the stature and qualifications of these three outstanding examples of fiddle virtuosity he looked forward to his forthcoming introduction to musicianship with a surprising degree of acceptance.

The first thing that happened to dampen his enthusiasm was the discovery that his violin teacher wasn't going to be Ariel, as one would have assumed, but a young lady, the daughter of Raymond Wann, for whom Mac had done some remodeling work. That may easily have been because there was additional remodeling Mr. Wann needed to have done, which could have formed the basis of 'a trade in kind' for the lessons. The Wann house was right on the way to school and very near the schoolhouse. One day a week Spud Murphy walked home from school, carrying his violin case under his arm and stopping at Goula Wann's for his music lesson. It was five-miles from school to the homestead but he liked the walk. It gave him plenty of time to be lost in fantasies of stagecoaches, red Indians, cowboys, the North-West Mounted Police, and for exploring along the way.

The second disenchantment came on the day of his first lesson, when he arrived at the Wann house just in time to witness the last half of Lola Stone's very first violin lesson. The reason she was that much ahead of him was because her grandmother drove her in the car. Her entry into the world of music coinciding with his, as it did, had both social and competitive consequences that complicated his life in many easily imaginable ways. Wetting Boogee's bed you can get over in time. Sharing a musical education with Lola Stone in a school with a total enrollment of only sixteen students, a number that defies anonymity, has enduring psychological consequences that are not so easily set aside.

The Sierra Ranch Hands came up to the homestead several times that fall, for practice sessions or just because the atmosphere of the Depression was closing in like a dark cloud over everyone's head in the city, and people needed to be doing things that brought them together. It seemed that music went a long way toward getting peoples' minds off their economic problems and focused on less painful subjects. The national unemployment figure in the spring of 1931 had passed eight million and was steadily rising in a work force of approximately fifty million.

In the fall Mac and Elsie collaborated in writing and producing a melodrama for the Willow Springs P.T.A. Christmas program. Spud Murphy played the juvenile male lead of Greg Grimsby whose parents had become so poor during the Depression that they hadn't enough food for Christmas dinner, and couldn't afford to buy little Greg a Christmas present, and were faced with the task of maintaining his belief in love, faith, trust, and justice, et cetera, in the face of the evil machinations of the wicked saloon keeper. Although intended to be a humorous farce, it turned out to be a real tearjerker. The audience was overcome with grief, which they all tried to hide when the lights came up, but at least for a while their feelings were directed away from their own hardships. It was so much a success in that regard that some of the cast wanted to take it on the road, but Mac vetoed that idea because he thought satire might be too difficult a concept for a lot of country folk to handle, considering the times, and he could never live it down if a production of his bombed, especially in Plymouth.

Seven

Every enduring friendship must have its defining moment. Such a moment comes when one's commitment to the welfare of another rises to a zenith beyond which no greater sacrifice on behalf of the other can be conceived. The defining moment of Grandma's relationship with Spud Murphy reached that pinnacle one Sunday afternoon when they were home alone and found themselves confronted with one of life's real tragedies. Surely, no greater test of love could ever have been devised.

As has been noted, Spud Murphy was the proud owner of a pair of six-shooter cap pistols. In the fall of 1931, when he had just turned six years old and was immersed in his Wyatt Earp years, fancying himself to be the reincarnation of that famous dispenser of frontier justice who by that time had been deceased for two years, having passed away in some sleepy little town on the outskirts of Los Angeles in Southern California. In discharging his responsibilities as a deputy U.S. marshal of Tombstone, in Arizona Territory, Spud Murphy found it necessary to be armed at all times. So he wore his six-guns even when practicing the violin and milking the cows. The only time he took them off was when he left for school or was sleeping or going to the bathroom.

Of course the word bathroom in this case is a euphemism. Baths were taken on Saturday night in a galvanized laundry tub by the kitchen stove. Aside from the washtub in the kitchen, the other utility that is ordinarily associated with a bathroom was provided by a "backhouse," and from that circumstance arose Spud Murphy's distress on this particular afternoon when he and Grandma were home alone

Backhouses often have multiple holes, for various reasons. Some say, as in the works of Mr. Riley, that it is to accommodate various-sized behinds. Another opinion, which Spud Murphy inclined toward, involved the economy of digging one long hole in the earth versus several small shorter holes. Obviously, a longer excavation requires that some flexibility be provided as to where one sits above the excavation so that the entire length of it is available for filling. Hence, more holes.

When Spud Murphy unbuckled his gun belt, he laid it on the seat close by his particular hole of choice, between that hole and the next adjacent one, and then he heisted himself up on the seat to do what he had come there for. The door to the backhouse he left open since there was no one at the homestead except himself and Grandma and he liked to keep an eye out for rustlers whenever possible. After some time had passed in contemplative observation, a cottontail came up the path that led to the backhouse door and sat there for a moment, looking in. Believing it to be the outlaw Ike Clanton, Spud Murphy grabbed for one of his six-guns from the gun belt that lay beside him and in the sudden exhilaration of the pending shoot-out knocked the whole works— gun belt, holsters, guns and all— into the hole and thence downward to the nether regions below.

Spud Murphy was aghast at what he had done. In utter despair, he began to cry. His treasured cap pistols were his most priceless of all possessions, more sacred to him than anything in the world and to his certain knowledge irreplaceable in those economic times. From inside the house Grandma heard him sobbing and found him on the back steps, Abdul sitting beside him and compassionately licking the tears off his face. When she had heard his sad tale, Grandma said, "Well, quit that crying and get me a lantern from the kitchen and a big water bucket out of the granary." While Spud Murphy did her bidding, she went to the woodshed and came out with a five-tined hand cultivator and a garden rake, both with long handles. An hour later, after the salvage operation was over and a lot of scrubbing and rinsing had been done with brush and garden hose, the bucket full of water was boiling on the wood stove in the kitchen, sterilizing the belt, holsters, and six-guns. It took a lot of rubbing with saddle soap and Neat's-foot oil to restore the belt and holsters after their hot water bath, and maybe they never again were quite as good for fast draw purposes, but for certain, a relationship of love had met its defining moment and survived with flying colors. That evening in front of the fireplace, when Mac heard the story of the afternoon's events, he memorialized it with a recitation of Mr. Riley's poem.

The Passing of the Backhouse

By James Whitcomb Riley

When memory keeps me company and moves to smile or tears,
A weather-beaten object looms, through the mist of years,
Behind the house and barn it stood, a quarter mile or more,
And hurrying feet a path had made, straight to its swinging door.
Its architecture was a type of simple classic art,
But in the tragedy of life, it played a leading part.
And oft the passing traveler drove slow and heaved a sigh,
To see the modest hired girl slip out with glances shy.

We've had our Posey garden that the women loved so well;
I loved it too, but better still I loved the stronger smell
That filled the evening breezes, so full of homely cheer,
And told the night-o'ertaken tramp that human life was near.
On lazy August afternoons it made a little bower
Delightful, where my Grandpa sat and whiled away an hour.
For there the summer mornings, its very cares entwined,
And berry bushes reddened in the streaming soil behind.

All day fat spiders spun their webs to catch the buzzing flies
That flitted to and from the house, where Ma was baking pies.
And once a swarm of hornets bold had built their palace there
And stung my unsuspecting Aunt – I must not tell you where.
My father took a flaming pole –that was a happy day –
He nearly burned the building up, but the hornets left to stay.

Homestead

When summer bloom began to fade and winter to carouse,
We banked the little building with a heap of hemlock boughs.

But when the crust was on the snow and sullen skies were gray,
Inside the building was no place where one would wish to stay.
We did our duties promptly, there one purpose swayed the mind;
We tarried not, nor lingered long, on what we left behind.
The torture of that icy seat would make a Spartan sob,
For needs must scrape the goose flesh with a lacerating cob,
That from a frost-encrusted nail suspended from a string–
My father was a frugal man and wasted not a thing.

When Grandpa had to "go out back" and make his morning call,
We'd bundle up the dear old man with muffler and a shawl.
I knew the hole on which he sat–'twas padded all around,
And once I tried to sit there–'twas all too wide I found,
My loins were all too little, and I jack-knifed there to stay,
They had to come and get me out, or I'd have passed away,
My father said ambition was a thing that boys should shun,
And best I used the children's hole 'til childhood's days were done.

And still I marvel at the craft that cut those holes so true,
The baby's hole, and the slender hole that fitted Sister Sue,
That dear old country landmark; I tramped around a bit,
And in the lap of luxury my lot has been to sit,
But ere I die I'll eat the fruits of trees I robbed of yore,
Then seek the shanty where my name is carved upon the door,
I ween that old familiar smell will soothe my jaded soul,
I'm now a man, but none the less, I'll try the children's hole.

When the Sierra Ranch Hands would come to the homestead,
it would usually be on a weekend and if it was good weather
they would stay overnight, rolling their bedrolls out on the
ground in the front yard. When they were getting their
instruments out and tuning up, Mac would tell Spud Murphy,
"Get your fiddle out, son," and then Ariel or one of the other

members of the orchestra would tune it for him. The first couple of times Mac told him to sit in, he was pretty self-conscious about his mostly discordant squawks and scratches, but they all encouraged him and treated him like he was really a coming fiddle player. He soon got over his self-consciousness and he was sawing away like he knew what he was doing, and it was not so long after that until he actually did know what he was doing. Ariel, being the orchestra's regular violinist, was Spud Murphy's main tutor, careful not to interfere with or detract from Goula's effectiveness as the primary source of his musical education, but helping him from time to time with the techniques and occasional embellishments that helped to make music out of his sawing. They all made their contribution to his musical knowledge at one time or another. One thing that Elsie saw to, however, was that no matter how much extracurricular exposure there was to the glamorous side of his musical world, the exercise regimen always came first and was never neglected.

After Spud Murphy had been Goula's student for about a year, Fritz Kreisler was booked at Sacramento's Memorial Auditorium for an evening engagement. Goula, wanting to breathe musical inspiration into her budding virtuosos, went to their parents with the proposition that they be allowed to attend the upcoming concert, in which case she would furnish transportation for the eighty-mile round trip and keep them out of harm's way on this pilgrimage. The students who made the journey were Frank and Roger McEwen, Lola Stone, and Spud Murphy.

Spud Murphy was elated. It was his first venture into the greater world without one or the other of his parents or his grandmother, and to go on a trip of that distance, especially with other children, and in someone else's car, was in itself inspirational. He felt like Magellan, setting out to circumnavigate the globe.

After standing in line with Goula and the others in despair that the seats would all be taken before they ever got inside, they finally found their way into the majestic edifice and gaped in awe at both the richly appointed grandeur of its foyer and the jostling throng of milling people waiting to enter the arched passageways to the orchestra seating, or climb the massive stairways to the balcony sections. He had never before thought a person could be made to feel so trivial and unimportant. It was remarked later by other concertgoers that he was seen actually holding Lola's hand among the press of this human tidal wave,

With the opening strains of Caprice Viennois, Spud Murphy drifted off into a peaceful slumber, waking at the concert's end with Goula tapping his shoulder and telling him "Wake up, dear, it's time to go home, now."

Elsie was a talented pianist but she rarely played with the Ranch Hands although the majority of their arrangements were done by her. Her stated reason for not playing with them was that she had a family to look after, but Spud Murphy suspected it had more to do with the competitive flame that frequently burned brightest when she and Mac got involved in any kind of collaborative effort of a musical nature. It seemed to Spud Murphy that Elsie was always suppressing her natural drive for recognition in order to more fully support Mac's aspirations.

Mac was a showman. In his "best of all worlds," music was normally an adjunct to some greater production. He had enough of a musical ear to distinguish or create what would serve as fundamental harmony— more than just a three-chord guitar picker, but even in his own words, not too far from that definition. Elsie, on the other hand, in addition to being a flawless pianist, equally brilliant whether the selection was "Rhapsody in Blue" or "Maple Leaf Rag," was also a perfectionist in the area of music theory. She saw it as her mission to be so, whether performing herself or communicating her musical transcriptions to the orchestra members. It frustrated her that Mac had, as he himself frequently admitted, "a tin ear." When they would start arguing about chord modulations and augmented sevenths and such, things were apt to get more than a little heated, with Elsie holding her own and inevitably making her point. Spud Murphy would put his hands over his ears, then, and if the debate went on long enough, he'd find a book to read and crawl behind the couch with it. Grandma, the musical theorist, would screw her face up into a look of violent distaste and leave the room.

The regular pianist with the Ranch Hands was Sally Bennett. She also played the accordion. Her husband, Harry, worked for the California State Testing Lab and took responsibility for helping Mac with the homestead in different kinds of ways. You couldn't really say Harry was a con man, but he certainly was a persuasive negotiator. It has been mentioned that he provided the equipment with which Mac was able to re-survey the homestead boundaries. At the same time Mac had been able to raise some much needed extra cash by re-establishing the boundaries of several adjoining properties for their owners.

Sally and Harry lived in an apartment in Sacramento where they kept a small, very old female Boston terrier named Spotty. Spotty was nearing the end of her life. She had a hard time controlling her biological urges and kept making messes in the apartment when no one was there to let her out. The Bennetts didn't want to have her put down, so they propositioned Spud Murphy to care for her on the homestead until she died a natural death. He didn't want to be paid for that, but they were insistent and Elsie said it would be okay, so every month he got a pay envelope with twenty-five cents in it. Mac helped Spud Murphy build Spotty a dog house next to Abdul's and about all Spud Murphy ever had to do after that was keep her water dish full and feed her and pet her a little bit now and then. He explained all the circumstances of her being there to Abdul, and Abdul treated Spotty with the respect and consideration that was her due because of her age. On the weekends when Spotty heard the Bennetts' car still far off just entering the flat, she would hobble down the drive as far as the well and meet them there. When she died it was very sad and Spud Murphy dug a grave halfway between the house and *the rock* and buried her there under a blue oak tree.

Spud Murphy's first public appearance as a violinist was in another of Mac's dramatic presentations, this one having to do with the mystic powers of the Eastern world as they are perceived in the arcane practice of telepathic communication. The entertainment value of the act relied heavily on artifice: role playing, lighting, mood music, makeup, costume and so on. The success of the ruse depended entirely on Mac and E.J.'s well-cultivated powers of memorization. The act followed a closely scripted routine.

The house lights dim to absolute darkness and the curtain rises on a darkened stage. With the curtain full open and the stage still in darkness a tiny bit of gunpowder is ignited at center stage and incense is wafted into the auditorium, simultaneously with the opening strains of "In A Persian Market," played on the violin by Spud Murphy, which continues through the chorus. The lights slowly come up sufficiently for one to discern the shadowed figure of Mac, turbaned and bejeweled, at center stage, with Pan-Cake-darkened skin. Spud Murphy is similarly made up but his skinny torso and spindly arms and legs are largely undraped and without adornment. He is upstage right, seated cross-legged with violin. E.J., very fair-skinned, is under a full spot with jeweled headdress, and is elegantly draped in a sari and decorously seated on luxuriant silver and gold brocade pillows, downstage left.

The music stops as an offstage male voice addresses the audience with an introduction to the mysticism of the Eastern world, the highly developed powers of concentration that are among the fundamental tools of mystics, and the need for absolute silence on the part of the audience while Princess Maharani is receiving the cerebral vibrations which contain the message being sent by the world-renowned Mullah, Mohammed Akbar Ahmad Muktar. After Princess Maharani is properly blindfolded by volunteer audience members, Ahmad Muktar goes about the audience receiving various objects and silently holding each article up for viewing by the audience before holding it tightly in his hand and concentrating his immense powers of thought transference so that Princess Maharani can identify the article. *What is it that I am now holding in my hand?* "I see....I see.....an elderly gentleman's gold-rimmed spectacles." *And what do I have here?* "That is a lady's watch." *And what kind of a watch, Princess?* "It is a lapel watch."

It took Spud Murphy a year to find out what the secret was-, because they never practiced the act in front of anyone, not even friends and family. After they dropped the act E.J. confided to Spud Murphy that the secret was in the words Mac used to phrase the question, which made a kind of code. Spud Murphy said, in a very deprecating way, "Well, anybody could do that. It's just too much work."

As for the audiences, some thought it was black magic and others thought it was vocal inflection or that the people in the audience from whom Ahmad Muktar got the articles were all plants or there was a hole in the blindfold, but a surprising number believed it was truly telepathic communication. Somehow, the real explanation rarely seemed to occur to people. It was, as Spud Murphy said, "Just a lot of hard work, memorizing what all those different words meant." After they were told how Mac and E.J. did it, they all said, "Well, sure, I knew *that* all the time. I thought you meant how it *really* works, how the Ay-rabs do it, you know."

Every summertime a primary focus of effort was toward getting up an adequate supply of stove and fireplace wood for the following winter. The main source of heat was the big cast-iron, wood-burning range in the kitchen. The homestead's range was an example of the enterprise and innovation that was always an identifying feature of homestead repair jobs. It happened that one cold December morning Mac got out of bed to go out behind the woodshed to relieve himself. Because of the frosty nature of the pre-dawn hours, he delayed until he could delay no longer, so that when he finally conceded to nature's call he was in quite a hurry. Due to the extreme chill of the night, Elsie had heated a flat iron on top of the kitchen range and taken it to bed with her, wrapped in an old flannel shirt, to ease the chill of the sheets and act as a foot warmer. Sometime during the night, when it had lost its effectiveness, she took the quasi-foot warmer from under the covers and put it on the floor at the foot of the bed.

Rounding the foot of the bed with cat-like speed and agility and aligned with unerring precision along the darkened route through the kitchen that would ultimately take him to relief, a route which he knew well from previous experience, Mac suddenly encountered the discarded flat iron while in mid-stride of what could easily have been mistaken for the approach to the football of a place kicker for the Green Bay Packers.

Mac was an accomplished master in the application of profanity and it probably could be agreed that on this occasion he had sufficient cause to employ such a talent, if ever a cause was needed for that purpose. When he finally could stop cussing and hopping around on his one remaining usable foot, he spotted the offending flat iron and lunging at it as if to crush it in his hands, he threw it with all his considerable strength in the direction he was aimed at the time, which happened to be precisely on line with the kitchen range. After the missile found its objective, it required a number of pieces of steel strap and a dozen or so stove bolts for Mac to stitch the fractured pieces back together enough for Elsie to be able to cook breakfast on it that morning.

Aside from the kitchen range as a source of indoor heat, there was also the living room fireplace, made entirely of large serpentine rocks that had been gathered during the pre-barley-planting preparations. The fireplace, when it was completed, was indeed a thing of beauty; and true to Mr. Keats's reflections on such matters, it was 'a joy forever' as well. Above the stone mantel were two pairs of manzanita pegs set in the mortar between the stone, each pair to hold a rifle. Spud Murphy asked Mac why there were two pairs, when they only had one rifle. Mac said, "Well, you can't tell, son, when another one might come along. It just pays to be prepared."

And finally, since the time of the flat iron incident, there was one more stove added, for which wood had to be cut. The new addition was a comfortable-looking little potbellied cast-iron stove that Mac installed in his and Elsie's bedroom, and from that time on, there was never, ever again a flat iron used to keep Elsie's feet warm at night or to warm up the bed, or for that matter, to be allowed in that bedroom for any reason whatsoever.

Oak was the normal fuel of choice, as it burned slow and put out heat at a consistent temperature. Oak was mostly saved for use in the fireplace. An oak fire could be banked up in the fireplace at night just before bedtime at eight o'clock and at four or five the next morning when you got up and all outdoors was white with frost, you would still have a bed of glowing coals there, even though the stoves in the kitchen and the bedroom would, by that time, be stone cold. On the other hand, if you wanted a cheery fire with dancing flames to read or play checkers by or just talk, you could throw a digger pine log dripping with pitch on the andirons. It wasn't wise to burn too much digger pine, though, because it produced so much creosote that the first thing you knew you'd have a whopping good chimney fire that would make such a roar in the chimney it would scare the daylights out of you. Worse than just the noise, lots of houses have burned down as a result of chimney fires. The biggest problem with digger pine, though, was that it was almost impossible to split into stove-sized pieces, what with its gnarled, twisted grain and numerous knots, so aside from the occasional need for a fireplace log, its use was pretty much limited to the smaller branches that yielded cordwood of a size to fit into the stove's firebox without splitting. As for toyon, or 'holly berry' as some called it, it was hard to start and keep burning and it didn't burn with much heat at all.

Far and away the hottest-burning cordwood came from the manzanita limbs, in which the homestead and the surrounding countryside abounded. When manzanita growth was fast and healthy, it cut fairly easy with a sharp cruiser axe, but when new cell growth stopped because of damage or disease or drought, the wood practically turned to iron and would wear the teeth right off the sharpest saw. You quickly learned not to let the manzanita dry out for too long before cutting it into stove lengths.

The woodshed was a good-sized building which held five cords of tightly stacked wood and still left plenty of room to move around in, and in addition, provided a whole wall full of shelves for vegetables and fruit and jams and pickles and venison all put up in quart mason jars. During the first couple of years, all the wood that was needed was that which went into the kitchen range, which was a fortunate thing, as it all had to be hand cut with a Swede saw, using a 'saw buck' to cradle the log or limb.

After the Essex was retired from active duty in the transportation service, Mac stripped all the body parts off her, leaving only the running gear, chassis, power train and engine. Then he fixed the right rear wheel so it couldn't turn and replaced the left rear wheel with a hub to which was attached a drive pulley. Directly above that pulley was another pulley fixed to an arbor-mounted shaft, at the opposite end of which was a twenty-four inch diameter circular cut-off saw. A pivoted carriage that tilted forward held the log or limb and carried it into the spinning saw blade to make the cut. Mac put blocks under the whole contraption to make it a semi-permanent installation right behind the woodshed.

There were no guards, or protective shields, or any other manner of safety devices incorporated into this rig and Mac forbade anyone on the homestead other than himself to operate it. Spud Murphy, probably for the first time in his life, did not disobey his father's injunction. It was patently obvious that the cutoff saw was a dangerous piece of equipment and he wanted no part of it. He worried about Mac working with his hands so close to the spinning saw blade. For once he was happy to be assigned the manual labor of stacking the wood in the woodshed and carrying it thence to the kitchen wood box.

One day toward the end of summer, with the temperature topping the one-hundred-degree mark, Mac, Ariel, Jack and Spud Murphy were working on the wood supply, cutting and stacking in the woodshed, when Mac happened to glance down the drive toward the flat and saw a stranger walking up the drive toward them. As he got closer Mac noticed that he was wearing a clean white shirt and his blue serge trousers were neatly creased. Mac put the transmission in neutral, turned the ignition off, and rolled a cigarette, waiting for the man to come up to him and state his business.

When Mac had originally positioned the Essex-turned-cut-off-saw behind the woodshed, he and Ariel had felled a good-sized digger pine with about a thirty-six-inch girth that was in the way of the saw location. When you cut a green digger pine down, the stump bleeds pitch like a stuck pig and it keeps on doing it for the next several years. On a good hot summer day it just boils out. The stump of the recently removed pine was in just such a condition.

As the stranger came closer you could see his shirt was soaked with sweat and he was puffing and panting to get enough air. The closer he got, the more Spud Murphy thought something must be wrong with his legs, because he was weaving and stumbling and having a hard time keeping his heading, which seemed to be fixed for the most part on the digger pine stump. He staggered the last few steps as he closed in on the stump, almost missing it completely at the last minute as he spun around and sat down. He looked up into Mac's eyes with a doleful expression and emitted a very loud hiccup into the still, country air.

Now, under normal circumstances Mac would have dismissed Spud Murphy immediately from such a scene, telling him to "make himself scarce," and whatever then transpired would have been unknown to Spud Murphy until Jack, if he happened to be in an expository mood, would enlighten him. Mac didn't send him off, however, and through that omission, Spud Murphy got a firsthand peek at what Grandma would call the wages of sin and the ills of intemperance.

The bootleggers always had someone standing watch at the still, twenty-four hours a day regardless of what else might have been going on, and the stranger, a new and untried employee, had been assigned that responsibility at the last minute because all the older hands, including the Ponds, were off to the state fair, which was having a ten day run in Sacramento. It's easy to see how the opportunity to sample a bit of the product may have been a little more than he could resist, particularly as a brand-new member of the organization. After a few nips from the bottle, he decided he, too, might as well go to town and take in the fair, since there was nothing happening at the still, and if Mac would kindly point him in the direction of the highway where he could thumb a ride to Sacramento, he would be off to the fair. After prying a flask from his pitch-saturated hip pocket, he saluted Mac with a "Much obliged to ye, sir, and would ye care now for a wee nip, to get ye by the day?"

Having dispatched Ariel to the still immediately on assessing the bootlegger's condition, Mac attempted to stall him until help arrived, but Ariel found no one at the still and the man eventually wandered off across the barley field and on beyond the brush line, heading in the general direction of the state highway. Somehow, the sticky mess of pitch on his blue serge pants had attracted an abundant crop of pine needles so from the rear he looked somewhat like a molting roadrunner. Mac reported the incident to Mr. Pond and Mr. Pond thanked him and told him not to worry about it.

It was September 1932, and America had over thirteen million unemployed, most of them standing around employment offices or in breadlines and sleeping on park benches or if they were lucky, on cots in the church basement. Spud Murphy had just turned seven and was starting the second grade.

Brother, Can You Spare A Dime?

Jay Gorney / E.Y.Harburg, 1932

They used to tell me I was building a dream
And so I followed the mob.
When there was earth to plow, or guns to bear,
I was always there, right on the job.

They used to tell me I was building a dream
With peace and glory ahead;
Why should I be standing
In line, just waiting for bread?

Once I built a railroad, I made it run,
Made it race against time.
Once I built a railroad, now it's done;
Brother, can you spare a dime?

Once I built a tower, up to the sun,
Brick and rivet and lime.
Once I built a tower, now it's done;
Brother, can you spare a dime?

Once in khaki suits, gee, we looked so swell,
Full of that Yankee Doodle-de-dum.
Half a million boots went slogging through hell
And I was the kid with the drum.

Say, don't you remember? they called me Al,
It was Al all the time.
Why, don't you remember, I'm your pal;
Buddy, can you spare a dime?

Seven

Once in khaki suits, ah, gee, we looked so swell,
Full of that Yankee Doodle-de-dum.
Half a million boots went slogging through hell
And I was the kid with the drum.

Say, don't you remember, they called me Al,
It was Al all the time.
Why, don't you remember, I'm your pal;
Buddy, can you spare a dime?

CHIEF RUNNING WOLF & FAMOUS WAR DOG 'SKIPPER'
Spud Murphy & Skipper   Summer 1929

PRINCE POTENTATE & LADIES OF THE COURT
Katherine   Spud Murphy   E.J.

JACK'S AIRPLANE   CALIFORNIA   1928
10 Year   Airmail   Anniversary

SACRAMENTO HAYWIRES

IN THE STUDIOS OF KFBK, THE "BEE" RADIO STATION SACRAMENTO, CA 1930
Ariel (Slim) Hinds, Yankee Mac, Sally Bennett, "Uncle" Reg Mason, Doug (Scotty) Brown

THE DAY WE LEFT E.J. AT SUNMOUNT   NOVEMBER 1929
Elsie   E.J.   Mac   Jack   Spud Murphy   Katherine

RANCH HANDS YANKEE MAC & THE SIERRA RANCH HANDS AT THE HOMESTEAD
Mac, Sally Bennett, Reg Mason, Doug Brown, Ariel Hinds, Bob Fellin

DOGHOUSE
Yankee Mac   Queenie   Ariel   Scotty

ABDUL & SPUD MURPHY

THE ROCK   Abdul & Spud Murphy   California c. 1934

THE SECOND GRADE CLASS of WILLOW SPRINGS SCHOOL
Boogee, Lola, Spud Murphy   October 1932

WILLOW SPRINGS GRAMMAR SCHOOL CALIFORNIA 1932
Back: Lola Stone, Helen Pond, E.J., Wendell Pond, Vernon Greilich, Willard Waters, Norma Waters, Winnie Littlefield, Norma Gomez, Jean Orr
Front: Roger McEwen, John Apedaile, Bill French, Johnny DeMartini, Frank McEwen, Norman Waters, Spud Murphy

May 1938

E.J. In getup of Crinoline's and Cutaway's Dancing Club

Spud Murphy   **OCTOBER 1941**   Sacramento, California
                    Jack   Mac   Elsie   Billy   E.J.

Pauline Irene (Voss) MacClanahan

GRANDMA   Chicago 1920

Eight

On July 28, 1932, General Douglas MacArthur led U.S. Army cavalry troops to rout unarmed and defenseless members of the "Bonus Army" out of an encampment they had occupied in Washington, D.C. The Bonus Army was the name given to World War I veterans and their families who were destitute and jobless as a result of the Depression and had come from all parts of the country to plead with the federal government for advance payment of a veteran's bonus. The bonus, for military service in World War I, had been approved by Congress with payment to be made in 1945. MacArthur succeeded in routing the veterans from their encampment in Anacostia Flats and in burning their shelters and hovels. In the process his troops managed to shoot to death two un-armed veteran bonus marchers, kill a three-month-old infant with tear gas, and bayonet a seven-year-old boy in the leg who was running back into the camp to save his pet rabbit.

Four months later, on November 8, 1932, Franklin Delano Roosevelt defeated Herbert Hoover in the presidential election of that year. On February 20, 1933, Congress passed the Twentieth Amendment to open the way for the repeal of Prohibition.

Twelve days later, on March 4, 1933, FDR was inaugurated as the thirty-second president of the United States. Almost ten months after its passage by Congress, ratification of the Twentieth Amendment by three-quarters of the state legislatures was obtained to repeal Prohibition on December 5, 1933.

Mac must have felt pretty good about FDR becoming President, because when the USS Constitution, otherwise known as "Old Ironsides," tied up at the wharf in San Francisco on public exhibition in the same month that the inauguration took place, he took a day off from work in celebration. The whole family rode the train to Oakland and took the S.P. ferry across the bay to see the famous warship that was such a national treasure. As inspired as Spud Murphy was by John Paul Jones and his famous reply to Captain Pearson of HMS Serapis when asked if he was ready to strike the colors of the *Bon Homme Richard* ("Surrender be damned! I have not yet begun to fight!"), the victories racked up by Old Ironsides over HMS Guerriere, HMS Java, HMS Cyan and HMS Levant in the War of 1812 were even more impressive. To stand on the deck that had been paced by Captains Isaac Hull, William Bainbridge, and Charles Stewart was an experience surmounting Spud Murphy's wildest dreams and expectations.

Old Ironsides

Oliver Wendell Holmes (1830)

Aye, tear her tattered ensign down!
Long has it waved on high,
And many an eye has danced to see
That banner in the sky;

Beneath it rang the battle shout,
And burst the cannon's roar;

Eight

The meteor of the ocean air
Shall sweep the clouds no more!

Her decks, once red with heroes' blood,
Where knelt the vanquished foe,
When winds were hurrying o'er the flood,
And waves were white below,

No more shall feel the victor's tread
Or know the conquered knee;
The harpies of the shore shall pluck
The eagle of the sea!

Oh, better that her shattered hulk
Should sink beneath the wave;
Her thunders shook the mighty deep,
And there should be her grave;

Nail to the mast her holy flag,
Set every threadbare sail,
And give her to the god of storms,
The lightening and the gale!

With spirits buoyed by hope for a return of prosperity under Democratic rule, Mac decided to buy a 1927 Model A Ford Roadster with a rumble seat that Spud Murphy thought was pretty snazzy. Mac thought it was a good buy and Roy Olson guaranteed it to be in top condition. Jack was only fifteen, but fourteen was the age at which to qualify for a driver's license in California if you lived on a farm in those days, and Mac figured Jack ought to have a car to drive. Elsie's Studebaker wasn't working out as a school bus. She didn't like to drive in the first place, especially after the wheel fell off the Essex and she knocked the battery out of it. The Studebaker was too cumbersome, stuck in the mud most of the time, and always breaking down whenever you wanted to go anywhere in it. Mac figured that what was needed for school transportation was a smaller, lighter car that was more economical to operate. With the Model A, Jack would be able to drop the grammar school kids off at Willow Springs and then catch the bus that went on to the high school at Sutter Creek. The high school bus stopped at Central House and that's where he would leave the Model A until he picked it up on the way home after school in the afternoon. That way, Elsie wouldn't have to worry about driving at all, unless the weather was good and the roads weren't all mud and she just wanted to go to Plymouth for something.

The Model A contributed to a lot of exciting episodes during the years that she spent on the homestead. The first of those happened soon after she became a member of the family. It was a day that for some reason E.J. didn't go to school. Maybe she was sick. Katherine was staying with the Bells, which was something she had to do until Aunt Mary and Elsie got over whatever spat they were having at that particular time. In any case, Jack and Spud Murphy were alone on their way to school. Even in such circumstances, with the passenger side of the front seat unoccupied, Spud Murphy would be riding, by preference, in the rumble seat. He liked to think of the Model A as being his limousine and Jack as his chauffeur and himself as Machine Gun Kelly or Baby Face Nelson, growling, "All right, youse rats, take dat, and dat," between bursts from his Thompson Sub-Machine Gun.

Just as they were about to ford the stream on the Ybright place near the Indian mounds, a stream that someone had christened "Possum Creek" (although no one could remember seeing a possum there), Jack brought the car to an abrupt stop. Rousing himself from where he was slumped down in the seat cradling the imaginary Tommy gun in preparation for getting off another burst or two, Spud Murphy looked over the side from the

Eight

rumble seat and along side the car were three good-sized rattlers, big enough to have ten or twelve rattles each.

Right after Mac had cleared out the den under the quartz outcrop with the bundled dynamite charge, one of his fellow workers at the S.P., on hearing of what he had done, volunteered to buy any more live snakes that Mac would care to bring him. At four dollars per adult rattler, adult being a snake with at least six rattles, snake hunting turned out to be a pretty lucrative business. Rattlesnakes with less than six rattles brought two dollars; king snakes, five dollars; gopher snakes, at least thirty-six inches long, one dollar; and horn toads, twenty-five cents.

Spud Murphy never caught any horn toads to sell; he considered them to be a different category of animal than the snakes and when he did occasionally bring one home, he always took it out behind the granary where there were a couple of large colonies of red ants and turned it loose, so it could get a good meal and hopefully stay around for a while. Mac made cages for transporting rattlesnakes and holding them in between his trips to the city. The king snakes had to have their own separate cage, or else they would kill and eat the rattlesnakes. Actually they ate them first, and the dying just happened as a result of that.

The gopher snakes were kept in their own gunnysacks, too, otherwise, the king snakes and rattlesnakes both would eat them. The king snakes were pretty rare and they made good pets. He would have let them go like the horn toads, except that they brought such a high price and Elsie needed every cent she could get to make ends meet.

Jack was getting out of the front seat and Spud Murphy climbed down from the rumble seat, being careful where he stepped when his feet touched the ground. There was a short handled pitchfork in the rumble seat and Spud Murphy climbed back up and got it for Jack, so he could pitch the three rattle snakes into Machine Gun Kelly's end of the limousine. He could

171

have put them in a gunnysack with which the Model A was equipped, but he figured he didn't need to. When he got them all loaded, Spud Murphy said, "I ain't sitting back there with them buggers," and democratically climbed into the front seat to sit with the limousine driver.

That afternoon when Jack got off the bus at Central House, he opened up the rumble seat to check on the snakes and they weren't there. He tipped the seat forward with the pitchfork and poked around under it and he still couldn't find them. Finally he got the idea to look under the front seat and sure enough, when he shoved it out on the ground and turned it upside down with the pitchfork, there they were, all three of them tangled in with the coil springs of the seat. It took him quite a while, working by himself, but he finally got them out of the springs and into the gunnysack. Spud Murphy never rode in the rumble seat again without tipping the seat up so he could look under it first.

The other single most interesting thing to happen with the Model A was when Jack moved to Ione for a year or so and E.J. started driving it. By that time Spud Murphy was about ten and was going to Plymouth Grammar School. E.J. would park the car near Johnnie Moyle's Garage on Main Street in Plymouth and catch the high school bus from there. After school, Spud Murphy would walk there from the grammar school and sit in the car in the driver's seat while he waited for the high school bus and his chauffeur for the ride home.

Henry Ford, in his industrious quest to remain the richest man in America, contrived some unusual ways of cutting costs on the automobiles he manufactured and sold to the gullible and uneducated American public. One of them, featured on the Model A, was to build the fuel tank into the cowl forward of the driver's seat. While that was a dangerous place to be carrying such a volatile product as gasoline, it completely obviated the need for a fuel pump, since gravity would operate to transfer the gasoline from tank to carburetor. At the point where the fuel line joined the tank was a small petcock that could be manually closed after the engine was stopped, to insure that gasoline did not leak through the system in case the carburetor float was stuck, as it usually was, or the float valve failed to work as intended. Conversely, if one wished to run the engine for more than five minutes or so, one needed to manually make certain the shut-off valve was open. At the homestead, it was unusual for anyone to ever close the valve, so as a consequence, it wasn't often necessary to remember to open it. As Spud Murphy sat in the car that day, waiting for his sister, he idly began, for possibly the hundredth time, a detailed inspection of the various instruments, switches, pedals and other components, and in the process of satisfying his curiosity, he happened to turn the fuel valve off.

During the Depression, conservation of resources was more often than not an absolute necessity and it was general practice to turn the ignition off and coast where possible to save gasoline. Having used most of the gas out of the carburetor bowl backing the car out of its parking place and heading it in the direction of home, E.J. shut off the engine and began a long coast that took her out of town, past McBride's, past Harold Swingle's place at the Spring Valley Road and midway of Mr. Purcell's farm to where a slight upgrade made it necessary to add a little power. When she put it in gear and let out the clutch, the engine started right up, but after running a hundred feet or so it coughed a couple of times and died.

After several unsuccessful attempts to start the car, E.J. decided it must be out of gas, which was quite unusual considering there was a gas gauge sticking up out of the gas cap right before her eyes in front of the windshield that clearly showed the tank was half full. After telling Spud Murphy to stay put and look after the car she set out across Frank White's pasture in the direction of the homestead to get some gasoline.

As soon as E.J. was out of sight Spud Murphy got down under the dashboard where he could get a good look at the valve. It was plain to see from the position of the valve handle that it was, indeed, turned off. He had a strong impulse to run after E.J. and tell her about the valve, but he managed to curb that wild rush to judgment until he was sure that the problem was cured. After waiting a few minutes and carefully aligning the valve handle to where it should be if it was on, he turned on the ignition switch and started the engine, which ran quite smoothly. After letting it run for a few more moments to be sure, while he thought over his options, he did honk the horn a couple of times, but when she didn't return or answer, he assumed she must be out of earshot.

"Well," he thought, "I guess I probably should give this old buggy a road test," so he slid over behind the wheel and drove down to Four Corners and got out and stood there leaning on the fender looking under the hood like mechanics do, but nobody came along to ask him if he was having problems so he could spit casually in the manner of someone chewing tobacco and say "No, jes tunin' her up," so then he drove home, thinking E.J. would probably be there by then. He arrived just after she finished siphoning a gallon of gas out of the Studebaker and was getting ready to walk the two miles back with it through Frank White's fields. As to the explanation for the engine stopping, Spud Murphy attributed it to being "Just one of life's little mysteries" as he himself had so often been told when people had something they wanted to conceal or just didn't want to be bothered about.

After the visit by the intoxicated bootlegger, it took about four months for the treasury agents to get around to investigating the rumor that a still was operating somewhere along the Cosumnes River in the Latrobe Road area. One day two shiny black sedans pulled into the homestead and a half-dozen men in dark business suits spilled out carrying guns, surrounding the house and the chicken house and Grandma's cabin where the Ponds were staying. Fortunately, Mac was home at the time, and just as fortunately, the Ponds were not. Mac was working at the forge, fashioning a pair of corral gate hinges and Spud Murphy was with him, tending the fire and cranking the blower. Jack and Ariel were crawling around on the stud wall plates, nailing rafters on the shop building that was under construction.

When Mac saw the treasury agents coming up the driveway, he said to Spud Murphy, "You get in the house and stay there. Tell Mama and the girls and Grandma to keep on doing whatever they are doing and just act normal."

After the agents occupied both the back house and the granary, using evasive action with guns held at the ready, they turned their attention to the shop building, where it looked for a minute like they were going to shoot Jack and Ariel right out of the rafters. The chief agent, holstering his government-issue forty-five, approached Mac, telling him to take them to where the still was. Of course Mac told them he didn't know of any such thing as a still.

They spent two or three hours discussing that, with *El Jefe* getting madder by the minute, during which conversation Mac pretended to be very polite and respectful to them, insisting on showing them two different concealed-weapons permits that he proudly carried in his wallet in commemoration of past glory days. One of them was from the state of Illinois, obtained at the time when he was the deputy sheriff in charge of security at the Cook County jail. The other was from when he was deputized by Sacramento County during his strike-breaking days for the S.P. Railroad. They weren't impressed much by either of these, finally suggesting they had just about enough of his obfuscation—for which even he would have acknowledged he had a great talent— and that they were about ready to take him into Sacramento and lock him up for obstructing justice. That seemed to nudge his memory enough for him to allow as how he may have heard of such an operation as they were describing, after all, but he sure never realized that it was for the purpose of making distilled spirits of any kind. Had he realized such was the case he would have notified them himself, being the dedicated ex-lawman that he was. Having at last acquired the cooperation that he sought, the chief treasury agent said, as a final expression of his authority, "And tell that stupid little kid in there with the broomstick and the cap pistols to quit running around pretending to shoot at my men through the windows. It's a damn disgrace."

The impasse was not quite as near resolved as the agent thought, because after hearing Spud Murphy's intelligence impugned, Mac turned toward the house and shouted, "Come on, Lizzy, get your girdle on! These boys want us to take a ride with them down to the river." When Mac called Elsie by his own private nickname for her, Spud Murphy knew Mac was just giving the agent the raspberry. After being told by the agent that no women were allowed, Mac said "Well, I don't know, then. I just never go anywhere without my little woman."

He lost that argument, too, but in the process he gained the bootleggers another half hour of time. Then he gained a little more by having the agents take a wrong fork at every opportunity that offered, so when they finally got to the Bastion place it was near dark and all they found was two completely empty warehouse buildings and nothing else except the strong lingering smell of sour mash corn whiskey. Spud Murphy in making his final inspection a few days later found several dead bluegills on the river-bank below the gorge and a case containing a couple of fancy-looking hydrometers that evidently was dropped in the haste of departure.

The Ponds moved out the following week. A week after that Spud Murphy woke in the middle of the night to hear an eighteen-wheeler as it passed the house on its way to its last stop at the granary. Next morning, on top of a sack of sugar and another of dried corn was a fifteen-gallon keg of whiskey. Taped to the whiskey keg was an envelope with the last month's rent payment. It was a sad day, to know that the Ponds would not be coming back. They were good, God-fearing people.

There was some thought given to settling Grandma finally into her cabin, now that the Ponds were gone. That was soon forgotten, though, when the sickness that always seemed to plague her increased in intensity after Christmas. Mac took her to Sacramento to the doctor, who put her in the hospital. After some tests he diagnosed her as having a particularly bad kind of cancer.

Those details and the further information that her sickness was probably terminal were not shared with Spud Murphy. She lived for four months after the cancer was discovered, dying on May 12, 1933. During the last month of her illness Spud Murphy was rarely allowed to see her. The living room where she was quartered was generally off limits to him. When she passed away, he watched in suddenly enveloping grief from a vantage point at the pump house as Trevor Weston's black hearse carrying her human remains slowly bumped down the driveway and disappeared beyond the grove of massive valley oaks as she left the homestead for the last time. Later, Elsie found him in the granary, sitting on a sack of barley with bowed head and staring blindly through his tears at the floor in front of him. She came to him and pulled him up to stand on his feet, raising his head with her hand beneath his chin. When their eyes met she said "God has sent his angels to take Grandma to heaven." He said "I know," and cried with his face buried against his mother's shoulder.

Spud Murphy had more than one wound to contend with in the following days. He missed Grandma greatly, but even worse than that was the fact that he was the only one not to have known that she was going to be taken out of his life just as Skipper, Queenie and Spotty had been taken, without his knowledge before-hand. One day, still struggling with the awful suddenness and finality of death, he confronted Elsie with his pain after he finished milking and was filling the large deep enameled pans that held the milk while the cream was rising until it was skimmed off for churning into butter.

As he strained the milk into the pans through a square of cheesecloth, he had a worried look on his face and he said to Elsie, who was working at the sink, "Mama, is it lying if you know something you should tell and you don't tell it on purpose?"

Elsie thought for a moment and said, "It depends on the 'should tell' part. Who's to say what should be told? Why are you asking, dear?"

"Well, somebody should have told me Grandma was going to die. You knew, and you didn't tell me. I didn't get to tell her good-bye."

"Well, dear, sometimes we try to protect the people we love from finding out things that would only make them feel sad."

"Why? What good does that do? They have to find out sometime, and then it's worse. You think it's good to keep feeling happy while your Grandma's dying? If I had known she was going to die, I could have thanked her for all the things she did for me, like the time I lost my pistols in the back house. Now I feel worse because I didn't get to tell her. I think grownups do things the way they do because it's easiest that way. Maybe it's just too hard to tell someone their grandma's dying. Maybe they're just putting off saying what they don't want to think about. Or what they're too afraid to admit."

At that Elsie said, "Oh, I'm so sorry, dear. I'm sure you are right. But it's too late now to undo what has already been done. Will you forgive me? I promise to never again do to you what I wouldn't want done to myself." As to the question of absolute truth, it is plain to see how easily the issue was sidestepped. It never came up again between them, which may have been fortunate enough in the matter of preserving Spud Murphy's self-image in the years to come.

With Grandma gone and the Ponds gone, Mac decided to use the materials from Grandma's cabin to add a bedroom onto the house for E.J. So Spud Murphy got to pull and straighten more used nails and stack more used lumber. Even the shake siding had to be salvaged, since the engine that had driven the drag-saw was now doing duty as a pump engine and was no longer available for logging. As was usual, Mac had been looking ahead when he laid out the three rooms of the main house that had already been built, so the new room for E.J. fit perfectly, in with what was already existing, without modification for either structural or aesthetic reasons. While he was building the addition, he wired the whole house for a six-volt lighting system. The lighting system was powered by a rebuilt Briggs and Stratton gasoline engine that had once been used to run a Montgomery Ward washing machine. The generator that charged the six-volt storage batteries was a DC model salvaged from the Essex. Most of the time, because of the noise the engine made, Elsie chose to use the kerosene lamps even though it was a pain to clean the soot from the chimneys and trim the wicks and fill them with kerosene every day.

E.J. was delighted with her new room, no longer having to live under-foot in the midst of all the family activities that nightly took over the living room, that privilege now being inherited by Jack, Spud Murphy, and Ariel, whose sleeping quarters shifted back and forth from the living room to the spacious but austere front porch, as dictated by weather and other considerations. And so, the family did finally come to be "all under one roof," as befit such a closely bonded household.

One of the great imponderables of homesteading is the matter of who wins, between the pioneers and the suddenly displaced denizens of woodland and meadow. Who determines the final disposition of things like chickens and ducks and their eggs that are the dietary staples of foxes, coyotes and bobcats; row crops like spinach, carrots, and corn that fall prey to the nightly incursions of deer and rabbits and raccoons; and fruit and nut trees, mercilessly plundered by squirrels, orioles and finches?

First to go was Jack's prize bantam rooster, followed shortly by a favorite bantam hen, both of whom wisely roosted high above the prowling foxes and coyotes in the branches of a pine tree, only to become the victim of a far wiser barn owl who under cover of night snipped off their heads with surgical proficiency and glutted itself and its fledglings on what it rightly saw as nature's provender. At first, nearly as many eggs went to skunks and as many baby chicks filled the bellies of snakes as ever satisfied the needs of the human occupants of the homestead. One night a forked horn buck reversed the score by entangling itself so severely in the newly stretched hog-wire fence that Jack and Ariel had erected to protect Elsie's garden that he had to be shot and was himself turned into venison chops and corned venison. It worked both ways.

For Christmas of 1932 Spud Murphy got a string of three, single-spring double-aught Victor traps. Mac showed him how to make the different sets for raccoon, fox, coyote and bobcat, using various baits and scents. Spud Murphy extemporized on his own, making a set for a cottontail by using a carrot for bait and caught a jackrabbit instead. He boiled the jackrabbit and tried to get Abdul to eat it but Abdul refused to have anything to do with it so he dumped it into the pig's feeding trough with a bucket of clabbered milk. The pigs proved to be not nearly so fastidious in their dietary habits as the dog had been.

One morning Elsie went out to the chicken house and surprised a coyote that had just killed one of her favorite Plymouth Rock hens. The hen was so mangled she decided to have Spud Murphy bury it in the dump. Spud Murphy knew the coyote would probably come back, no matter where he buried it, and dig it up again. Or worse, Abdul might dig it up and get a taste for chickens. He tied Abdul up on the back porch and, taking the chicken up on the ridge almost to the fence line, he dug a hole near a greasewood bush, deep enough to bury the chicken. Above the chicken he set the trap with plenty of chicken blood on and around it. The chain on the trap wasn't long enough to reach the greasewood bush so he extended it with some twine such as came tied around the forty-pound ice cakes that Mac brought home from Sacramento for the ice box. The other end of the twine he tied fairly high up to a springy but very strong branch of the greasewood bush. He covered the trap with fine dirt and humus from under a manzanita, which would not choke the action of the trigger or the pan of the trap, and smoothed the whole area out so you couldn't tell anything unusual was there at all. Then he set the other two traps along the east fence of the homestead in the same way, using only the chicken blood and tying the trap chains with twine to the bottom strand of the barbed wire fence.

The next morning at milking time, with Mac and Ariel already on their way to work in Sacramento and before Spud Murphy went out to the corral to attend to the milking, he walked up to the ridge to check his traps. Suspended off the ground, tangled up in the middle of the greasewood bush, was a thirty-pound bobcat, hopping mad and aching for the chance to fight something. It was powerless to do much more than spit and snarl and glare and otherwise carry on in a most menacing way, because of the springy nature of the spiny branches in which he was lodged. Spud Murphy grabbed Abdul— who was likely thinking of the last bobcat he had tangled with in the middle of a manzanita thicket, and trying to decide whether he wanted any more of that particular breed of animal— and dragging him along by the scruff of his neck, lit out running for home. As he passed the quartz outcrop and headed down to the house he was yelling at the top of his lungs, "Mama, bring the rifle! Hurry! Bring the rifle! I caught a big cat in my trap! I think it's a mountain lion. Bring the rifle before it gets away!" Elsie took the .22, inserted the ammunition clip, and headed up toward the outcrop, Spud Murphy at her side but careful not to get ahead of her. Abdul was ahead, still somewhat undecided, but bolstered by the reinforcement of Elsie and the rifle.

When they got to where the bobcat was caught in the trap, Elsie said, "Oh, my! He is a big one!" and chambering a cartridge, raised the rifle to her shoulder and shot the bobcat neatly between the eyes.

Spud Murphy skinned out the pelt and wanted to have it tanned and the head and cape made into a headdress like Hugh Glass and Jim Bridger and some of the other mountain men wore when they went to William Henry Ashley's fur rendezvous at Green River, but Mac said it was worth good money and better to sell it as it was plus getting the few dollars bounty that the county predator control would pay. The investment in traps was repaid in any case with enough cash to buy a day or so's ration of corn-meal and beans. Unfortunately for the bobcat, it paid the full price for the loss of Elsie's Barred Plymouth Rock hen while the coyote got off scot-free.

Eight

In July, on Spud Murphy's eighth birthday, his present from Mac and Elsie was a .22 caliber rifle. It wasn't much, as rifles go, just a four-dollar single-shot from the Montgomery Ward catalog, but he had practically worn that page of the catalog to dog-eared obscurity, pining for that one gift above any other of the catalog's offerings. He knew it was the best that Mac and Elsie could afford, if in fact they could afford even that. After a cleverly conducted thirty-day campaign in which the catalog illustration was always visible from wherever Mac might happen to sit, when it did finally become his, the cheaply made rifle represented to Spud Murphy the equivalent of the finest Sharps Model 1874 buffalo rifle that was ever made. Fortunately, there were no buffalo around to try it out on, only spinach- and carrot-eating jackrabbits, skunks and raccoons and baby-chick-eating rattlesnakes. Before any of that ever happened, though, there were a lot of gun rules and hunting safety regulations to be learned, even though they already had been absorbed over the months at the homestead by observation and common sense.

Mac said the one most important rule to learn was that a gun must always be assumed to be loaded. Just to make the point, he slipped a fired shell casing into the chamber when Spud Murphy wasn't looking, leaving the action open. When Spud Murphy took back the gun, out of sheer good fortune he noticed the cartridge and extracted it before closing the bolt, thereby winning some points and saving himself from a big, long lecture on the importance of looking in the chamber before closing the bolt. Rifles were always stored in the house with the action open. There was never a question of whether they were loaded or not. You just always handled them as though they were.

The second most important rule was to never crawl through a barbed wire fence or climb over any fence with a gun in your hand and to never lean it against the post or the wire while you crawled through. Always lay it flat on the ground, out of the way of where you're crossing, and then reach through and bring it towards you after you had crossed.

After the lessons came the sighting-in and the target practice. Mac took a brake drum from one of the dismantled vehicles and suspended it on chains in front of a pile of overburden—a legacy of the World War I chromite-prospecting activities— that would make a good backstop. In front of the brake drum, he made a frame to hold a target. Any shot that hit the target would also hit the brake drum, thereby making the noise of a loud gong. The target was about a hundred yards from the front porch, about the farthest distance from which you would expect to shoot a coyote, for which the county paid a bounty of ten dollars.

The final brush with a mountain lion came two or three years later as an indirect result of ownership of the .22. Spud Murphy was deer hunting one chilly fall morning after transferring to Plymouth School in 1935. Buzzards circling over a spot often indicate that either something has died there or possibly is about to die. From the meadow at the Bastion place he noticed buzzards circling upriver over the Michigan Bar miner's ditch where it followed a hillside between the Eiler place and the Bastion place. He began stalking whatever was attracting the buzzards. As he worked his way on his belly up the slope through the dry meadow grass and scattered brush, he caught a glimpse of a four-point buck browsing on the hillside above the ditch. He crawled on ahead to the ditch and cautiously continued to the top of the berm that formed the ditch bank on the lower side. He had the deer in sight when he happened to glance down along the ditch-bottom. Staring up at him from a distance of fifteen feet was a large mountain lion, who had evidently made the same assumptions about the habits of buzzards that had been in Spud Murphy's mind. On seeing Spud Murphy the mountain lion swapped directions and in three giant bounds was out of sight around a bend of the ditch. The buck left in a hurry, having been alerted by the commotion, followed by Spud Murphy, and finally, the last to leave, the ever-hopeful buzzards.

When the price of gold had doubled in January 1934, Mac's interest in prospecting took on new meaning. At that time he staked out two twenty-acre placer claims which he registered with the U.S. Land Office— one in his name and one in Elsie's— situated on opposite banks of the gorge where the river narrowed and tumbled among the huge boulders that choked the contorted riverbed. For the next two years he had neither time nor money to establish any kind of sustained mining activity, but he designed and built—in what time he could devote to it—a highly efficient centrifugal pump for use on a suction dredge for mining the gravel in the riverbed.

After the Bonus Bill was passed by Congress in January 1936, he could afford to spend more of his time on weekends working in the shop at the homestead, constructing the remaining elements necessary to complete a floating suction dredge powered by the same old four-cylinder Star engine of many previous assignments. Some of the parts he fashioned at his anvil while Spud Murphy turned the blower that fed oxygen to the glowing bed of coals in the forge. Many more of the smaller pieces he made on the lathe and milling machines at the S.P. shops, bringing them in his lunch bucket past the collaborative guards who stood watchfully at the gate. In the newfound opulence resulting from payment of the bonus money, he even paid to have some of the larger pieces rolled by a steel fabricator. When the dredge was complete with pump and suction hose and sluice box and winch and clamshell bucket and cables and sheaves, he disassembled it all and hauled it to the river where he reassembled it on a floating barge made of fifty-gallon oil drums.

The personal satisfaction of conquering the mechanical aspects of the construction of the dredge probably yielded a greater return to Mac than ever could have been equaled by the value of the gold that was recovered. But it was in the operation of the dredge, as measured by gold recovery, that Spud Murphy finally found a task, other than the one of milking cows, at which he was more adept than his father.

Mac designed the suction nozzle to be worked along the fissures in the bedrock of the river bottom to capture the gold that had settled there over the years as a result of the high specific gravity of the gold and the hydraulic action of the river current. It was a back-breaking, hit-or-miss proposition to try to control the nozzle from the deck of the dredge in depths of water that ranged to as great as ten or twelve feet below the surface. Spud Murphy was not only an excellent swimmer, he was also blessed with tremendous lung capacity, enabling him to stay under water for exceptionally long periods of time. On the first day of operation he watched as Mac struggled to control the nozzle. Finally he said, "Give me the nozzle, Dad—I can do it easier. I can dive with it." Not only was the nozzle simpler to handle by that method, Spud Murphy could see at close range under water exactly where the gold-bearing sands were trapped in the crevices of the river-bed. His efforts were such a success that thereafter the job of operating the nozzle along the bedrock fissures of the river bottom became his, permanently. It was a small victory, but it gave him a sense of contributing, a personal feeling of which he was in short supply at that time.

Nine

There never was a year, of the nine that they spent at the homestead, when drought was not a matter of concern. The shallow well on which they were dependent, tediously excavated by hand by Mac and Ariel and Jack in the hard rock formation that underlay the shallow soil, was slowly forsaken by the diminishing trickle of water that seeped through the fissures in the rock, until, by the end of August, survival meant hauling water by fifty-gallon barrel from Leighton's spring. What water that the homestead's well did produce went first to the kitchen and to the animals on which the family was dependent for meat and milk and butter and eggs. Wastewater from domestic use was piped to the vegetable garden for irrigation. In the worst of drought years, the garden that had been a profusion of vegetables of every sort in spring sometimes withered without an autumn harvest. In those years the skeletal corn-stalks died with barely formed cobs, barren of kernels. Over all hung the suffocating blanket of oppressive heat.

Worse than just the discomfort of the hot, dry summers or the crop loss from lack of water was the danger of fire. A wildfire could start in many different ways, but in the foothill country of the Mother Lode it most often started from human activity of some kind, anything from a discarded cigarette butt, or a hot exhaust pipe, to a spark created by a pick striking a quartz boulder. It just doesn't take much to set dry grass afire.

In the fall of 1934, just after the school year started, a brush and grass fire got started near Shingle Springs late one afternoon and by the next morning it was putting out a lot of smoke but it didn't seem to be going anywhere. Elsie sent Jack off with the Model A to deliver E.J. and Spud Murphy to Willow Springs and to get himself to Central House to catch the high school bus to Sutter Creek. She climbed up on *the rock* to watch the progress of the large column of smoke from the fire. As she watched, she noticed that the column, while still a long way off, was getting noticeably closer. By noon a substantial breeze had picked up. The smoke appeared to be coming out of the river bottom, having advanced six or eight miles through the morning hours. For an hour or so the fire was stalled by the Cosumnes River and then it jumped the river and came roaring up out of the river bottom on a direct line for the homestead.

The nearness and speed of the advancing smoke so frightened Elsie that she panicked. It was her intention to get in the Studebaker and drive to Barneys for help and to try to contact Mac at the S.P. shops. In her hurry she stumbled over the loose boulders at the base of the rock and fell, cutting a huge gash completely across her knee. She stopped at the house long enough to rip a sheet and wrap strips of it around her leg and knee to stop the bleeding. Then she got in the Studebaker and headed with all haste to Barneys. She got no farther than the flat, however, where she found Elmer and Waldo Barney and a dozen others already there, backfiring the grass along a line that ran from one edge of the flat to the other, directly in the path of the oncoming flames. They had been watching the course of the fire's advance, and when it jumped the river they came up to the flat, which was the next logical place to stop the fire after the river. If they didn't stop it there, it would no doubt burn the house and all the out-buildings at the homestead.

By the time Jack and E.J. and Spud Murphy showed up on the scene it was four o'clock. The wind had died down and the fire was pretty well under control, although Spud Murphy got to follow along the backfire with a McLeod, helping to keep it under control until it burned itself out. Mac got home at about the same time, having been notified of the threat to the homestead as a result of Mrs. Barney's calling the S.P. shops, but he had to turn right around and drive Elsie to the hospital in Sacramento to get her knee stitched up.

After that episode, Mac built a hundred gallon water trailer with a positive displacement hand pump that could be pulled behind any of the vehicles to put out spot fires caused by flying embers and for general protection around the house. Checking daily that it was full of water and ready to go at all times was another chore that was assigned to Spud Murphy.

In the late summer of 1935, Spud Murphy went about his chores finding his thoughts directed more and more in hindsight to the six weeks of summer that he and E.J. had spent in Sacramento while Elsie was in the hospital giving birth to a baby brother. Elsie was thirty-seven when the baby came along. Because of her age or for some other reason she had a hard time during her pregnancy and spent almost the entire last six weeks in the hospital, leaving Spud Murphy and E.J. mostly to their own devices in the apartment that Mac rented at 18th and "F" Streets for their stay in the city, while they waited for the birth of the baby. They couldn't even visit Elsie during the times she was actually in the hospital except for the half hour in the evening while Mac was visiting and then they could only stand outside on the sidewalk and wave to her through the window.

What stuck out so clearly in Spud Murphy's mind was the difference in responsibility between country and city life. Other than helping E.J. with washing dishes and making beds, there weren't any chores for Spud Murphy to do. Reading and his violin were all he had to keep him occupied. With more time on his hands than he had ever thought possible, Spud Murphy fell in with two other boys about his age who were city-wise, and roamed the neighborhood with them while E.J. stayed in the apartment and washed and ironed and sewed and read or visited with Elsie if she didn't happen to be confined in the hospital at that time. If Mac had realized what the situation was he would probably have hired Spud Murphy out to somebody for the summer at no cost, just to keep him in shape and out of trouble.

The three boys often played in a nearby city park, climbing into the upper branches of a giant elm tree and hiding there, pretending to be Indians waiting to ambush the cavalry who appeared from time to time in the form of a policeman strolling his beat in the neighborhood. They silently launched imaginary arrows at him from their imaginary bows, and when he had strolled out of sight and hearing they scrambled down to scalp and do a victory dance over his imaginary corpse. Ordinary civilians who walked through or tarried in the park were either settlers on their way west or buffalos and in either case did not require the same degree of subterfuge in their slaughter, it being sufficient to slink behind the trees and shoot them in the back. At other times they were outlaws and wore cap pistols tied down to their thighs for the fast draws necessary in their pursuit of the local stage coach which ran down "P" Street on the trolley tracks.

There was a large Victorian mansion in the neighborhood and wonder of wonders, right there in the back-yard, protected by an imposing wrought-iron fence built especially to keep kids out, was an uncommonly large and inviting swimming pool, diving board and all. One morning they noticed the owner and his family loading their car with all sorts of luggage, then driving off as though they were leaving on a very long vacation. After an impromptu council of war, the three delinquents all ran home for their swimming trunks and after reaffirming that no one was left to guard the oasis they hoisted each other over the fence and spent most of the rest of the day in possession of the swimming pool. The next day it was the same and the next as well. On the fourth day the owner returned in the afternoon: it was only owing to their extreme agility, abetted by unbounded fright at the consequences of getting caught (and the three different directions in which they took their departures), that they all managed to escape his clutches and thereby the ultimate disgrace of being taken into custody by the never-too-distant strolling cavalry. After his brief experience of unconstrained emancipation in Sacramento, it was with great sadness that Spud Murphy returned to the homestead at the end of the six weeks with Mac, Elsie, E.J., and a new baby brother.

DESTITUTE LABOR IS TOLD TO STAY OUT OF CALIFORNIA

IMPOVERISHED IMMIGRANTS WILL BE DEPORTED TO HOME STATES

A virtual ultimatum to the destitute migratory workers of the nation to keep out of California was issued at San Francisco today by H.A.R.Carlton, director of the federal transient service.

The Associated Press quotes Carlton as announcing indigent workers have been pouring into California at the rate of 1,000 a day and as declaring:

1--The federal transient shelters in California no longer will be operated as hotels for migratory workers.

2--No Works Progress Administration jobs will be given to transients registered in this state after August 1st.

3--Destitute persons entering California will be deported back to their home states upon arrival.

Sacramento Bee, August 24, 1935.

From a distance, Spud Murphy's small figure was almost indistinguishable as he toiled up the hillside, a small insignificant brown form barely noticeable against the vast panorama of mottled grays and browns of the brush-covered serpentine ridges that rose beyond him. He sat on a boulder, bending over to knot the ends of a broken lace of his frayed tennis shoe, pulling carefully on the rotten fabric so as not to break it again. His bare back and shoulders were baked a chestnut brown from long exposure to the summer sun, so he appeared, except for his blond hair, to be more native Indian than white. The clothes he wore consisted only of patched, faded, denim jeans and a pair of canvas tennis shoes to protect his feet.

Half an hour behind him the river wound through the hills in long, lazy bends, reduced in places to barely a trickle in this last, determined stand of summer. Blue gills and bass had long since found the deepest pools, listless, almost dormant, suspended in time, waiting to be reborn by the winter rain and snow-melt that in spring rushes down the narrow canyons from the blue-gray mountains that loom on the eastern horizon. With its tepid and sometimes stagnant water, the river offered the only reprieve at all during the long summer months from the oppressive heat that clung to the earth from morning till dark, stifling the voices of even the normally raucous blue jays. But the river lay behind him, forgotten in his distress at the worrisome and unsettling news that had cast its threatening shadow over him.

The rock on which he rested was in the meager shade of a withered buckeye where the trail forked, one branch following Cascara Creek, dry for most of its course in late summer, but nourished at least in part by a year-round spring a quarter mile further up the ridge, whose trickle of water was soon lost in the dry stream bed. This was the same spring of previous adventures that was secluded in a grove of live oaks at the lower end of the flat.

In spite of the obvious advantage that it offered of a welcome drink of water, the creek fork always seemed to Spud Murphy to be too dark and cloistered where it passed among the live oaks. For the lower part of its ascent it was also choked with impenetrable thickets of greasewood, manzanita and toyon. Mostly in its disfavor was the absence of any vantage point along it from which to pause and look down on the vistas of the central valley that stretched to the western horizon, there to ponder the uncharted mysteries that lay beyond.

The other trail sloped up a barren feeder ridge to the left and it was in that direction he turned. Although it was a long, hot climb to the ridge, once there he could enjoy the openness of the horizon falling away below him as he looked back in the direction of the river and beyond. The eye could contemplate a broader sweep of the world, and for reasons that were fundamental to the nature of his being, he seemed always to be in need of all the perspective he could get. It was typical of Spud Murphy to notice that in this, his tenth year of life, what was of monumental importance to him seemed to be barely of passing interest to his elders.

For the last four years of his short existence, actually representing almost half of his lifetime, *school* had meant a one-room building in the sparsely settled part of the county in which the homestead was located. Willow Springs Grammar School, in fact, defined the community, and the community was where he had grown up, where he had learned the customs and ways and modes of permissible behavior, and where he didn't have to worry about being *different.* Next to the river and the homestead, school was the most important place in his life.

Mrs. Littlefield, universally known as "Teacher," was a nurturing and caring friend, mentor and counselor, guiding her pupils through the maze of education with patience and understanding, proud of every accomplishment that they demonstrated, and as considerate of their developing personalities as a mother. Spud Murphy's only two friends were there, where the three of them together made up one whole class of the one-room school. Together, they stood for more than just three times as much as was the worth of any one of them alone. Spud Murphy felt safe there, protected from the fears of strange surroundings and unfamiliar people. It was a safe haven in a world that was otherwise unpredictable and unforgiving, even at times including his own home. It stood with the river as the only bulwark against the tyranny of the world, natural or contrived, over which he had no control.

Tomorrow, those who controlled his life were going to thrust him out into an unforgiving world of strangers: to a school that was not his, wherein not one single person was even known to him; to a school in the town, that had too many children who had different ways, and where he was an outsider. It was for economic reasons, they said. He did not know about economics. Economics was a grown-up concept. He was not a grown-up. He only understood the difference between a place of safety and one of danger. Those are concepts understood by children. They said, "You'll get used to it. The change will do you good." "No," he thought, "you have not done this for my good. You have done it for your own good."

He picked up the single-shot .22 from where he had placed it on the ground by the rock and started up the ridge trail, following a set of tracks left in the early morning hours by a buck that would be maintaining a wary lookout from the shelter of the blue oaks and digger pines that fringed the crest of the ridge above. Abdul detached himself from the shadowed leaf mold under a nearby manzanita and trotted alertly ahead up the trail, occasionally turning his head back over his shoulder to see that he was being followed.

When Spud Murphy got home Elsie and E.J. were sitting on the front porch in the shade, his mother in a rocking chair with Billy lying on her lap. E.J. was sitting on the steps stitching a design on a small cloth stretched on a frame. They watched him come up the drive and when he mounted the steps Elsie asked, "Did you have a good time?"

"Yeah. I shot a rattler at the Bastion place. A little one."

E.J. asked, "How many rattles?"

He reached in his pocket and his hand came out with the rattles he had cut from the dead snake. He held them out for her to see and said, "Five and the button." She wouldn't touch them and wrinkled her nose in distaste. The baby's eyes were following him and he held the rattles for him to see and shook them but the baby was more interested in Spud Murphy's face than the rattles and Elsie said, "Put them on the mantel for daddy to see when he gets home."

He sat on the step by E.J. and said, "Mama, how old's the baby going to have to be before he can do things like coming with me to the river?"

"Oh, I don't know, dear. He's only two months old. I'm afraid an awfully long time."

"Yeah. I'll probably be in high school by then. I wish he was older."

E.J. said, "Say 'yes,' not 'yeah.' And if wishes were horses, beggars would ride."

Elsie said, "I'm sorry, dear. We just have to accept things the way the Lord provides."

"Yeah, Yes."

Spud Murphy went in the house and put the rattles on the mantel. He hung his rifle on the pegs that stuck out from the rock chimney above the mantel. In the kitchen he looked in the wood box and brought an armful of wood from the woodshed to top it off. He took the milk pails from where they were turned upside down on the drain board and headed for the corral. All three cats jumped off the back porch when he went out carrying the milk pails and followed him to the corral where the cows were waiting not so much to be milked as in anticipation of their evening feeding. He went into the granary and got a flake of alfalfa which he dropped in the feed box of the stanchion before he opened the corral gate enough for Patsy to shoulder through it and then closed it after her and closed the stanchion, too, when she shoved her head in it to get to the alfalfa. After washing her udder he kicked her hock until her foot was back so he could get his knee inside her leg and his head buried between her flank and her belly so she couldn't kick and then he pulled the stool under him.

The small town of Plymouth, once known as Pokerville, came into being because of the gold mining activity in the central section of the Mother Lode. It played a role as a transportation gateway and supply center more than it did as the site of significant gold deposits, although there was a considerable amount of placer mining activity there in the 1850s and 60s. In the following decades some hard rock quartz deposits were developed in the area. The hard rock mines that sustained the town as the cattle industry developed in the later part of the nineteenth century were located on the east side of the town. There was also a stamp mill that occupied the bank of a creek on the west side of town opposite the mines, which at various times was used to reduce the ore that the area produced. In its lifetime, Plymouth Consolidated Mines yielded $13 million of gold, but by 1935 it had long since passed its peak. It wasn't nearly as productive as the Argonaut or Kennedy in the hills near Jackson, or many other mines in the region. The Keystone mine at Amador City, for instance, produced $24 million before it suspended operations. None of these mines, or the stamp mill either, would have been operating during the Depression if President Roosevelt had not increased the price of gold from seventeen to thirty-five dollars an ounce in January 1934, as an adjunct to other political and economic steps taken to ease the economic ills of the Depression. With the increased price of gold, hopeful men could labor to fill the small ore cars that were pushed by hand up the tracks into tunnels in the hillsides, returning with ore from drifts that followed the elusive veins of gold, bringing it to the tipple where it could be loaded into trucks and hauled to the stamp mill.

The population of Amador County contained its share of hard-working Italian and Eastern European 'turn of the century' immigrants. Their children constituted a large segment of the students that attended the Plymouth grammar school. Specific individuals amongst them tended to be undisciplined at times, a condition that Spud Murphy would find difficulty understanding or coping with.

E.J. parked the Model A on Main Street near Johnny Moyle's Garage, where the high school bus would stop to pick her up. Amador High School was in Sutter Creek, several miles south of Plymouth on Highway 49. As Spud Murphy got out of the car with his lunch pail, she said, "Stay on Main Street and walk up the hill past the highway. You'll see the grammar school on your right when you get to the top of the first rise. I'll be here this afternoon after school. If you get here before I do, just wait for me." He followed two other children who were obviously going to the school, staying a discreet distance behind them. They looked back once and saw him, but didn't offer to wait for him and he didn't try to catch up.

Spud Murphy was awed by the size of the school building. It had three classrooms and was a dirty white color. His old school was white, but it was a clean, freshly painted white. Parents of the students worked on weekends to keep it looking that way. This school looked as if nobody cared about it. It was just big. Big, and ugly.

There were groups of children gathered in small clusters in the schoolyard, waiting for the bell to call them to class. He kept his distance and stood with his back to them and none of them volunteered to come near him. After a while a teacher came out. She spoke to some of the girls and they said, "Good morning, Miss Joseph." From the corner of his eye, Spud Murphy saw her looking at him.

Nine

When the bell rang he followed a boy as big as himself into a classroom. He realized then he was in the wrong room, but he stood there by the door, unsure of what to do. The teacher said, "Good morning, children." The children answered her in unison, "Good morning, Mrs. Davis." She saw him standing by the door and said, "What grade are you in, boy?"

"Fifth, ma'am."

"Then you want Miss Joseph's room." She told him to follow the porch around and take the next door he came to into the building.

When he entered Miss Joseph's room, all the children were seated. Every eye turned to him as he was asked the same question and gave the same answer. Miss Joseph showed him which desks were for the fifth grade and he slid into one that was not taken. There were eight fifth-graders, including himself. The third and fourth grades were also in that room.

At recess time, one of the boys in his class came up to Spud Murphy and introduced himself in a friendly way, saying, "Hi. My name's Julius. You can come and play marbles with us if you want to. We're playing keepsies, though."

Spud Murphy had never heard of the game of marbles. It was not a game that was commonly played at Willow Springs. If Boogee ever had any marbles, he didn't bother mentioning it to Spud Murphy. Nor did Spud Murphy know what 'keepsies' meant. Curiosity caused him to follow Julius back to the circle of boys kneeling on the ground. Not wanting to divulge his ignorance, he avoided mixing in. He pretended boredom, lingering on the outer fringe of the circle in a show of disinterest while he figured out the rules of play. The only aspect of the game that he didn't understand was the reason anyone would want to play for 'keepsies' after he found out that meant risking the loss of one's marbles. He had difficulty recognizing the justification for keeping someone else's marbles when there was so much difference in the abilities of the players. He vowed privately that if he were ever lucky enough to possess a collection of such perfect glass creations he would treasure them, and never risk losing them in a foolish child's game.

At lunchtime he ate alone, sitting on the edge of the long porch, remaining aloof from the other boys and several of the girls who collected in a knot under a huge water oak that dominated the schoolyard. After lunch, they chose up sides for a game of softball. When Julius, who was one of the team captains, chose Spud Murphy as one of his picks, later even than some of the girls, Spud Murphy said he didn't want to play. Mr. Davis, the school principal, was the umpire, and the pitcher for both teams, as well.

After lunch period was over, Spud Murphy found himself subjected to the cruelest torture that could possibly have been visited on a member of the human race. Miss Joseph sent the entire fifth grade to the blackboard for an arithmetic quiz and began calling out pairs of fractions to be added. With each pair of fractions, the first student to write the correct answer on the blackboard got to sit down. The winner of the first round was Ruth French; of the second, it was Jimmy Castro. And finally there was only Spud Murphy standing alone in front of the class, staring through tears of rage and frustration at a blackboard on which appeared such a stupid and useless expression as $1/4 + 2/7 = ?$

Unknown to Spud Murphy, the Plymouth fourth grade class of the previous spring had been introduced to the concept of the *least common denominator*, as a condition of receiving promotion to fifth grade. Willow Springs Grammar School, on the other hand, influenced by the less stringent requirements of Teacher, emphasized language arts in its final fourth grade thrust toward learning, setting aside for the following year the introduction of the least common denominator. The result was

Nine

that Spud Murphy, who was quite capable of diagramming compound sentences containing prepositional phrases and adverbial clauses, was totally mystified when it came to finding the sum obtained by adding the fractions two-sevenths and one-quarter.

After making him stand at the blackboard for the next thirty minutes while the rest of the class went on to a geography lesson, Miss Joseph finally sent Ruth French up to show him the secret of the least common denominator, as though it were beneath her own standing to suffer such an ignorant lout, which was the most humiliating thing to which Spud Murphy could have been subjected if you tried for a thousand years. Although he ended up with the right answer with Ruth's tutoring, he still didn't understand the process, and he would have been at a loss if Miss Joseph had tested him with another problem. Fortunately, she didn't. By the end of the week, with E.J.'s help (no mathematical genius, herself), Spud Murphy knew enough about fractions and the arithmetic functions that went with them to be, from that time on, the pace-setter in Miss Joseph's weekly arithmetic drills.

On the second day of school Spud Murphy was one of the first down the hill, anxious to get to the car and wait for E.J. Still feeling the sting of his public humiliation of the day before, he had not yet warmed to anyone other than Julius, Ruth French and Jimmy Castro, and he had very few words even for them. He was anxious to get on with his arithmetic studies, determined to prove himself to Miss Joseph and the whole fifth grade before Mac found out about his shameful performance.

Plymouth's Main Street intersected State Highway 49, running north and south along the length of the Mother Lode at the very east edge of town. If you continued east on Main Street from that intersection, you would find the street name changed to Oleta (or Fiddletown) Road. Julius lived with his mother, Hilda, his dad, Sisto, and his younger brother, Raymond, on top of a small rise on the north side of Fiddletown Road about a hundred yards or so past the highway intersection. About a quarter mile past Julius' house was the Plymouth grammar school on the south side of the road. After that the road forked, the right fork going on to Fiddletown, and the left fork going to the Shenandoah Valley. In the front yard of Julius's house was a huge Mission fig tree.

As Spud Murphy crossed the highway, something hit him on the back of his head. Instinctively his hand went to where he had been hit and came away with the soft pulp of what remained of an over-ripe fig. He turned around and was immediately eye-to-eye with the taunting sneer of a stocky fourth grader who Spud Murphy had already sized up as being something of a school bully.

It doesn't take a whole lot of experience to recognize when you've been challenged, and the response to such a situation is something you generally don't take a whole lot of time to think about. Although Spud Murphy had never been in a fight before in his whole life, he instinctively lashed out with his fist and delivered a pretty good punch to the leering face of the fig-thrower. The other children passing through the intersection instantly became a ring around the two pugilists and there, right in the intersection, where Main Street crosses Highway 49, they tore into each other. Traffic in all directions came to a stop and grinning men sat in their trucks and yelled encouragement to both combatants. It was still a draw when a huge hand grabbed each of them by their shirt collars and separated them. Both hands belonged to Mr. Davis, the principal of the school and teacher of its sixth, seventh and eighth grades, who must have had a sixth sense to have known to leave his car at school and walk down to the intersection. He calmly said, "I will see the two of you before school tomorrow," and released them

Nine

When Spud Murphy got home, Mac noticed the bruises on his face. Without saying a word, Mac took Spud Murphy's hands and turned them over so he could see the knuckles. When he saw they were skinned, he simply grunted in a mildly approving way and let them fall. The next day Spud Murphy got off with a lecture from Mr. Davis, but the fig-thrower was not so lucky. Mr. Davis physically threw him right through the door of the boys' anteroom, nearly knocking the door off its hinges.

The whole incident could have been forgotten as far as Spud Murphy was concerned, but the fig-thrower wouldn't let it be. The girls didn't help any, either. They gathered around him as though he were some kind of hero to have struck out the way he did. The fig-thrower was a bully and as with most bullies, had a certain following, mostly male, but not too many real friends. Only Julius and Jimmy Castro could be said to be strictly neutral. When the fig-thrower challenged Spud Murphy again, he agreed to fight after school on Friday, this time in Julius's backyard where they wouldn't be interrupted by the ever-vigilant Mr. Davis. When Friday came Spud Murphy told E.J. that he wanted to walk home after school so she would not wait for him.

It seemed to Spud Murphy as though every kid in school showed up for the fight. They formed a ring in Albianis' backyard, and the two combatants squared off. It never was a contest, although it went on for a long time. The fig-thrower got in the first blow. He was wearing a large ring and blood flowed down Spud Murphy's face from a cut over his eye. Spud Murphy never got in a telling punch and he took a real licking. Worst of all, his frustration and the emotion of combat released his tears so they flowed down his cheeks continuously. He wouldn't give up in spite of the pounding he was taking. The two neutrals finally stopped the fight and everyone dispersed.

Somehow, the whole town except for the three teachers knew about the fight and even they may have known more than was said. Spud Murphy had to walk the length of Main Street before he struck off across country on his five-mile walk for home. Several of the bystanders on the sidewalk gave him a knowing grin or nodded at him. When he reached Colburn's drugstore, the young woman who worked there stopped him and called him inside. She gave him a wet cloth to wipe the blood and grime off his face and some ice for his bruises and she made him a milk shake. The drugstore was empty except for him and the girl, but he sat at the end of the counter, as inconspicuously as he could, and neither one of them had much to say. When he finished drinking the milk shake, he thanked her and left. On the way home he realized there was something he had to do before his father saw him. He walked up to the first white oak he came to and bloodied his knuckles on it.

Mac was not a man of imposing size. He just had this intense look about him, the look of a scrapper, Shanty-Irish through and through, a man who would tolerate no nonsense. Spud Murphy, always aware of Jack's propensity for getting into trouble and the price he paid for it, plotted every step of his path through childhood on a course designed to avoid testing the limits of his father's temper. It was not done to curry favor. It was done to avoid, at all cost, the penalties for disfavor. It is easy to see why Elsie may have said that he was such an easy child to raise. Without question, at least through the period of his early years, he was Mac's favorite as well. During those years he felt the fury of his father's wrath on only three occasions.

The first two times, Mac just hauled off and backhanded him in mid-sentence when he interrupted a conversation. He was standing at Mac's side and, although he certainly knew better, he suddenly felt compelled to get his two-cents' worth in. Mac's backhand caught him on the ear and the side of his jaw and he saw an explosion of stars and his ear didn't quit ringing for a week. The first time it happened Mac was talking to Mr. Pond and the second time it was Thelma White. There never was a third time.

The final incident happened on the morning of his eighth birthday in 1933, after he had just been given his .22 rifle as a birthday present. He was doing the morning chores and while the water pump was running to fill the storage tank, he ran up to the corral and turned the valve on to fill the watering trough in the corral. Because it was his birthday and they were going to have a picnic at the swimming hole at the Ball place in the afternoon, he was excited and in a hurry to get his chores done. He ran from the corral to the woodshed to fill the wood-box in the kitchen. While he was doing that he heard the pump motor speed up, indicating the well had run dry, so he ran down to the well to shut the pump off and then went back to the house to finish with the wood box. He forgot all about the water trough that was by now overflowing in the corral. He was cultivating a hill of beans a half hour later in the vegetable garden when he heard Mac's yell from the corral: "Spud Murphy! What the hell are you doing? Damn it, boy, you've run every drop of water we had out on the ground!"

The instant he heard Mac's voice, Spud Murphy remembered the water trough in the corral, but of course, by then it was too late. As he stood dismally surveying the sea of mud in the corral, he heard Mac say, "You lousy dim-witted little moron, if it wasn't your birthday, I'd get a whip and take the hide right off of you!" Spud Murphy, on hearing that, came perilously close to asking what his birthday had to do with it, but for once he managed to hold his tongue.

As he simmered in rage with his own frustrations, he thought, "Well, what could you expect the man to say after all the things that have been dumped on him, and then seeing his idiot kid pull a stupid stunt like that? At least I didn't get beat up on, and that's got to be something."

At the outset of the Depression in 1929 Mac had put all his ambitions and plans for personal fulfillment on hold and threw himself, heart and soul, into a battle to carry his family through a national economic catastrophe while at the same time engaged in a desperate struggle to save the life of his dying child. In his bid to accomplish those ends he homesteaded the land they lived on and performed a hundred small miracles, such as building from scratch the forge with which to shape his tools, using the scraps from someone else's junk pile. He became all things to those who depended on him for whatever needs might be, whether it was food to nourish the body or music to nourish hope. He was an electrician by education, a machinist by trade, a musician at heart, a prospector by caprice and a carpenter and farmer by necessity— and he excelled in all of those things. In the darkest years of the depression when the railroad spread its reduced work-load amongst its employees so that there were only two days a week in which to work his trade, he still provided for them all: no one of his family ever missed a meal for reasons of an insufficient larder.

He was a machinist par excellence, a specialist in the rebuilding of safety valves and feed-water pumps and train control systems on which the huge steam locomotives that crawled up the slopes and through the mountain passes of the transcontinental railroad depended for their safety and performance. He never failed the men of the train crews whose lives depended on the perfection of his machine work.

When Mac was at the homestead, Spud Murphy was expected to be at his side every minute, helping with whatever work there was to be done, learning from Mac's vast store of knowledge in whatever time was available between school and regular chores. As often as not, what was a stimulating challenge to Mac was devastating boredom to Spud Murphy. The focus of Spud Murphy's thoughts would forever be on exploration and adventure. If the subject had been forest lore or exploration or the conquest of distant lands, Spud Murphy would certainly have been the most avid of students. It is not easy to be apprenticed to a master craftsman who is proficient at all that he turns his hand to when your heart is in the romance of far away places. It is doubly hard when the master craftsman is one's father. Nor was it in Spud Murphy's nature to willingly become the instrument of his father's ambitions. He was compliant to Mac's wishes because that was what was expected of him and it would have been unthinkable for him not to be.

Mac was not a tolerant or patient man. In his intemperate moments he used words as if they were lashes, funneling his own frustration with the world and its inconsistencies into biting sarcasm, belittling any effort that led to less than his own ideal of perfection. To his notion, tolerance and forgiveness were unredeeming weaknesses. He saw the world as an eternal adversary, the best defense against which was an unrelenting calcification of his own personal opinions and standards. Too often Spud Murphy bore the sting of Mac's words in Mac's resolution to form his son to his own standards. But the worst of Mac's shortfalls in Spud Murphy's mind was Mac's overweening absorption with himself and all who bore the family name. While it was true that Mac was a near genius, it was equally true that he was an inveterate braggart, infatuated with his own self-certitude and boastful of his triumphs.

Spud Murphy, being a male and brought up in a conventional family relationship, looked to his father as his role model. Unfortunately, most of Spud Murphy's sensibilities seemed to be the product of Elsie's genetic contribution and her primacy in providing the nurturing elements of his early years. It was unfortunate because it created two opposed, polarizing forces within himself that always kept him at odds with himself. From Elsie's encouragement there sprang within him the romance of life and a curiosity about the world that existed beyond his horizons. It was she who forgave him his chores and sent him off to explore the freedom of the woods and the river, at times when Mac was not at the homestead. It was with her encouragement he discovered the seductive charm of literature and vocabulary and history. It was against her poise and grace and forbearance that he contrasted his father's often-violent frustrations with the material reality of the world.

For more than a year Spud Murphy and Elsie stayed alone as full time residents of the homestead. For all that time he was her constant companion, helping her salvage the lumber that Mac would use on the weekends in building the house; turning the soil for a garden and planting, cultivating, and harvesting: hauling water for their domestic needs and for the growing livestock population. In the evenings, even after the house was completed and the family reunited, she taught him to read and to wonder about the mysteries of the universe among the constellations and the galaxies. She endowed him with a curiosity for events and circumstances that lay far beyond the limits of the directly observable world that was within the range of his physical senses.

She was an uncommon woman, in that— despite the intolerable impoverishment of the times, despite her personal grief brought on by her daughter's illness and the lonesomeness she must have felt, she treated Spud Murphy not as a child but as a potential adult, recognizing and encouraging his efforts to assume an accountable role in life. She avoided ever lecturing on that subject, however, relying on circumstance to provide the opportunities to reinforce his responsible behavior. She never belittled or reprimanded. When at times he was remiss, her reproof was administered in a thoughtful, kindly way.

Nine

The conflict that arose within him from the contrasting natures of Mac and Elsie was not something that Spud Murphy could identify from his immature perspective. It nonetheless seethed within him, unresolved. In the end he accepted it as a condition of life and withdrew from honesty in his relationships with all. After a time, not Mac nor Elsie nor his teachers nor any sibling nor peer was privy to his deepest feelings and emotions. He reacted to people based on what he thought they expected of him. He saw the expression of his own feelings as secondary to the greater goal of peace in his relationships with those around him. He became an expert in the art of subterfuge and deception. The surprising thing was that this duplicity netted him an unexpected bonus. Instead of being confronted for the insincerity of his sham, his accommodation to others was perceived to be rooted in some sort of virtue that was of small consequence to him. The point had long since come to be the avoidance of confrontation at any cost.

Ten

On a cool spring day in April 1936 Elsie called the family to lunch and Spud Murphy sat on a long wood bench at the table in what would normally be E.J.'s place. He sat there in her seat, for no reason other than to be a pest. E.J., now almost sixteen and firmly ensconced in her position as the family angel, grinned back at him and sat on another bench opposite him in what would normally be his seat, without appearing to have any ruffled feathers whatsoever. Next to her on the same bench, shaking his head at Spud Murphy's perversity, was eighteen-year-old brother Jack. Mac was not at home, it being a workday at the S.P. shops.

Elsie brought a huge bowl of chicken soup that had been boiling on the stove and set it on the table. Then she went into the living room and brought nine-month-old baby brother Billy in his bassinet and set the bassinet on the bench beside Spud Murphy. She said to all of them in general, "I don't feel well. Watch the baby for me so I can lie down in the living room and get a few minutes' rest while you're having lunch."

Spud Murphy was the last to fill his bowl with the hot soup. He took a spoonful and blew on it to cool it and sat looking down at the baby in the bassinet making unintelligible gurglings and laughing and waving his hands above him. He saw a tiny hand find the rim of the bowl and pull. The bowl tipped and came off the table and Spud Murphy saw it all in slow motion and his mind was telling him to make the bowl stop but he sat frozen and couldn't move. The bowl was upside down in the bassinet and scalding soup was all over his baby brother and the soft gurglings had been transformed into terrible, racking screams of pain.

Spud Murphy stumbled to his feet, but Jack was around the table and at the bassinet before him. He had Billy in his arms and then Elsie was there and took Billy, unpinning his diaper as E.J. brought towels to wrap him in. Jack ran to bring the car to the door, and when they were getting in the car Spud Murphy heard his mother say, "Get to Barneys and call your father at the S.P. shops. Tell him we'll go straight to the county hospital in Sacramento." Spud Murphy wanted to go with them but Elsie said, "No." E.J. took his hand and they stood there together crying and watched the car drive down the road and out of sight. Frozen in his mind were the images of the tiny hand, the tilting bowl of soup, and the knowledge that he had failed to act in time to prevent the scalding chicken soup from pouring on his nine-month-old baby brother. Billy was in the hospital for a couple of weeks and recovered with just a little tendency to be pigeon-toed and flat-footed from the effect of the scarring on his legs and feet. It was enough of a reminder that Spud Murphy was never able to forget or forgive himself for his slow-witted reactions.

HOUSE VOTE OVERRIDES ROOSEVELT'S BONUS VETO

WASHINGTON, Jan. 24--(UP) The house impelled the soldier bonus toward payment today by overriding by a vote of 324 to 61 President Roosevelt's veto of the baby bond payment bill, almost immediately after the unique hand-written six-sentence veto message was read.

The bill which provides payment to veterans of about $2,000,000,000 in bonds of $50 denomination cashable after June 15th now will go to the Senate where concurrence to the house action is regarded as virtually inevitable.

Sacramento Bee, January 24, 1936

Early in the year, Congress passed the bill providing for payment of the World War I Veteran's Bonus over the President's veto, making payment available in June 1936. Intended to lift the spirit, if not the immediate resources of a despondent and impoverished society, it began at once to have an effect on the level of Spud Murphy's personal fortunes. It was manna from heaven, a grain of hope that brought the scales at least partly to balance for seven long years of Mac and Elsie's hardship and denial. With the nearly one thousand dollars Mac received, he made down payments on a brand-new 1936 Ford pickup and a Baldwin baby grand piano.

It isn't always possible to foretell the results, good or bad, that follow from a seemingly unexpected event such as the receipt of the bonus money. It really was unexpected, because the veterans, for the most part, felt they'd never see a nickel of it, the way they'd been horsed around. Of course, Mac was happy about getting the pickup, and a new one at that. Elsie, too, was overjoyed with her beautiful new piano. But Spud Murphy, experiencing only the immediate joys and pains of an uncertain world over which he had very little control, saw himself as the real beneficiary of Congress's wisdom. Even to his unsophisticated mind it was clear that his parents' suddenly improved financial position brought about an equally sudden relief from the domestic tempests that had resulted from spending years living on the verge of bankruptcy. It was a relief that he had prayed for many times on the occasions when Mac's frustrations were vented in rage at either Elsie or Jack. The eruptions of Mac's temper frightened him so much he would have welcomed anything that would have put a stop to them.

The old saw is that "money can't buy happiness." Spud Murphy thought that may be so, but he was certain that the lack of it could surely bring an awful lot of unhappiness. Whether it was the symbolic acknowledgment of the nation's gratitude that was represented by the payment of the bonus, or the pride of ownership of the new pickup, or the satisfaction of being able to buy Elsie her long coveted grand piano, or maybe a little of all of those things is not what mattered. What mattered was that Mac found less need to blow off steam. But a short temper remains that, always present under the surface with frequent small eruptions to remind one of the greater torment that lies within.

With the acquisition of the piano and the concerns of pregnancy behind her, promising a return to a more predictable lifestyle, Elsie focused her attention once more on Spud Murphy's musical education. In the three years of violin lessons since second grade, he had developed a proficiency that led both Mac and Elsie to believe that he had enough talent to justify, in light of their rekindled hopes of prosperity, a more advanced music teacher. A more complete explanation of the situation was that the 'more advanced' teacher Mac had in mind was Edward Weida, an expatriate German violinist of some local (Sacramento) renown who was concert master with the

Sacramento Symphony Orchestra. By coincidence Mr. Weida was also an employee of the S.P. Railroad and as such was Mac's supervisor in the Motive Power Division. He took Spud Murphy on as a student, pro bono, as a favor to Mac, although it is true that Mr. Weida also held out great hope for Spud Murphy's musical future.

To Spud Murphy, music lessons were just another price to pay for the benefit of unruffled domestic relationships and the privilege of being allowed to play with the Sierra Ranch Hands. He kept that notion strictly to himself, however, especially after he came to appreciate the logistics involved in having a weekly music lesson on a school day in a city forty miles away from one's schoolroom. One part of those logistics involved not ever having to go to school on Fridays as long as he earned top grades in school and was a credible violin student.

Spud Murphy really enjoyed going on gigs with the Sierra Ranch Hands who by 1935, had been renamed the Sacramento Haywire Orchestra. They took him along on every possible opportunity if it was an event at which the presence of a ten-year-old fiddle player was socially acceptable. There were some intermediate situations, though, such as stag nights at the American Legion hall in Oak Park, when they hid his chair back in the wings so the audience couldn't see him. Which seemed to satisfy the conventions, without really getting in the way of his being able to watch the stripper doing her number on the stage. Anyway, the strippers always did their thing with the lights turned down a little and who wants to look at a kid in such circumstances, anyway? The Fridays-off-from-school part was negotiated by Mac and Elsie in discussions with the school authorities, in this case being Mr. Davis, the principal, and Miss Joseph, the fifth grade teacher at Plymouth, with Mrs. Littlefield (Teacher, Willow Springs) always in consultation. Which might explain why the very first class assignment of the new school year happened to be the blackboard quiz on fractions. A way of starting things off on the right foot, perhaps?

The deal was that, in return for being the smartest kid in the county, Spud Murphy would get to ride with Mac to Sacramento every Friday morning in the new pickup and in the afternoon when Mac got off work he would take Spud Murphy to Mr. Weida's house for his violin lesson. For the eight hours in between the ride to Sacramento and the music lesson he was his own man, free to roam the city as he pleased. This last was never articulated in the terms of agreement, but Spud Murphy just assumed that if he thought it was, and didn't talk too much about it, there was a better chance of it being so.

It was summer vacation when this regimen came into being, so there was no problem of interference with school activities. On the first morning when Mac pulled into the S.P. parking lot with Spud Murphy on board, Spud Murphy piled out and ran around to Mac's side to get his instructions. Stepping down from the truck cab with his lunch pail, Mac said, "All right, son. Listen carefully. Right over there by that guard shack, where you see all those men going by those two goons in uniform, is the shop gate. At eleven o'clock sharp when the whistle blows for lunchtime, I want you standing there at that gate waiting for me and I will come to get you and take you inside where I work, because that's where we eat lunch. After lunch you can find your own way out and then be back again at the gate at three-thirty sharp, when the whistle blows at quitting time."

Pointing, he said, "Up that way about six or seven blocks you'll find the City Library. It's a big building across from the post office on "I" Street. I expect you can find some reading material there to keep you busy. Around the corner next to the library on 9th Street is the Roxie Theater. I saw your mother give you fifteen cents at breakfast. That'll get you into the matinee after lunch, if you want to see a movie. Back this other way is the riverfront. There are lots of boats there from different places. Just stay out of the river and away from where they're working.

"Watch your step, and don't be late for that eleven o'clock whistle. Keep your head on your shoulders."

Spud Murphy watched Mac walk through the gate past the two "goons," and when he was out of sight Spud Murphy ran back around to the passenger's door of the pickup and crawled back in and slammed the door shut.

It took him almost a half-hour to decide that he couldn't sit in the pickup all day. He thought of trying to find 18th and "F" Street and his two friends from last summer but finally decided it might be just as easy to try to find the city library as Mac had suggested.

The commercial area of downtown Sacramento from the riverfront to where the railroad shops were located was a strange and interesting place. It was not as threatening as it first appeared, once a person got adjusted to the steam exhausts of the locomotives that were sidetracking or entering or leaving the railroad yards; the clanging bells and coupling noise of engines in the switch-yards; and more clanging bells of the city's trolley cars, with their whining electric motor and wheel-on-rail sounds and the automobile traffic and honking horns on the streets and people sweeping sidewalks and the constant stream of humanity bearing down on a person. By the time he had uncertainly navigated the distance from the S.P. employee parking lot to the library on 9th and "I" Streets, Spud Murphy's spirit of adventure and exploration had returned somewhat to supplant his initial feelings of being swallowed up like Jonah by the alien commercialism of the city. In a very short time he became used to it and found himself looking forward to an infinite number of Fridays in the city, even though he was sure he would never understand why everyone was in such a hurry there.

And there was the riverfront, where you could sit on the edge of the dock for hours watching the boats and barges move along the river, many of them with the names of other home ports neatly lettered on their bows and transoms, some being from places he had read about, and others that he had never heard of before, like "San Pedro" and "Astoria". Occasionally, large sailing yachts were moored to the docks, resplendent in gleaming brass and dark polished mahogany and bleached white piping, celebrating the prodigality of their owners while simultaneously mocking the dull, weathered hopelessness that was so much a part of everything else that was normal to the times.

One block south of the S.P. depot was "J" Street. Centered on that thoroughfare, beginning on Front Street and separating the railroad yard from the rest of Sacramento, was a skid-row collection of saloons and pawn shops and small cheap hotels and narrow, dingy coffee shops— the kind they called greasy spoons— and small trade stores; hardware shops and second-hand stores and even a blacksmith shop and a saddlery, both of which did a land office business in spite of the Depression, or perhaps because of it. Most of the gaudier hotels with freshly painted signs such as "The Nevada Hotel" and "The Jade Rooms" were not hotels at all but only houses of prostitution, and young women often looked down on the street from second-story windows, or stood like other merchandise on display beside their doors. After school resumed in the fall and they became aware that he still continued to pass by on what then should have been a school day, they asked him why he wasn't in school and their friendly eyes sparkled with quizzical amusement at the country politeness of his explanation. They came to know him and called him by his name and sometimes engaged him in conversation, remembering the almost, but not quite forgotten, images and dreams of their own age of innocence, often not too long past.

He never entered any of the shops without invitation, but he never tired of looking at the merchandise through the windows that fronted on the street, examining with both his eyes and his imagination the known and the unknown, ranging from the utilitarian to the elegant. His passage through this drab, down-to-earth neighborhood with its exotic appeal seldom delayed him for long from reaching his destination, which in the morning was always the city library that Mac had directed him to, a block past the skid-row section and within the downtown city proper.

In the library, Spud Murphy learned where all the western novels and adventure books were shelved, and he read Will James, Zane Grey, Ernest Haycox, Edgar Rice Burroughs, Jack London, Nordhoff and Hall's *Bounty Trilogy, Captain Blood,* and *Scaramouch* by Rafael Sabatini, and *Beau Geste* by Percival Christopher Wren, who had actually graduated from Sand Hurst before he fought with the French Foreign Legion. Like the prostitutes and many of the shopkeepers, the library lady came to know him by name and treated him with special consideration, setting aside books for him that she thought he might enjoy. After seeing him every Friday for more than a year, she asked him if he would like to have a library card so he could take books home if he wished. When he told her he didn't live in the city or even in the same county, she said, "I think we can manage that all right. I shouldn't worry about it." Aside from the pride he took in having his very own library card, it really didn't make any difference in his reading. He still came to the library every Friday morning.

By eleven o'clock he was back at the gate at the railroad yards. When the whistle blew Mac showed up as promised, and after the first time of having to go in with Mac, the guards at the gate let him go alone to the machine shop where Mac worked. He sat on a stool at Mac's work bench next to the big South Bend lathe that was the stock-in-trade of Mac's craft and ate the bacon sandwich Elsie had put in Mac's lunch box for him and watched Mac and Fred Bishop and another machinist play three-handed pinochle over lunch or they would play whist if there happened to be four of them. When the half-hour lunch period was over and the whistle blew again he used the fifteen cents Elsie always gave him and hurried to the Liberty Theater on lower "K" Street or the El Rio that was next to the city library and for the three and a half hours that it took for a double feature to run he sailed the Caribbean with Captain Blood or rode the "breaks" of the Missouri River on a fast horse with Jesse and Frank James and otherwise lived in vicarious exaltation whatever life that Friday's movie bill of fare offered and that was not at all like the real life he lived at the homestead.

It was fortunate that Spud Murphy was not one who needed constant reinforcement from the members of a peer group, as was the case for many boys of his age. If he had been, Fridays could have meant a lot of lonesome hours for him. Far from ever finding himself with lonely hours to spend, his problem was always exactly the opposite. He treasured the solitude in which he found himself, free to reach his own unchallenged conclusions about the whys and wherefores of his evolving world, although such singleness of perspective often had the effect of setting himself at odds with the rest of the world. His opinions were at least his own, however, and were easily discarded or modified if it really was necessary. In any case, if it was an issue that needed immediate verification, he had the hour's drive home after his music lesson in which to solicit Mac's opinion.

In the meantime, he reveled in the opportunity to engage himself in uninterrupted reflection, or even fantasy at times, in either the world of exploration and adventure or the materialistic world of discovery and invention. The city was full of strange and fascinating *things* that stirred his sense of curiosity and imagination. Too full, almost, for him ever to have time to sustain an interest for very long in any single thing. But then he had no grand vision of ever becoming a contributing part of the commerce of this or any other city, as if he ever could, or would want to. The fact was, the subject never entered his mind. One could easily say that except for that which had yet to be explored, he was totally without lasting ambition in any given direction. The ambition that was assigned to him by others, primarily his father, was far more than he ever had a use for.

He never once gave thought to being more than an interested observer, enthralled with the enormity and audacity of the city, swallowing whole its magnificence, its complexity, its grandeur. He liked its people and the fact that he was treated by them as an equal, a responsible member of society, and not a responsibility to be endured or a child to be scolded or instructed. Only the policeman, whose job it was to patrol the sidewalk and by right of his uniform and badge could question him on the subject of his not being in school, ever saw or treated him that way, and then only in the beginning, before each understood the other's role.

All week long, every week, he looked forward to Friday and was careful to keep his grades above the grades of his classmates so that he didn't jeopardize his weekly ventures into the adult world. Before and after school he did his chores with alacrity, and most importantly, he practiced his music, every boring exercise that he found so tiresome. When summer came and school let out on vacation, even the enticement of the river on a hot afternoon could not lure him away from his Friday freedom to explore the magic of the city streets.

Spud Murphy was a year and a half younger than Julius. Even so, they just naturally gravitated to each other. Notwithstanding their attachment for each other, they were unlike in many ways.

The attraction was more one of opposites, like the opposite poles of a magnet. The most obvious difference between them was the ease with which Julius fell in with the company of others as opposed to Spud Murphy's preference for 'going it alone.' There were many other ways in which they were as different as night and day.

Julius was good at games and sports. Whether it was marbles or softball or riding the half-wild burros that belonged to the Forest Service or the matter of who was the fastest runner, it was all the same. If Julius didn't actually come in first, you could bet that he wouldn't be far behind. Spud Murphy, on the other hand, couldn't win a game of hopscotch against a quadriplegic.

Julius was also quick-witted in emergencies. There was the time in the seventh grade, on a frosty morning before school with a fire roaring in the big potbellied stove in Mr. Davis's room and the draft wide open, when all the girls were standing around the stove as close as they could get, trying to stay warm, and the hem of Helen Wickland's ankle-length dress got sucked into the draft and, in the time that it took for her to feel the pain and jump back from the stove, the fire was already up around her waist. Spud Murphy was standing not ten feet away from her and there were other boys as close, or closer, but it was Julius who was right behind her when she ran screaming out of the classroom through the boys' anteroom, trying to escape the terrible pain of the flames by running outdoors. He caught her when she was half-way around the school building and rolled her on the ground and put the fire out. One of the students brought a coat and he wrapped her in it and by then an adult who came to drop off a child for school, drove her to the hospital. Julius got some burns out of it, but what mattered was that he saved Helen's life.

In some ways they did prove to be very much alike. Neither one could pass up a challenge or a dare. They each had a gleam in their eye that most of the time spelled trouble. Julius won more of his challenges than Spud Murphy ever did, but he also caught more of the backlash for his errant ways, maybe because he was too honest. His father, Sisto, was a strict disciplinarian who enforced the rules and regulations with his belt. Along with whatever trouble Julius could manage to get himself into with his own foolishness and shenanigans, there was always his younger bother Raymond ready to help him into more.

Julius and Spud Murphy would often sit together at Spud Murphy's desk to study. More than likely, their 'studying' consisted of drawing pictures of various army air corps pursuit planes such as Boeing P-26A Pea-Shooters in combat with Fiat G.55 Centauros of the Italian Air Force during Mussolini's 1935 conquest of Ethiopia, or Curtis P-36 Hawks shooting down ME109s (which was rather an unlikely event) in the final days of the Spanish Civil War. The secret was to hide the particular work of art in whatever book they were supposed to be studying whenever it looked as though Mr. Davis was sneaking up behind them. Once or twice they got so involved in the aerial battle or in trying to aggravate Ruth French, who sat right in front of Spud Murphy, that they forgot to keep an eye out for Mr. Davis, who caught them red-handed from behind and knocked their heads together. He sent them to the front of the room to stand on a bench facing the blackboard with their noses about six inches from the board. Julius never could keep his mouth shut whenever he was caught doing something wrong. He was always prompted to say, "I wasn't doing anything," in a hurt, whiney tone of voice, to which Mr. Davis would respond, "I know. So get busy and do something," and give him a swat on the rear end with whatever was handy, most likely the largest textbook that was on his desk at the moment.

Above all else, except perhaps for horses, Julius and Spud Murphy valued their rifles and the opportunity to target practice. The ammunition to pursue that sport costs money, and neither of their families could spare the cash to satisfy their endless yearnings to make a tin can jump up in the air or hear the whine of a bullet as it ricocheted off a serpentine boulder. Both Mac and Sisto were war veterans. As such, they were also members of the American Legion, Post 108 of Amador County, which made Julius and Spud Murphy eligible for membership in an organization called the Sons of the American Legion. The attraction that caused them to join that organization was the free ammunition the legion supplied for target practice. The justification for it was the possibility it offered for forming a junior rifle team to compete in target matches with junior rifle teams from other American Legion posts. To the best of Spud Murphy's knowledge there were no other junior members of Post 108 from which to make up a team, which suited them quite nicely. Evidently there was no other post around with a junior rifle team either, because he had no recollection of ever firing a match. No matter, the two of them became an officially recognized rifle team anyway, short-handed as it was, and that, praise be, qualified it for an unlimited allotment of free ammunition for target practice.

.22 long-rifle ammunition, at thirty-one cents per box of fifty across the counter at Wheeler Bros. General Merchandise, was exactly the commodity of which these two buffalo hunters were most in need. The only restriction that came with this free ammunition was that it had to be used on the outdoor target range the Legionnaires set up at the football field at Amador High School. You couldn't just take it home and start potting tin cans and jackrabbits with it and ricocheting it off rocks the next day. Well, better that than nothing.

What really drew them together more than anything else was Julius's innate softness of heart, which from the start refused to allow him to abandon a socially dysfunctional new kid in school who badly needed a friend, and who obviously didn't have a clue about how the social system, or pecking order, or whatever else you wanted to call it, worked in the scruffy little mining towns of the Mother Lode, such as Plymouth. Spud Murphy could see he needed all the help he could get, and if this scrappy kid with an Italian name wanted to get on his side, he sure wasn't going to object. By the end of the first week, it was obvious they were going to hit it off well together.

Sometime during the second half of the 1930s, Spud Murphy went over to the Ybright place, thinking he would find Old Bill and ride him down to the river. He had a length of twine with which to make a hackamore of sorts and an apple core so Bill would feel better about carting him around. Next to the Cosumnes River and the gorge, Ybrights was Spud Murphy's most favorite place, because it still retained some of the look of what a ranch should be. The whole country was full of old abandoned ranch houses and homesteaders' buildings all the way from the old Slate Creek School and beyond to the Ball place. Even the famous desperado Joaquin Murrieta had an old stone building where he was supposed to have hidden out along with Three Finger Jack, halfway up the ridge on the north side of the river, the El Dorado side. Except for Ybrights and the Eiler place, there just wasn't enough left standing of any of the old buildings to amount to much.

The Slate Creek School house was still pretty substantial, but there wasn't anything there except the one-room building where Harp Taylor had been one of the students when Ima was the teacher, but that was before they were married. The first time Spud Murphy saw the building, which was before he joined up with Hugh Glass and became a trapper, there was a skunk pelt nailed up over the door and not being sure just what it was, he asked Jack about it. Jack told him that there was an Indian who used to stay there from time to time and the hairy thing nailed over the door was the scalp of a homesteader. Jack said the

Indian still lived around the area somewhere, he just didn't know quite where.

On this particular day when he got to Ybrights, he got quite a surprise because along with Old Bill and Wallace there were a couple of young-looking saddle horses, one a pint-sized little buckskin gelding and the other a stout-looking dark bay mare. Spud Murphy couldn't get anywhere near the buckskin, but the mare took the apple core out of his hand and then checked out all his pockets for another one. Spud Murphy leaned on her shoulder and patted her neck and rubbed her nose. Then he went over to the shed and squatted on his heels looking at her, wondering where she came from. After awhile he fitted the hackamore to her and rode her up to Black's Flat and back. Spud Murphy never ran Old Bill, seeing as how he was so old and worn out, but after he got through the Wooden Gate he touched his heels to the mare and they went up through the flat like the wind.

Spud Murphy was quite a while finding out who had provided this glorious addition to his remuda. Never having bothered to discuss his occasional use of the neighbors' horses with Mac or Elsie, he didn't think it would be prudent to risk raising their curiosity at this late stage by bringing the matter up at all. Perhaps a month or so later he was riding the mare up Cascara Creek on the way back from the Ball place. As he passed in a dreaming state of mind through the live oak grove, which no longer held any threat to him, he came face-to-face with another rider stopped on the trail watching him approach. Spud Murphy wondered if they still hung horse thieves, 'cause if they did, he figured he was done for, for sure. Not having any other plan in his mind, he just sat the mare off the side of the trail like he didn't have a worry in the world

"Howdy," said the stranger.

"Howdy," said Spud Murphy, looking the stranger directly in the face.

"Nice horse," said the stranger.

"She'll do," said Spud Murphy, and being that he was looking the stranger straight in the eye as he said it, he couldn't fail to see the hint of a smile that crossed the stranger's face at his reply. The stranger's horse stepped forward, moving off the trail to let Spud Murphy ride by. As he passed, Spud Murphy noticed the Harrington & Richardson .22-caliber eight-shot revolver the stranger carried in a holster on his hip. That night at dinner he mentioned seeing a man on horseback down at the flat, without bringing up the fact that he also had been on horseback. After Spud Murphy described him as being lanky and not too old but kind of weather-beaten, Jack said "That sounds like John Taylor. Was he wearing a pistol?" Spud Murphy said "He had an H & R .22 revolver in a holster." Jack said "How do you know what make it was, moron?" and Spud Murphy answered, "Because it's just like the one in the Monkey Ward catalog. Who's John Taylor, anyway?"

Elsie explained that John Taylor was one of Harp Taylor's sons, which didn't help much, but out of the conversation finally came the information that Harp Taylor was a man who drove the Shell Oil Company truck delivering fuel oil and who was also keeping some horses down at Ybrights. It suddenly became clear to Spud Murphy that the jig was about to be up.

But as time went by, nothing happened; no one said anything about the matter. No posse showed up with a hanging rope. Sheriff Lucot did not come down from Jackson asking about his whereabouts. Abdul did not have to roust out any strangers that were found snooping around the corral. When a month passed with nothing happening, Spud Murphy went down to Ybrights with a whole apple that had just one bite out of it and a length of twine, just in case. He never got caught red-handed stealing horses again in all the remaining time he spent on the homestead, although he continued to ride the mare when he had the opportunity and he also ran into John Taylor on the Ybright place many times after that, but never again when he, Spud Murphy, was sitting on a horse of any kind. It seemed that John Taylor's powers of perception were almost transcendental, allowing him to intentionally avoid Spud Murphy whenever the latter happened to be on a "borrowed" horse's back.

When Julius found out that there were more horses to be ridden, he wasted no time in getting permission from his parents to spend a day with Spud Murphy. After the morning chores were done, Elsie gave Spud Murphy the rest of the day off and the two ne'er-do-wells made a beeline over the top of the hill to the Ybright Ranch.

In addition to being the place you most likely would find the horses, the Ybright place had other attractions such as an old two-wheel trap in a shed and a regular four-wheel buggy in another shed. You couldn't do much with the trap without putting a horse between the shafts, which they didn't attempt only because there were too many easier things to do and there just wasn't enough tack of one kind or another laying around from which to jury-rig a harness. The buggy, however, was another matter. All you needed was a couple of ropes to steer with and you were in business. After you pulled it up the hill and lined it out, you simply released the brake and practically flew down the hill past the house for a hundred and fifty yards or so. You just didn't want to lose hold of the steering ropes on the way down.

A creek flowed down through the ranch about a hundred fifty feet in front of the Ybright house. It was the same creek where Jack and Spud Murphy caught the three rattlesnakes that got loose in the rumble seat of the Model A. except that was further on down where the road crossed the creek at a ford. Spud

Ten

Murphy never knew for sure if the creek's real name was Possum Creek or if that was just a name Waldo Barney or Jack gave it trying to be funny. He spent a lot of time looking but he never saw anything remotely resembling a possum anywhere along it. Spud Murphy's private name for it was pigeon creek because, three or four times during the ten years he lived on the homestead, thousands of migrating pigeons roosted there overnight on their way to wherever pigeons go when they migrate. The county already had one Pigeon Creek, though, so they didn't really need another.

Possum Creek ran a little water most of the year, drying up toward the last part of August during the drought years, which was most of the time, except for a couple of pools that were fed from under-ground. One of the pools was right in front of the house, and there was an old bathtub for a watering trough there. Every night the quail would come down at about dusk, regular as clockwork, and if it was quail season you could sit there as still as a church mouse with a .22 and get a couple of them for dinner. If you sat real still, they'd practically walk right over you. Upstream from the watering trough was a small almond orchard of about fifteen or eighteen trees, in a fenced enclosure. Five or six of the trees were the bitter-tasting kind that it takes to pollinate the flowers of the eating variety, and they were always loaded with big, healthy-looking nuts that had the most awful bitter taste you could ever imagine. The edible nuts from the other trees were mostly harvested by the squirrels, but you could sometimes find a few they missed, or hadn't gotten to yet. If you couldn't find any edible almonds, there were always pine nuts in the big healthy cones of a digger pine on the creek bank.

If you were setting out to design an amusement park for ten-to- twelve-year-old boys, you couldn't have done much better than Ybrights, considering the thrill of riding down the hill in an out-of-control buggy, the nut concession, the roomy house with its shady porch, a remount contractor who was so agreeable he didn't seem to mind having his horses stolen occasionally, and the pleasant nature of the shooting range and its associated facilities.

Eleven

Even before the S.P. shops returned to full employment, Mac had given up the radio program rather than burden himself with the aggravation of having to solicit sponsors. He explained how during that time, which was the darkest part of the Depression, the uncertainty of such a venture, coupled with the pressing demands of getting the homestead up and running simply ruled against wasting his time on it. As a result, he took greater advantage of opportunities in other venues, playing weekly engagements in clubs and on special occasions for fraternal and social groups and private parties. The George Manhart American Legion post in Oak Park was a venue they played frequently. Spud Murphy well remembered an engagement there, which included both a tap dancer who did her number to "The Sidewalks of New York" and a fan dancer who did hers to the soulful strains of 'Poor Butterfly'.

Poor Butterfly

**Music by Raymond Hubbell
and
Lyrics by John Golden (1916)**

Poor Butterfly...'neath the blossoms waiting...
Poor Butterfly...for she loved him so...
The moments pass into hours...
The hours pass into years...
And as she smiles through her tears...
She murmurs low...

The moon and I... know that he'll be faithful...
I'm sure he'll come...to me by and by...
But if he don't come back...
Then I'll never sigh or cry...
I just must die...
Poor Butterfly...

Another venue for which Spud Murphy had fond memories because of the elegant atmosphere, was the 1937 New Year's Eve dance at the St. George Hotel in Volcano. Ariel said, "Well, that just shows you what a couple of gents wearing tuxedos will do for the ambiance." Mac placed the kitty right in front of Spud Murphy's chair. It was a pretty shrewd thing to do, because the tips were doubled from what would have been a normal take. Spud Murphy wondered if anyone there was so foolish as to think he was actually going to share in that take, or in the wages, either. It never bothered him not to get paid for playing. If he'd had the money and they'd told him to, he would have been glad to pay the other orchestra members for the privilege of sitting in the bandstand with them. Occasionally, Ariel gave him an opportunity to solo, which was special, such as on the intro to an easy number like 'Girl of My Dreams' or 'Sleepy Time Gal.'

Dance gigs didn't offer anything to challenge Mac's promotional talents, so with Elsie's help he organized a group of young people from the Willow Springs area that were good round dancers and taught them the figures and movements of square dancing. They performed the 'old time' dances of the nineteenth century and earlier and successfully competed in the square dance contests that still are among the featured events at county fairs all across America. They gave themselves the name *Crinolines and Cutaways* after those prominent articles of formal wear that were in vogue during the nineteenth century, at which time the European quadrille and the American square dance reached their greatest levels of popularity. *Crinoline* was the coarse fabric made of cotton and horsehair used in European fashions of that era to stiffen ladies' hats and other garments. It lent its name to the petticoats made from it that were worn by fashionable ladies of the times. A *cutaway* was a man's formal coat with the front edges below the waist cut back and sloped, to form tails behind. As was usually the case with Mac's productions, the Crinolines and Cutaways turned out to be a cut above the normal country square dance club, featuring highly skilled dancers wearing stylish costumes more normally seen in elegant European ballroom dancing.

The Crinolines and Cutaways drew on the styles and manners of English and French tradition more than they did their American counterparts, except for the employment of a "caller," which is an American improvisation. The reason for that concession was not hard to find, inasmuch as there was only one choice possible in the selection of a *caller* for the *Crinolines and Cutaways* and that, of course, was Mac. It was the perfect role to spotlight his unique showmanship. Elsie and Spud Murphy and occasionally Ariel provided the music. A 'set' for a quadrille consisted of four couples. Although the dancers varied from time to time, four of the regular couples were Ralph Wait and E.J., Tom and Goula Wait, Norval Stuart and Eunice Barney, and Jack Holmes and his wife Vivian. Occasional dancers were Norma Waters, Betty Facht, and the Drake brothers, Donald and Francis, and others whose names are lost in the dim recesses of time.

In addition to the quadrilles and square dances, individual round dances— such as the varsouvienne, gavotte, polka, waltz, schottische, and minuet— were sometimes used to fill out the program at exhibitions. On the occasion of at least a couple of such exhibitions, Spud Murphy underwent the extreme humiliation of being seen openly dancing in public with a girl. His partner on those occasions was Peggy Facht, the eleven- or twelve-year-old femme fatale of the Crinolines and Cutaways' youth division. Their specialty was the Spanish three-step and except for Peggy trying to lead most of the time they were professional indeed.

The valley of the Cosumnes from Michigan Bar to the Highway 49 bridge crossing and beyond had been well-scoured during the gold rush and the following years, most recently by the Chinese miners around the turn of the century, who left the valley well gleaned to the extent that the placer mining technology of those times permitted. With the doubling of the price of gold following President Roosevelt's January 1934 edict, renewed interest caused the mining industry to revisit many of the more productive sites in the Mother Lode that had discontinued operations in 1930. One of those with a reawakened interest was Ed Wolin, who was married to Hazel Anderson. Hazel's grandmother, Jennie Ball, held title to the Ball place of Spud Murphy's early days of exploration, having succeeded her deceased husband, William Proctor Ball.

Eleven

Ed figured that the yield from reworking the Chinese diggings on the Ball place that were presumed to be exhausted at the pre-1934 price of gold would be enough at the increased price to make dredging a worthwhile proposition. The stickler in the operation was that Jennie wanted eight hundred dollars for the mineral rights to her property, eight hundred dollars that Ed didn't have, and she wanted payment up front. To raise the eight hundred and also acquire a needed dragline, Ed took in two partners. After rebuilding the running gear and undercarriage of the dragline, which was completely worn out, he walked the rig all the way from Michigan Bar to the Ball place on the Cosumnes River.

Although Ed's take was considerably diminished by the partnership arrangement, it did get him started. With these associations and others over the next four years he participated in dredging most of the river from the Latrobe Road to the gorge, including the Lorentz, Hinkston and Ball properties, the mining claims of Russ Coulard and his wife, and other mining claims on the El Dorado County side of the river.

One of Ed's associates in the gold mining operation was Ernie Lilly, who wanted to dredge the river above the gorge, on the old Bastion and Eiler properties. The Eiler property and the Bastion place were both owned by Joe Garibaldi, who stood to profit along with Lilly if any gold was produced from either of those two properties. Lilly and Garibaldi had some notion of taking the dredge up through the gorge and they approached Mac about granting them a temporary easement. Taking the dredge upriver through the gorge would have been a foolish undertaking, with an awful lot of rock to shoot with the attendant risk and expense, which is probably why Ed bailed out of the deal, but Mac gave Lilly and Garibaldi the easement they wanted in exchange for permanent access through Garibaldi's property from the homestead to the two mining claims Mac had staked in the gorge. The easement was never used, and Lilly eventually moved another dredge overland onto the Eiler property in 1939, by way of Spring Valley Road.

During the summer of 1939, Floyd Stone was running Ed's dredge on property owned by Mrs. Hinkston. While he was working the dredge alone, there was a problem with the drive motor on the stacker conveyor that Floyd attempted to fix without shutting down the conveyor. In some way, when the problem was taken care of and the belt started moving again, Floyd's arm was caught by the moving belt and the power of the motor tore his arm out of the socket at his shoulder.

Weeks later Spud Murphy happened to meet Mrs. Hinkston at the Wire Gate where the "lane" split off from Lorentz Road and she told him about her returning from a trip to Sacramento on the day of Floyd's accident and how she began to have strong feelings of panic as she left the city limits. Her panic increased as she drove home on Highway 16. She said the car kept speeding up as though somebody else had his foot on the accelerator, making it go faster. She had a strong premonition of some terrible accident happening that caused her to drive faster. When she got home, she found Floyd hanging from the end of the conveyor by what was left of his arm and shoulder. Spud Murphy had a great deal of difficulty reconciling Mrs. Hinkston's account with what he felt to be true of claims of miraculous intervention.

Spud Murphy heard about the accident right after it happened, long before hearing Mrs. Hinkston's account, however, and on the Friday a week after the accident, instead of going to an afternoon movie with his fifteen cents, he bought two streetcar tokens and rode the "P" Street car to Sutter Hospital on 29th and "K" Streets and asked to see Mr. Stone. A nurse showed him into Floyd's room and said he could visit for a while as long as Floyd was resting quietly and wasn't being disturbed too much. After she left, Floyd had Spud Murphy walk around the bed to his right side where the detached arm was laying beside him with tubes connecting it to his shoulder. Floyd said they were trying to make the arm grow back onto his shoulder, but that was causing him a lot of pain and he wished they'd just forget about it. Later when he got out of the hospital he had an empty sleeve on that side of his body that he folded up neatly and stuffed in his shirt pocket so it didn't flap around. Spud Murphy stayed until it was time for him to catch the streetcar back to the S.P. shops. When he left, Floyd thanked him for coming and Spud Murphy made a promise to come back again whenever he could. He got back to the S.P. shops just in time to meet Mac at the gate.

Afterward he wondered why he had gone. He never realized life could offer such a depressing experience. On top of that, he barely knew Floyd at all and had little in common with him. Having gone to school with someone's daughter isn't exactly the same as being his lifelong friend. It had been all right, of course. Floyd talked to him as though he was a grownup, explaining about how the accident happened, how they thought they might get the arm to grow back on, and how hard it was to have to stay in bed all the time. Spud Murphy wondered why he had done it, why he had spent a whole afternoon with this man who was the same to him as a complete stranger. He wished he had gone to the movie in the first place, as he normally would have done. It just seemed when the idea to go first occurred to him that it was the right thing to do. Then he thought of Lola taking her first violin lesson at Goula's house and he knew it was the right thing to do.

Under the laws pertaining to mining claims, a claim is good for only one year and then it has to be renewed, extending it for another year. The way most prospectors did that was to dig a certain size excavation showing they were working the claim and attach a photograph of the excavation to their application for renewal. The excavation wasn't necessarily made because you were looking for gold there. It was just a hole dug where the digging was easy as a requirement of the law to hold the claim year after year until the dredge could find its way there. It was called "assessment work," somewhat akin to "busy work" in Spud Murphy's eyes.

Spud Murphy was doing assessment work on Mac and Elsie's claims one day when Ed showed up and asked if Spud Murphy would like to do the assessment work on some other claims along the river. There were seven of them. Each one had to have an excavation two feet deep by two feet wide by eight feet long. Ed said he would pay fifty cents for each excavation. Spud Murphy would have done them for nothing if Ed had asked, just to be neighborly, but he didn't mention anything about that after Ed offered to pay. Three dollars and fifty cents for seven claims would buy ten boxes of .22 shells and eight bottles of soda pop at five cents a bottle and he wouldn't even have to share with anybody if they didn't find out except Julius, and that only because he was Spud Murphy's best friend. Later, after they saw what the dredge did to what had been the finest swimming hole in all of Amador County, they decided not to ever again let capitalists profit from their labors even for the promise of soda pop or .22 shells. As a way of evening the score for Ed's duplicity, they locked up his small shop trailer and threw the key into the dredge pond. Then they drove his Fordson tractor up Cascara Creek some ways and hid it in a grove of cottonwoods. They were so mad over the loss of their swimming hole, they probably would have joined up with a band of environmentalists if anyone would have thought to start one up in those years.

Shortly after the end of summer vacation in September 1938, Mr. Davis announced to the eighth grade that those students who intended to enter the annual American Legion oratorical competition should speak with their parents about entering it and then advise him so he could make himself available to assist them as needed. Mr. Davis quietly let it be known to Spud Murphy that he in particular would be expected to enter the competition.

Since the days of Thomas Paine and Patrick Henry and right up to the invention of television, and after, America has thrived on the notion that fiery oratory and debate, especially on a patriotic theme, is the essential ingredient of political leadership and the glue that holds the Republic together and steady on its course. Aimed, like TV itself, at the persuasion of the uncultivated masses, it is often more a flowery art form than a Socratic discourse intended to provide meaning and understanding, although there are always a few minor exceptions to such a sweeping statement. It was only natural that school-children in the 1930s were easily persuaded to work at improving their rhetorical skills in mimicry of the older members of society. The hope was strong that they, too, might someday be capable of manipulating the emotions of others in their eternal quest to persuade or dissuade their fellow-man in order to elevate their own cause. Encouragement of that effort was the purpose of the American Legion oratorical competition.

The rules of the competition required the student to choose a patriotic speech from published reprints of notable speeches made to the general public since the founding of America, commit it to memory, and recite it in an evening performance before a panel of judges in an auditorium full of parents, legionnaires, eighth grade teachers, grammar school principals and a few other non-partisan fair-minded individuals.

Spud Murphy's entry into the contest had a strange effect on Mac. In almost every activity of a competitive nature that Spud Murphy had ever undertaken, Mac had at some time stepped in and taken it out of Spud Murphy's hands in the interest of showing Spud Murphy how to do a better job of it. "Let's learn to do it the right way, son," he'd say. The soapbox derby the legion sponsored was like that. When Spud Murphy went to Mac asking for some hints on how to go about getting started, Mac just took the whole project over and built a scaled-down version of a current Indianapolis race car, which Spud Murphy was embarrassed to enter, because one look at it told you no ten- or twelve-year-old kid had anything to do with its construction. It came in last in the race but won the five-dollar prize for the best-looking entry. Spud Murphy could only complain bitterly to Julius, when they were alone, "I thought it was supposed to be a race, not a beauty contest." He wasn't angry at Mac about losing the race, he was angry with himself for being too chicken-livered to stand up for what he knew was right.

In the oratorical contest, Mac couldn't just take over and do everything himself because selecting the speech was the least part of it. But he tried. He said, "My favorite patriotic speech is Patrick Henry's 'Give me liberty or give me death' speech." Spud Murphy so wounded him by saying "Naw. Never did like that speech much," that Mac punished him by acting disinterested after that, whenever the subject of the competition came up.

For openers, Spud Murphy didn't have a clue on how to start on such a project, but Mr. Davis found a book for him that was a limited compilation of patriotic speeches by well-known public speakers. He also passed along the information that the speech he had heard most often at past competitions was Lincoln's Gettysburg Address. He also happened to mention that it seemed to be the favorite of a lot of other people, including the judges, because it had been a frequent winner in past competitions. (It is to be noted that teachers often take as much pride in the good works of their students as do the parents of the children themselves.)

Spud Murphy took the book home and went through it from cover to cover. He decided that Mr. Davis and all the historians were right. There was no other speech that had the impact of the Gettysburg Address. That Friday when he was at the library in Sacramento, he told the librarian about the oratorical competition. She immediately asked him, "Why don't you do the Gettysburg Address?"

He said, quite firmly, "Because everybody does that one. I want to do something different. And the Gettysburg Address is too easy, anyhow. I already know it by heart. There wouldn't be anything left for *me* to do. It would be almost like cheating. And if I did lose, I'd feel like an idiot."

The librarian said "Wait," and went to the stacks, reappearing shortly with a large volume entitled "The Works of Robert Green Ingersoll,—volume I." She said, "Look in this book. If you don't find what you're looking for, I'll get you the next volume." As Spud Murphy skimmed through the various essays, he became convinced that he had at least found the right essayist. Interspersed between the essays were evaluations of their author's creativity and speech-making artistry. It was not long before he came across a laudatory review of one of Ingersoll's speeches by a reporter for the Chicago Times:

NOMINATION OF EDWARD G. BLAINE FOR PRESIDENT

Nomination Of Republican By Robert Green Ingersoll

The nomination of Blaine was the passionately dramatic scene of the day. Robert G. Ingersoll had been fixed upon to present Blaine's name to the Convention, and, as the result proved, a more effective champion could not have been selected in the whole party conclave.

As the clerk, running down the list, reached Maine, an extraordinary event happened. The applause and cheers which had heretofore broken out in desultory patches of the galleries and platform, broke in a simultaneous, thunderous outburst from every part of the house.
Ingersoll moved out from the obscure corner and advanced to the central stage. As he walked forward the thundering cheers, sustained and swelling, never ceased. As he reached the platform they took on an increased volume of sound, and for ten minutes the surging fury of acclamation, the wild waving of fans, hats, and handkerchiefs transformed the scene from one of deliberation to that of a bedlam of rapturous delirium Ingersoll waited with unimpaired serenity, until he should get a chance to be heard.

* * *

And then began an appeal, impassioned, artful, brilliant, and persuasive.

* * *

Possessed of a fine figure, a face of winning, cordial frankness, Ingersoll had half won his audience before he spoke a word. It is the attestation of every man that heard him, that so brilliant a masterstroke was never uttered before a political Convention. Its effect was indescribable. The coolest-headed in the hall were stirred to the wildest expression. The adversaries of Blaine, as well as his friends, listened with unswerving, absorbed attention. Curtis sat spell-bound, his eyes and mouth wide open, his figure moving in unison to the tremendous periods that fell in a measured, exquisitely graduated flow from the Illinoisan's smiling lips. The matchless method and manner of the man can never be imagined from the report in type. To realize the prodigious force, the inexpressible power, the irrestrainable fervor of the audience requires actual sight. Words can do but meager justice to the wizard power of this extraordinary man. He swayed and moved and impelled and restrained and worked in all ways with the mass before him as if he possessed some key to the innermost mechanism that moves the human heart, and when he finished, his fine, frank face as calm as when he began, the overwrought thousands sank back in an exhaustion of unspeakable wonder and delight".

Chicago Times, June 16, 1876

And from another, more contemporary, reviewer:

"But it was his private speaking career that made him famous. Tour after tour, he criss-crossed the country and spoke before packed houses on topics ranging from Shakespeare to Reconstruction, from science to religion. In an age when oratory was the dominant form of public entertainment, Ingersoll was the unchallenged king of American orators. Ingersoll was the friend of presidents, literary giants like Mark Twain, captains of industry like Andrew Carnegie, and leading figures in the arts. He was also beloved of reformers, like Elizabeth Cady Stanton. Other Americans considered themselves his enemies. He bitterly opposed the Religious Right of his day. He was an early popularizer of Charles Darwin and a tireless advocate of science and reason. More, he argued for the rights of women and Negroes...(He) also praised the virtues of family and fireside. And he practiced what he preached."

There was no question in Spud Murphy's mind but that Robert Ingersoll was the man whose banner he wished to follow. Now, all that remained was to find the right essay. After lunch, instead of going to the Liberty or Roxie Theater, he went back to the library. The librarian, smiling at his persistence, handed him the next volume of the series. Within the first ten minutes of searching, he found the essay he wanted. He recognized it by its title alone. When he read its message, his judgment was confirmed. He showed it to the librarian and she agreed there could be none better. The librarian checked the book out to him and he took it home and carefully transcribed the chosen essay to foolscap.

Vision Of War

By Robert G. Ingersoll

The past rises before me, as it were, like a dream. Again we are in the great struggle for national life. We hear the sounds of preparation -- the music of boisterous drums -- the silver voices of heroic bugles. We see thousands of assemblages, and hear the appeals of orators. We see the pale cheeks of women, and the flushed faces of men; and in those assemblages we see all the dead whose dust we have covered with flowers. We lose sight of them no more. We are with them when they enlist in the great army of freedom. We see them part with those they love. Some are walking for the last time in quiet, woody places, with the maidens they adore. We hear the whisperings and the sweet vows of eternal love as they lingeringly part forever. Others are bending over cradles, kissing babes that are asleep. Some are receiving the blessings of old men. Some are parting with mothers who hold them and press them to their hearts again and again, and say nothing. Kisses and tears, tears and kisses -- divine mingling of agony and love! And some are talking with wives, and endeavoring with brave words, spoken in the old tones, to drive from their hearts the awful fear. We see them part. We see the wife standing in the door with the babe in her arms -- standing in the sunlight sobbing. At the turn of the road a hand waves -- she answers by holding high in her loving arms the child. He is gone, and forever.

We see them all as they march proudly away under the flaunting flags, keeping time to the grand, wild music of war -- marching down the streets of the great cities -- through the towns and across the prairies -- down to the fields of glory, to do and to die for the eternal right.

We go with them, one and all. We are by their side on all the gory fields -- in all the hospitals of pain -- on all the weary marches. We stand guard with them in the wild storm and under the quiet stars. We are with them in ravines running with blood -- in the furrows of old fields. We are with them between contending hosts, unable to move, wild with thirst, the life ebbing slowly away among the withered leaves. We see them pierced by balls and torn with shells. In the trenches, by forts, and in the whirlwind of the charge, where men become iron, with nerves of steel.

We are with them in the prisons of hatred and famine; but human speech can never tell what they endured.

We are at home when the news comes that they are dead. We see the maiden in the shadow of her first sorrow. We see the silvered head of the old man bowed with the last grief.

The past rises before us, and we see four millions of human beings governed by the lash -- we see them bound hand and foot -- we hear the strokes of cruel whips -- we see the hounds tracking women through tangled swamps. We see babes sold from the breasts of mothers. Cruelty unspeakable! Outrage infinite!

Four million bodies in chains -- four million souls in fetters. All the sacred relations of wife, mother, father and child trampled beneath the brutal feet of might. And all this was done under our own beautiful banner of the free.

The past rises before us. We hear the roar and shriek of the bursting shell. The broken fetters fall. These heroes died. We look. Instead of slaves we see men and women and children. The wand of progress touches the auction-block, the slave-pen, the whipping- post, and we see homes and fire-sides and schoolhouses and books, and where all was want and crime and cruelty and fear, we see the faces of the free.

These heroes are dead. They died for liberty -- they died for us. They are at rest. They sleep in the land they made free, under the flag they rendered stainless, under the solemn pines, the sad hemlocks, the tearful willows, and the embracing vines. They sleep beneath the shadows of the clouds, careless alike of sunshine or of storm, each in the windowless Palace of Rest. The Earth may run red with other wars -- they are at peace. In the midst of battle, in the roar of conflict, they found the serenity of death! I have one sentiment for all soldiers living and dead: cheers for the living; tears for the dead.

Spud Murphy had several months before the competition, but he didn't wait to memorize it. He recited it endlessly, mostly to E.J. so she could check him for accuracy, word by word as it was written on the foolscap until his recitation was letter perfect, and then when the competition was drawing near, he recited it to Elsie, working in the kitchen, and finally to Mac, on the road to Sacramento, so each of them could coach him on style and delivery and articulation. When none of them could stand to hear it one more time, he recited it to Katie, Patsy, and Rosie as he did the milking.

When the evening of the competition came Spud Murphy had a momentary spell of apprehension, but after it was over he had won the competition so decisively as to be able to afford feelings of sympathy for all the losers, especially those who had obviously worked hard and chosen essays that were not the Gettysburg Address. Mac puffed up and went strutting around after it was all over, letting everybody know which kid up there on the stage was his, and how smart a young fellow 'my boy Spud Murphy' really was.

On the Friday following the competition, Spud Murphy returned all the Ingersoll books to the library and told the librarian about his winning and all the details of the various speakers, and she hugged him right there in the library and said, "Spud Murphy, I'm so proud of you I could cry." At school, Mr. Davis shook his hand and had him recite the speech in class for all the sixth, seventh, and eighth graders to hear.

The most beneficial and lasting consequence of the competition for Spud Murphy was the introduction it provided him to the writings of Robert G. Ingersoll, particularly those essays he discovered later in the course of his life, having to do with religious matters and agnosticism, not that he was prepared at this early stage of his life to declare himself an agnostic, or even put much effort into thinking about it. There just wasn't much point that he could see in making it an issue. And until there was, it simply presented another possibility for his private consideration that he had never previously thought about. In the meantime, he was relieved to learn that others beside himself were having trouble understanding some of God's logic.

In Spud Murphy's opinion, one of the faults of attending school in Plymouth was that it didn't have a Boy Scout troop. Aside from the things Elsie taught him and what he learned from Mac about woodsman ship and machinery, most of the real important things he knew had come from Jack's Boy Scout's Handbook and from the back issues of Boy's Life. For example, he would never have known a thing about the Chippewa tribe, or the Sioux either, without one or the other of those two publications. And there was much more, such as tying knots and dog training and horsemanship and all sorts of things of that nature. It was with a great deal of happiness that he one day received from Julius the news that Plymouth was about to get a Boy Scout troop.

It happened that a young man with scout leader experience had drifted into town recently and was working as a mechanic in Johnny Moyle's Garage. All the boys twelve years old or older who wanted to join the Boy Scouts were supposed to come to a meeting in an old vacant storage building across Main Street from Roos Brothers' Store and bring fifty cents so that scout handbooks could be ordered. Spud Murphy was ecstatic. On the day of the meeting, Elsie gave him the fifty cents and he stayed at Julius's house after school, eating dinner there. After dinner he and Julius walked down the hill toward town to the meeting.

Not much happened at the meeting except that everybody turned his fifty cents over to the scout leader, who said he would set a time for another meeting when the handbooks came. A couple of weeks passed and no books came and on the day after payday at Johnny Moyle's Garage the scout leader didn't show up for work and after that he was never seen in those parts again. It came as a great shock to Spud Murphy that something as noble of purpose as the Boy Scouts of America could permit itself to become the dupe of such a mean-spirited swindler. Spud Murphy never sought to join the Boy Scouts again, preferring to rely on the public library as his information source for the esoteric studies of Indian lore and other such preoccupations that were meaningful to him.

E.J. graduated from Amador High School in 1938, at the age of eighteen, surprising all the medical experts with their gloomy predictions. It is true that most of what she accomplished in her life she did through personal determination and because of a positive attitude. She enrolled in Sacramento Junior College immediately after graduation from Amador High. She was probably in the best physical condition of her life during the two or three years that included the time between finishing high school and the first year or so of college. In those years she never weighed more than 105 pounds but every ounce of her was pure grit and sweet disposition, regardless of what discouragement may have stood in her way.

The other significant event of 1938 was the marriage of Ariel to Lavonne Peterson. Lavonne was a diminutive but vivacious redhead who made a perfect match for the easygoing, dry-witted Ariel. Ariel was a favorite of Spud Murphy's and so it was natural that Spud Murphy might have had reservations about any woman Ariel chose to marry. Lavonne was special in her own right. She fit into the family along with Ariel as though she belonged there.

Spud Murphy liked Ariel because of the laid-back way about him. He didn't get upset if you screwed up the obbligato accompaniment to the chorus of Goodnight, Angel. He would mostly crack a big wide grin and chuckle, and then he'd say something like, "Now there's a way of playing that song I never even thought about," and they'd go on to the next thing. And talk about chuckling. A lot of instances of people chuckling are mentioned in different peoples' accounts, of one aspect or another of life, but Ariel was the only one Spud Murphy could say that actually knew how to chuckle. If you ever heard a real chuckle, you never would confuse it with a laugh again.

When E.J. was attending college, she lived with Aunt Isabelle, who, after the death of Grandma, was even more attentive to the spiritual needs and the general well-being of her foster son and his brood. Aunt Isabelle lived in a small apartment near the Episcopal Cathedral at 26th and "M" Streets. "M" Street was later renamed "Capitol Avenue." There was a noticeable show of devoutness in most members of the family, prompted in part by E.J.'s lingering flirtation with death, but otherwise firmly founded in Aunt Isobelle's, Elsie's, and E.J.'s strongly religious belief systems. The family had a cordial relationship with Bishop Porter of the Sacramento diocese and Deaconess Clark and Dean Pearson of the cathedral clergy.

Jack was seldom at the homestead after his high school graduation. He graduated a year ahead of E.J., but the uncompromising discipline that Mac dealt out mostly with his hands and with so little regard for Jack's self-esteem led him eventually to a rebellious confrontation with the law. That misfortune plagued his life for two or three years, and perhaps even longer than that. When he wasn't misbehaving, Jack was also a Sacramento Junior College student. With his enrollment in junior college, he became eligible for pilot training under a fully subsidized federal program designed to train civilian pilots needed in the eventuality of war. After he got his pilot's license, he invited Spud Murphy to come along for a ride in a two-place Taylorcraft.

They flew over the homestead and Spud Murphy took pictures from the airplane that didn't show much more than the landing gear and the wing struts of the airplane itself. When they had used up all their film, Jack practiced doing stalls and spins, which not only scared the liver out of Spud Murphy but also caused the contents of his stomach to rise up in protest, until he finally had to stick his head out the window and let fly all over the side and tail of the airplane. Before that happened Jack had told Spud Murphy several times to be sure to let him know if he was getting sick, but Spud Murphy was not about to ask Jack for quarter in that regard until the facts became too obvious to hide. After all, what would the arch-enemy Barron Von Richthofen think if his adversary was so unnerved as to be seen puking all over the side of his airplane, for cripes' sake?

Eleven

Jack worked for the California Pear Growers' Association for most of 1938. His job included delivering pear wrappers to the association members around Placerville and in Lake County and the Delta. When he had a trip to make to Placerville or Lake County, he would usually ask Spud Murphy to ride along for the company. The days of hassling each other were over, along with a lot of other things relative to attitude that you don't really need in a Depression, or even in your everyday life, without a Depression.

After the pear wrappers were delivered, they would sometimes load the pickup with pear culls to take back to the homestead for feeding to the animals, including the cows. Culls are fruit of one kind or another that has no market value, either because it is bruised, over ripe, or maybe it's just too small or a little misshapen. Bartlett pears have to be picked green, otherwise they bruise too easily. In the slower paced days before the war, they were ripened before they got to market by wrapping each pear in an individual wrapper so it was never in the direct sunlight or touching another pear. They ripened in their wrappers in lug boxes at room temperature. If Spud Murphy saw the way pears and other fruit are put in the bins green at the super markets today, and left for the housewives to take home and ripen, he'd probably think that the store people put them out that way out of the generosity of their heart, for people to take home free and feed to their pigs.

At the homestead there was a fenced yard around the shop and a lean-to added onto the shop building, where the culls were stored, so the cows couldn't get at them and founder from eating too many. Cows are dumb in that way, and don't know when to quit. They're like a kid watching a cookie sheet of hot fudge cooling on the windowsill. No will power.

It happened one day that everybody had somewhere to go, and with no one around to keep an eye on her, Patsy got the gate opened into the pear storage yard. She ate nobody knows how many pears. When Spud Murphy got home with Mac and Elsie, Patsy looked like the Hindenburg with her huge belly inflated with gas and a small head and four legs sticking straight out at different angles. Spud Murphy never knew why Katie and Rosie didn't get into the pears, too, unless it was just Patsy's nasty, dog-in-the-manger disposition that kept them out. If it had been either of the other two cows that had gotten in, they would have died for sure. Spud Murphy thought Patsy was done for, just from looking at her, but Mac sent him to get the ice pick out of the ice box and knew right where to stick her so she would deflate like a helium balloon at a kid's birthday party.

Twelve

They left the homestead at the end of the school year in the spring of 1939, after Spud Murphy had graduated from grammar school. They left so Spud Murphy would have the educational advantages of a large city high school. They left because E.J. and Jack had already flown the family nest, pursuing their educational interests at Sacramento Junior College. They left because the eighty-mile round trip from the homestead to work and back each day was an obstacle to Mac's aspirations for professional recognition and because Elsie yearned for the cultural and social advantages of the city. They left because they had accomplished what they had come for, and it was time to return to the environment that their natural instincts and their predispositions inclined them toward. They left because E.J.'s health was restored beyond anything that could have been foreseen or imagined and there was no further reason for staying.

The Depression, while not yet over, was at least in the final stages of its demoralizing tenure, only recently alleviated somewhat by the manufacturing and transportation demands of the coming war in Europe, which would start with the September

1 invasion of Poland, after the March 14 occupation of Czechoslovakia provided a preview of what was to come. Thousands of men in America were being reemployed nationwide in the daily build-up of defense production and in the rebirth of the transportation industry. In recognition of their own economic revitalization, Mac and Elsie rented a three-bedroom flat at 28th and "S" Streets which lay within the grid of the old city as it had been laid out by John Sutter in the 1840s.

The flat that Mac and Elsie rented was the lower of two such units that, together with a full basement, made up the building. The basement was divided equally by a partition, the domain of each flat including one-half of the basement. The half-basement provided space for Mac's workshop. The lady who owned the building lived with her sister and brother-in-law in the upstairs flat, about six feet above Spud Murphy's head (if he was standing up straight with his shoes on). Next door to the west was the office of Mr. Clifford, a masonry contractor. Next door to the east was Mr. Clifford's brickyard. Spud Murphy mentioned to Elsie that, compared to living at the homestead, moving to the city was like moving into an ant colony. Or, on second thought, into a nuts and bolts storage cabinet where you had different size nuts in different bins over you and on each side.

Although the Depression was slowly yielding its grip on the economy to the increasing need for war materials, there were still soup kitchens for those less blessed, and jungles along all the major rail routes from which hobos still foraged out into the community seeking handouts. Ariel shrugged his shoulders and said, "Well, I guess old habits are just hard to break, sometimes." Every community had plenty of souls who had lost so much to the depression they had given up the notion of ever contributing to the economy again, even though it could easily be seen that the darkest times had passed. The legacy of the Depression for many was a distrust of the old order of capitalistic despotism. For others, it was a cynical uncertainty about capitalism's replacement, seen as a liberal dole. But to most, the changing economics brought relief from hard times at last, regardless of what politico-economic color it was painted. A promise of spring, if not spring itself.

For one thing, the railroads were returning to a measure of activity as great as they had enjoyed in the 1920s, with the war in Europe demanding shipments of all manner of goods and shipping space at a premium. San Francisco had two new bridges nearing completion that would stimulate renewed commercial opportunity and were at least symbolic of the progress that was to follow. The Golden Gate International Exposition, otherwise known as Treasure Island, was in full blossom, steadily losing money, but raising hope and bolstering morale.

The homesteaders, staying in touch with their patriotic roots and needful of bidding a celebratory farewell to the departing Depression, boarded the train to San Francisco as they had on previous occasions, drawn this time not by a glorious icon of America's naval history, but by the Golden Gate Exposition and the promise of twentieth century technology to be discovered in her future.

The price of admission to the fair was fifty cents, and if one had a car, parking cost two bits more. In keeping with the cultural values of California, the first thing to be seen on entering the '*Gayway*' from the parking lot was Sally Rand's 'Nude Ranch' and probably the next thing after that was one of the Pan American Clippers waiting to board passengers for Honolulu or Manila or Hong Kong.

If there was anything that exemplified the escape from the stagnant backwaters of the Depression, it was the advent of the luxurious Clipper Ship service of Pan American Airways. The California Clipper, a Boeing B-314 seaplane, had seats for seventy-four passengers, sleeping berths for thirty-six, a luxurious lounge, and elegant dining facilities. Initiating service in 1936 with crews of ten for each plane, the Clippers crossed the Pacific Ocean from San Francisco to Hong Kong in forty-eight hours flying time, at a cruising speed of 183 miles per hour. The cost for a one-way fare was $950. For comparison purposes, an average journeyman worker in the building trades at the time earned about $1,500 per year. A new Pontiac Coupe cost around $600. The Clipper Ships were symbols of America's soon-to-be-regained prosperity. So what if you couldn't afford to travel on it? Maybe someday. And in the meantime, you could dream, couldn't you?

Spud Murphy was glad for the change of scenery from chaparral-covered hills to paved city streets. He was tired of the eternal drought of the foothills, the bleakness of the homestead, the monotony of farm chores, and the hopelessness of life seemingly without a future. He thought it was pretty pathetic that after attaining the age of thirteen, the greatest accomplishment you could point to was that you had finally worked your way up to having a room that was yours, with a door you could shut, even though you did have to share it with your three-year-old brother. But there were no cows to milk, and no chickens to feed or butcher. Instead there was the excitement of having new surroundings, any new surroundings. A momentary respite from the monotonous sameness of life. A week before leaving the homestead, Spud Murphy put a lead rope on Rosie, the last of the livestock to be disposed of, and walked her to Plymouth, where he delivered her to the Albiani's.

When they moved, it was in the early part of summer. They moved piecemeal, not completely severing their ties to the homestead. They went back and forth between city and country as interest or necessity dictated, to look after security and maintenance matters, and to bring their belongings to their new place of abode, piling them high in the cab and in the bed of the '38 Ford pickup— like short-haul Joads from Steinbeck's *Grapes of Wrath,* only in reverse. As they loaded up for the first trip that would leave the homestead vacant and unoccupied, after they had sold or given away all the livestock, Spud Murphy realized that Mac intended to leave Abdul behind and made a point of asking him about it.

As if it was some small thing that had just slipped his mind, Mac said, "Hell. We haven't got room to put him, now. Well, we'll get him next week. He'll be all right. He's got food and water to last him."

Spud Murphy had a lot of misgivings about leaving his dog. It was just something you'd never think of doing. A premonition arose in him, something in Mac's voice telling him that Mac had no intention of bringing Abdul, that he was being lied to. Abdul stood at the yard gate in front of the deserted house and, with questioning eyes, watched them until they were out of sight.

When they returned the following weekend, Abdul was nowhere to be found. Spud Murphy searched the forty-acre homestead in vain, searching for any sign of him, even a newly dug grave. He walked to the river and back, calling Abdul's name all the way. Mac said, "He'll be back. Just wandered off somewhere. When he gets hungry, he'll be back." Spud Murphy thought, "No, you're not telling me the truth. He won't be back and you know it."

Another week passed and they went to the homestead and Abdul was not there. On the next weekend they found him sitting at the wire gate at the head of the lane where the narrow road to the homestead leaves the main county road, two miles from the homestead. A glance at Mac's face told Spud Murphy his father was not happy that the dog had found his way to the homestead again, so apparently whatever plot Mac had cooked up to prevent that from happening, had failed. Abdul was just sitting there, watching the pickup approach him down the county road. He was little more than a skeleton, his skin hanging loose on his frame like an oversize coat on a starving man, the once healthy fleece a matted, tangled mess of cockleburs and twigs and blackberry thorns. His pads were torn and bleeding but he jumped on Spud Murphy and licked his hands and Abdul's tail was a madly waving celebration of love and reunion.

When the pickup was loaded and they were ready to leave for Sacramento, Mac said, "He's learned his lesson. He won't run off again. We'll take him in with us next week." Spud Murphy kept his head turned away from his father all the way to the city and his cheeks were streaked with tears. He felt as though his heart had been cut out of him. He never saw Abdul again, and the bitterness never left his heart.

Later he found out from Elsie that she and Mac had known when they leased the flat that the landlady wouldn't allow dogs on her property, although she had one of her own. Like the unfortunate bobcat that got caught in the trap, Abdul and Spud Murphy fell victim to higher authority for reasons never explained to them. Again he wondered, as with Grandma's illness, why people who professed to love you did not deal openly with the truth.

From the very beginning, living in Sacramento day in and day out was a far different proposition than going to the S.P. shops once a week with Mac to have a violin lesson. The city itself lost much of its magic, as a city is prone to do when it becomes a common haunt, and was no longer so much a place of mystery and wonder on its own account. Mystery and wonder were still there in abundance; you just had to look harder to find them. Spud Murphy never went back to skid row anymore, just to wonder at the mystery of the place, and the people who made it their home, or to the Liberty or El Rio or Roxie Theaters, although he could have been to any of those places within a brisk twenty-minute walk from the flat. Somehow, familiarity destroyed the beguiling attraction they had previously held for him and what he had once considered to be his own exclusive domain he didn't care to share with others. He did return to the public library frequently and sometimes for hours at a time, although now the library card he proudly carried was no longer just a conspiracy between himself and the librarian for checking out the books he wanted to take home to read.

When Spud Murphy first met Bill, he thought Bill must be the neighborhood blabbermouth, which was a logical conclusion to arrive at, considering Bill's naturally acquisitive nature. Not that similar traits are at all unusual in other city-bred boys of Bill's age. What was unusual, at least to Spud Murphy, was that Bill had some kind of inner information-retrieval system to tell him exactly when the new boy in the neighborhood would be walking up to Vickers Market on an errand for his mother, so that his path would take him right past Bill's front steps at the exact moment that Bill would happen to be sitting on them. That seemingly natural coincidence provided the opportunity for them to exchange monosyllabic grunts, which in terms of human speech translated to "Hi." At that point Bill could in clear conscience get up from the steps and fall in beside the new boy and ask the all-important question: "Going to Vickers?" On such complex protocols are the long-term allegiances within the brave and unburdened generation founded.

Bill was a year older than Spud Murphy. He was an only child and, in Spud Murphy's mind, a little spoiled because of it. Bill's father, Ray, drove a Channel Pie Shop truck, delivering bakery goods to many of the restaurants and grocery stores in the Sacramento area. His mother was a rather small lady with pink cheeks and an exaggerated southern drawl, who was born and raised in Louisiana, as was Bill's father. Bill's mother reminded

Spud Murphy of a china doll, both in appearance and in the way she passed her time (Sitting on the shelf). After leaving Louisiana, Bill's family lived for a few years in Visalia before moving on to Sacramento. Their house was on "S" Street, a block and a half east of Spud Murphy's parents' flat.

It was Spud Murphy's responsibility to keep the workshop clean and the grass around the flats mowed, and to do whatever other odd job Mac or Elsie needed him to do. Outside of those chores, and the hour each day he spent practicing his violin, the rest of the time was his own. Bill usually didn't have any chores to do at all, but he had a paper route for the Sacramento Bee, an evening paper that came out on the street at about two-thirty. Spud Murphy helped Bill fold the papers, so they would stay intact when they were fired with unerring accuracy from a speeding bicycle, in a fashion intended to fall just short of knocking the subscriber's screen door off its hinges.

Spud Murphy spent most of that summer in company with Bill. They helped each other with what few chores either of them were assigned. They spent the rest of their time shooting buckets at a half-court basketball setup that some considerate person had provided in years past on the paved parking lot of the Farmers' Free Market, which was situated directly across "S" Street from Vickers. On Wednesdays and Saturdays— when the Farmers' Market was open and full of farmers with farm produce spread out on the long tables, and every housewife in town was there shopping for fresh fruit, and garden vegetables, and eggs, and other farm produce— Bill and Spud Murphy would go to the city park at Twenty-eighth and "Q" Streets and toss a football around with a couple of other boys who lived nearby. Once in a while they were joined at the park by still others who wanted to get up a game of "touch" football; while Bill was comfortable with the larger group, Spud Murphy was not, and he would usually come up with some reason why he should be at home. After making his getaway, he would spend the rest of the day reading.

As summer wore on and the days got hotter, the two boys spent more of their time in the public swimming pool at McKinley Park where they could swim all day for fifteen cents or in the YMCA pool in downtown Sacramento which was free because they both had membership cards. Swimming was the only activity in which Spud Murphy was complacent in the presence of a crowd. He was confident in the water, regardless of the number of swimmers or onlookers.

Not long after Spud Murphy and Bill struck up their friendship, they were sitting in Bill's kitchen where Spud Murphy was explaining to Bill about spearing frogs in the Cosumnes River. Ray was reading the paper in the living room, but he must have had one ear on the conversation in the kitchen, because he got interested in the prospects of getting a good mess of frog legs, a delicacy he hadn't been able to enjoy since leaving Louisiana. Spud Murphy took it upon himself to invite Ray and Bill to the homestead for the purpose of harvesting a few of the Cosumnes River's vast supply of frogs, contingent on Mac's approval. When Spud Murphy asked him for permission, Mac not only sanctioned the idea but decided to come along himself. That wasn't exactly what had been in Spud Murphy's mind, having wanted himself to be the grand poobah of the expedition, so to speak. In any event, like it or not, that's the way it turned out.

Late one Friday afternoon Spud Murphy rounded up the flashlights and extra batteries and the coffee pot and makings and they headed for the homestead with Ray and Mac up front in the pickup and the two boys riding in the back. At the homestead they picked up the frog gigs and a couple of gunnysacks to hold all the frogs they were going to catch. A frog gig is a five-tined spear with barbed tines so that when you spear the frog he won't slip off the tines and jump back in the river before you get him in the gunnysack. You do your frog gigging after dark from a small flat-bottomed boat called a punt. The bright light of the flashlight immobilizes the frog where he's sitting with just his eyes sticking out of the water, waiting for a water bug of some kind to come along to be eaten. The frog can see fine in the dark to catch the water bug, but the flashlight shining in his eyes blinds him so he can't see the gig coming. Poor frog.

When they got to the river and pushed the punt out of the willows into the river, it was still not dark enough for the flashlight to have much effect on the frogs' vision, so they decided to pole up the river to a sandy beach where they could build a fire and boil some coffee while they waited for dark. Mac was poling from the stern, with Ray and Bill seated on a thwart amidships while Spud Murphy poised on the bow thwart with the painter in his hand, ready to leap ashore in dramatic imitation of George Washington routing the red coats after crossing the Delaware River. At the exact instant that he sprang from the bow of the boat, he became aware that the end point of the trajectory on which he had just launched himself was already occupied by a large and ugly rattlesnake, somewhat coiled, but seemingly oblivious of the wrath that was about to descend upon him.

Spud Murphy was barefoot. Afterward he would swear that he flew right over the snake, having touched neither earth nor snake in passing. After the snake was decapitated with a short-handled axe that was in the punt, an autopsy of its remains revealed that the large swelling noticeable a third of the way down its length was a recently ingested, medium-sized cottontail, which might explain why Spud Murphy didn't get snake-bit. Aside from that surge of adrenaline release, it was an uneventful but enjoyable evening, with lots of frog legs to fry and a warm feeling of camaraderie in Spud Murphy's heart.

Twelve

That was the summer Spud Murphy turned fourteen. On the Monday following his birthday, he and Elsie took the recently acquired '34 Ford Sedan and drove to Jackson in order for him to take his driver's test. The reason for him going back to Amador County to get tested was that only in the case of a person having a rural address could a fourteen-year-old be issued a valid driver's license. Mac figured that the homestead could continue to be Spud Murphy's address at least long enough for him to get his license, since he had been driving the Model A ever since the fuel valve trick he'd pulled on E.J. when he was ten-years-old. During that time he had become an excellent driver, and probably a better mechanic than some, as well. It wasn't any big, easy deal getting a license in Jackson, however, because Jackson had some of the narrowest, crooked, steepest streets in the state, and parallel parking in front of the county courthouse to make passing the driver's test as difficult as possible. Spud Murphy passed both the driving and the written tests without trouble. Bill immediately hit Ray up to let him do the same thing, but Ray told him, "Not a chance." Spud Murphy tried to keep his smug self-satisfaction from showing, but it was a hard thing to do.

Toward the end of summer vacation, Spud Murphy and Bill spent a week at the homestead on their own and quite miraculously, they both survived, although there were some tense moments. Bill's family was substantially better off than a lot of folks during the Depression, including Spud Murphy's family, partly because they only had one kid to feed and they didn't spend their money on grand pianos and fancy violins. It was also because Ray lived a far simpler life than Mac and always got a full week in at work from the beginning to the end of the Depression. Bakery goods, unlike steam locomotives, are in demand no matter how tough the times are. Due in some measure to his father's affluence as well as his very indulgent approach to raising his son, Bill had both a .22 caliber automatic rifle and a 20-gauge pump shotgun. You could say that when it came to armament, he was pretty well fitted out.

The first mishap occurred while they were taking a rest at the spring at Cascara, having just climbed up the trail from the Ball place. Spud Murphy heard a covey of quail approaching the spring through the dry leaves and grass. He signed to Bill to be quiet and not move. Bill was sitting on a little berm that paralleled the trail with his rifle across his knees, pointing up the trail in Spud Murphy's direction. Spud Murphy was sitting on the same berm about fifteen feet further up the trail. The quail were slowly working their way to the spring when one suddenly popped out on the trail, midway between Bill and Spud Murphy.

Bill must have been sitting there with his finger on the trigger and with the safety off. When the quail popped out onto the trail, he pulled the trigger in a reflex action. With the sound of the shot Spud Murphy felt the tug of the bullet as it whipped through the leg of his pants. Looking down, not sure if he'd been shot or not, he found two holes in the fabric of his jeans, showing where the bullet had passed through his pants about an inch in front of his shin and midway between his knee and his ankle. He said, "For cripes' sake, Bill! You damn near shot me!"

The very next day Bill had his twenty gauge and he was following behind Spud Murphy along the ridge-line above the homestead when a whole covey of quail exploded out of a manzanita thicket about twenty feet in front of them and the exact same thing happened, except this time Bill blew the heel off one of the practically brand-new Redwing boots Spud Murphy had just gotten for his fourteenth birthday. Spud Murphy was so unnerved by the time he figured out what had happened all he could think to say was, "Dammit, Bill!" in about the most disgusted tone of voice he could come up with. From that day forward he didn't get a lot of hunting in, because he wouldn't let

Bill get behind him. He spent most of his time from then on keeping track of the direction in which Bill's gun was pointing.

One morning after breakfast they boiled some navy beans and shot a cottontail, which they skinned and gutted and cut up into pieces. They buried it with the beans and some molasses and other seasonings in a three-pound coffee can, with holes punched in the lid to let the steam out, in a pit of coals they made in the back-yard. They covered the can with coals and dirt and dug it up that night, hot and steaming, for their supper. Each night after dinner they sat at the kitchen table in the light of a kerosene lamp and smoked Wings cigarettes they had filched from their fathers' supplies and drank cups of scalding-hot black coffee. They shot quail at the spring at evening time, drilling them neatly in the head with their .22 rifles and roasting them on sticks over an open fire. They walked to the river and pulled the little flat-bottomed punt out of the willows and gigged frogs in the dark by flash-light in the broad slow stretch of river below the gorge, taking them home in a gunny-sack and rolling their skinned, twitching legs in flour and salt for deep frying.

They took lead ropes and went to the Ybright ranch each day, where Harp Taylor and the Barneys continued to pasture horses that weren't ever used, and easily caught two with sour apples growing wild in some earlier homesteader's now-deserted orchard, offering them from the palms of their hands. They fashioned Indian bridles and rode the horses bareback across the river and to the bandit Joaquin Murrieta's supposed hideout in El Dorado County, avoiding all the signs of civilization along the way. They rode upriver to the falls of the Cosumnes, and to Spring Valley Road, and to the top of Sugar Loaf.

They didn't milk any cows, or plant or cultivate any gardens, or split any more wood than was absolutely necessary to cook the current meal. They didn't make their beds, or wash their dishes, or take a bath, except for swimming in the river every day, and when Elsie picked them up after a week, their clothes were dirty, they were unkempt,... and they were barely speaking to each other.

Thirteen

Spud Murphy's spare time increased enormously as a result of the move back to Sacramento. What time wasn't spent in company with Bill, Spud Murphy used to appease his insatiable thirst for tales of exploration and adventure. He continually had his nose buried in a book and sometimes in more than one. Elsie fielded so many requests for word definitions she finally bought him a used dictionary of his own for his birthday. He did his reading while sprawled on the bed in the room he shared with four-year-old Billy. He would pretend that he didn't hear Elsie's occasional summons when she needed help with a chore or there was an errand to run, until she came in patient persistence to his room. His hearing always improved when Mac was around to do the calling.

The Sacramento School District had its own ideas about education that were totally at odds with those of Amador County. When school started in the fall of 1939 and his former classmates were starting their freshman year at Sutter Creek High School, where E.J. and Jack had been students, Spud Murphy was relegated to the ninth grade at California Junior

High, in what should have been his freshman year of high school. The Sacramento high schools didn't have freshman classes. Bill was out of the picture now, a sophomore at Sacramento High. Spud Murphy went to school among strangers, as had been his lot in the fifth grade at Plymouth. Fortunately, the city had a more civilized code of behavior than the foothill counties and didn't subscribe to the same practices of initiating new students. That is to say, you didn't need a bodyguard just to get to and from class without getting smacked in the back of the head with an overripe fig.

To Spud Murphy's notion the school was a huge affair, in terms of the number of students and in the size of its campus and its general complexity, which helped him remain almost entirely anonymous for the year he spent there. Elsie asked him if he wanted her help enrolling in his classes and he told her he would be glad to have all the help he could get. Her main interest in offering to help him was to make sure he enrolled in the school orchestra, which was an after-school, extra-curricular activity. Spud Murphy would probably have avoided it if he could have followed the dictates of his own heart. The music teacher scheduled him for a tryout during the first week of classes. After the tryouts she assigned him to second chair in the first violin section. A girl who was a holdover from the previous year got the first chair assignment. She was so enamored by her appointment she clearly thought that everyone having less stature than second chair should prostrate themselves before her ladyship, in adulation of her virtuosity. Why Spud Murphy was singled out for preferential treatment by her was beyond his knowledge, unless it was simply because the queen felt she needed a consort. He didn't want the honor and politely went about ignoring her most of the time. When he couldn't ignore her, he tried to irritate her as much as possible by asking her if she planned to become a fiddle player when she grew up, which was a tactic he learned from Mac and which seemed to ruffle her feathers a bit. When she tossed her head in a snit (to use one of Grandma's favorite words), he said, "What's wrong with that? You can probably make it if you work hard enough at it." He was appalled at his own rudeness, but her arrogance was more than he could stand. Instead of avoiding him, as he hoped, she kept coming back for more.

School was a couple of miles across town from the apartment. Elsie gave him money to buy bus tokens for the city bus, but after a few days of taking the bus he decided to walk. The bus tokens were seven cents each and it took one token each way, which made a total of seventy cents a week. When he quit riding the bus, he told Elsie, but she continued to give him twenty-five cents a week of what was saved by his walking. She said it was to buy an occasional luxury such as a soda pop, or a Popsicle, or even a Saturday matinee at the Alhambra Theater once in a while. The Alhambra had a majestic theater organ and an organist who played for an hour or two every Saturday morning before the matinee. Spud Murphy thought that circumstance might have influenced Elsie's generosity in financing his attraction to the silver screen. Her older brother, Duncan Macdonald, was the organist for the Episcopal church in a city in Indiana and for a theater there, as well.

With Elsie's prodding, Spud Murphy attended one of the weekly dances that were held on Friday in the gymnasium during homeroom period. After standing by the door and watching for about five minutes, he slipped out unnoticed and returned to homeroom, where he had been reading Rudyard Kipling's Captains Courageous. That evening at dinner, Elsie asked him if he had a good time at the dance. He said, "Yeah, it was okay, I guess."

"Did you dance?"

"No."

"Why not?"

"I don't know. Nobody asked me, I guess."

E.J., listening to the conversation, said, "You dummy. The boy is supposed to ask the girl."

"Yeah, I know. But they were all so busy dancing, I didn't feel like bothering any of them."

He carried his lunch in a paper bag, folding it carefully after lunch period so it would fit in his back pocket and serve again for the next day's use. Halfway through the school year he qualified, by virtue of his grades, for a job on the serving line in the cafeteria, dishing hot food onto stainless steel trays for the students whose parents could afford to give them the money to buy their lunch. The benefit of working in the cafeteria was that you got your own lunch free. He quit when he learned that there were students who needed the job more than he did because they weren't getting any lunch at all.

He had perfect attendance and got straight A's in all his classes, including orchestra. And to his great surprise, he actually sank a couple of baskets to help his homeroom team win the intramural basketball championship for the ninth grade. He thought that it was such a joke, he made the mistake of telling E.J. about it. She told Elsie, who told Mac, who went strutting around, telling everybody else in the world how "My boy, Spud Murphy, pulled one out of the fire for his home-room basketball team." When he happened to run into Bill one day at Vickers' Market, Spud Murphy told him about Mac's making such a big deal out of it. "Good lord!" he said in disgust. "He acts like I was Jesse Owens, or Jim Thorpe, or somebody. Doesn't he realize it was just a fluke?"

Summer came and Spud Murphy graduated from junior high. He and Bill went back to shooting baskets at the Farmers' Free Market and tossing the football around at the city park. When his mother sent him to the grocery store, he always managed to pirate five cents from the grocery money she gave him for an orange soda pop. He would drink the soda pop in the store so as not to have to pay the extra two-cents' deposit on the bottle. After a while his guilt began to bother him, so he acquired his own source of income, thanks to Mr. Clifford's brick-yard and masonry business, cleaning the mortar off used bricks and doing other odd jobs such as mowing the lawn and sweeping out the office. Used bricks were important in the masonry business because they had a reclaimed appearance which people thought gave masonry construction a 'rustic' look. More important, in a Depression when wages were low, used bricks were actually cheaper than new ones, in spite of the extra amount of labor necessary to clean them up.

When Spud Murphy started working for Mr. Clifford, he was earning more money than Bill made on his paper route, which prompted Bill to quit the paper route and get part-time work pumping gas after school, at the Associated gas station at Thirty-Third Street and Folsom Boulevard, across Folsom from Arata Brothers' grocery store. Almost every evening Spud Murphy could be found there at eight o'clock, helping Bill close the station.

They walked down Alhambra Boulevard in the growing darkness of a summer evening, their hands shoved deep in their jacket pockets and their shoulders hunched and their heads slouched forward as though they were bent on discovering those universal truths that have been the goal of scholars since antiquity, and with the expectation that the sidewalk five feet in front of their scuffing feet might yield the solutions to all of earth's mysteries.

Always probing, Spud Murphy broke the silence. "Do your folks know you smoke?"

"Naw. Maybe my dad. My mom would throw a fit."

"You get along good with your dad. He lets you do whatever you want, doesn't he?"

"Yeah. He's pretty easy-going. My mom runs right over him sometimes but it doesn't bother him any."

"How come you talk back to her so much?"

"Just that she won't leave me alone. She wants to tell me what to do all the time like I was five years old. She gets on my nerves."

"I couldn't sass my mom. My dad would probably beat the hell out of me if I did. I don't think I'd want to anyway. She's got enough problems without me adding to them and she doesn't pick at me." Bill said, "Well, you're lucky." They walked in silence until they reached the Farmers' Market. They got their cigarettes out and Bill struck a match on his thumbnail and cupped it in his hands and they lit up. They sat on a produce table hunched over with their legs swinging over the side and stared at the glowing tips of their cigarettes.

Presently, Spud Murphy said, "I don't know if I'm lucky or not. Sometimes I think I am and sometimes I think I'm not."

"You mean because of your dad?"

"Yeah."

"Not much you can do about it."

"No." That put an end to the conversation, until Bill said, " Do you want to meet Dean Smith? He's the kid I told you about that plays the accordion. He wants to meet you. He's starting a band."

Spud Murphy said, "I already got one of those." After which he added, "Yeah. I suppose so. I'll meet him."

Dean lived a few doors from Spud Murphy, on the corner of 29th and "S" Streets. With a guitar picker and a drummer already in his ensemble, Dean thought it would add a note of sophistication to have a fiddle player, too. He harbored the expectation of furnishing the music for the weekly dances at the high school. On Dean's invitation, Spud Murphy joined them for a few nights of practice, even furnishing the score of Jimmy Dorsey's arrangement of "Green Eyes," but he found that the guitar picker couldn't sight-read, let alone transpose. On top of that, he decided Dean was far too amateurish and undisciplined. None of the band members was interested in working seriously to increase their repertoire which at the time was limited to the "Beer Barrel Polka" and a couple of others of that genre (which did sound pretty good on the accordion and violin but didn't furnish much of a selection for a high school dance). After a few practice sessions Spud Murphy dropped out.

Sometime in midsummer, about the time of his fifteenth birthday, Spud Murphy showed up at the gas station and he and Bill sat on a couple of stools inside the station sharing a bottle of pop that Bill snitched out of the cooler. As usual, they were hashing over the injustices they had to cope with as the price of living with their parents, which, as far as Spud Murphy was concerned, were mostly the problems he had with Mac's insensitive attitudes. Bill pulled a pack of Wings out from under the counter and held it out to Spud Murphy.

"Hey, Bill! You can't smoke in here. This is a gas station. You'll blow us all to hell."

"Naw, nothing will happen. Everybody does it, all the time. There's even an ashtray under the counter. If somebody comes and I have to pump gas, I put it out." He struck a kitchen match on the underside of the counter and they lit up and blew smoke rings and watched the gray-blue smoke trail upward from the cigarettes they held between their fingers.

Bill said, "I bet you didn't know that half the football team got suspended for getting caught in a whorehouse last fall, after the Turlock game. It was in yesterday's paper."

"At Sac High?"

"Yeah. It's crazy. They were all seniors and the school authorities waited a whole year, 'til after they graduated, to expel them. They'd already got their diplomas. They call it a retroactive expulsion."

"Maybe it will affect their eligibility for a football scholarship."

"Yeah. Maybe so."

For a while they sat silently, contemplatively watching the twining trails of the cigarette smoke. Spud Murphy could tell from the way Bill was squirming around that he had something else he was itching to say. It finally came out.

"You didn't know I went down there, too, did you?"

"You went where? To the whorehouse?"

"Yeah."

"You didn't! Did you really?

"Yeah."

"Which one?"

"The Utah Rooms. On Third and Jay."

"I know the one. When? Were you scared?"

"A couple of weeks ago. One night after I closed the station. One of the nights when your dad's orchestra had a gig and you were playing with them. I just decided all of a sudden to go."

"Were you scared?"

"Well, it was different." Then, pensive, "A little, maybe."

They sat in silence. Spud Murphy wanted to ask questions but didn't know how to ask them without exposing his ignorance. Finally, for lack of anything else, he said, "Most of them are just a bunch of old hags. I don't know if I'd want to do that, anyway."

"You sure don't know much, do you? You get to pick the one you want. Some of them are real good-looking and I wouldn't say that any of them are hags. And it only cost a dollar and a half. But you're probably too young, anyway. I don't think they would take you at fourteen. That's pretty young."

"I'm old enough. I'm going down there."

"Boy, you sure changed your mind in a hurry. Must have been 'cause I told you I was there? Well, just remember. It's the Utah Rooms. You better not get caught, or your old man will really raise hell. I could go down there with you, if you want. Not to go in, or anything. Just to be there in case you wanted company."

"Nah. I don't need any company. But thanks, anyway."

Spud Murphy waited until Friday, knowing Mac and Elsie were going to be at the homestead for the weekend, after Mac got off work. At about eight o'clock he took a bath and put on his best jeans and a clean shirt. He folded up a black string tie he used on orchestra nights and carefully put it in his pocket. Then he found a bottle of Jack's after-shave and rubbed some of it on his cheeks and chin. As he was about to leave the house, E.J. asked him where he was going.

"To Dean's house. We're practicing."

"Well, you're not going to practice very much without your violin."

"I thought I'd try the drums, for a while."

"Oh. Well, have a good time, and don't forget to come home."

It took him twenty minutes to walk downtown and get to the red light district. He saw the Utah Rooms' sign and passed it by, going all the way to the waterfront where he stood looking across the river for another twenty minutes, with his heart beating in his throat. The prostitutes were all housed in second-floor flats above the commercial shops that were at street level in the lower story. After staring for a while into the semi-darkness and occasional lights that were on the Yolo side of the river, he turned and walked back up "J" Street, intending to go to the Nevada Hotel, but a woman and a man were standing at the bottom of the stairs, talking with muffled voices, and he lost his nerve. He went on by, passing the Utah again and midway of the block ahead he saw the blinking neon sign of the Chicago Hotel. When he got there, away from the streetlight, he noticed that the sidewalk was deserted and he stepped through the open doorway and falteringly ascended the stairs.

By the time he reached the top step, he felt like he had just climbed Mount Everest. His breath was coming in short gasps and his heart was pounding and when the grotesquely overweight woman who was slumped on a worn settee on the landing at the head of the stairs lowered her book enough to see him and ask him if he was lost, he couldn't find his voice to answer.

Sizing him up she said "Oh, hell! No, I guess you ain't lost. Well, sonny, if you got a buck and a half just follow me and we'll see what we can find for you." He misunderstood her and thought she was going to go in a room with him and he wanted to say, "No, I changed my mind," but his voice box was no longer working and he blindly followed her down the hall until she opened a door and motioned for him to enter.

Inside the room was a double bed with sagging springs and mattress and painted ornamental metal bedposts from which the paint was falling off in flakes. The mattress was covered by a worn-through embroidered spread that had once been white, but was gray with age. Against the wall was a dresser that had been painted too many times with paint slopped over the mirror and drawer pulls. Sitting on the dresser were a chipped enamel washbasin, a water pitcher, and a stack of towels. A chamber pot stood on the floor beside the dresser. Street noises could be heard through an open window that looked out on the darkened street below and was framed with graying lace curtains that matched the bedspread. When his eyes had taken in all of the oppressing bleakness there was to see, he realized the woman had left, closing the door behind her. He was alone in the room. He stood with his knees braced and trembling, wanting to sneak out the door and leave but afraid to, trapped between his ego and his fear of getting caught. Time passed, and he thought maybe she had sent for the cops and he would end up in jail with his parents having to bail him out or maybe they would just leave him there and his name would be in the paper like the members of the Sacramento High School football team. With his mind trying to process all the imagined consequences that lay before him, the door opened and a girl came in. She was a nice looking girl who didn't seem to be much older than himself. It turned out, however, that she was much wiser in the ways of the world, which was the essential element necessary to his educational enrichment at that particular moment.

After the family's return to Sacramento, Mac seemed to find ever-increasing reasons to vent his explosive anger. Spud Murphy thought it should have been just the other way around, with financial burdens becoming less of an issue and the long drive to work no longer necessary. The S.P. was the perceived source of most of Mac's immediate frustrations, for what he considered to be its vacuous management policies and inefficient shop procedures. But those, it seemed, were just excuses to vent his anger. The real reasons for his temperamental flare-ups were rooted in his bitterness at having remained too long anchored in a backwater during the period he thought should have been the most productive part of his life, driven as he was by the wealth of talent and ambition that was his heritage. His anger was simply the aftermath of the Depression. At a critical time in the pursuit of his own ambitions he had found it necessary to devote his resources solely to the struggle to provide a living for his family, and he resented it. A man shouldn't have to give up one for the other.

The brunt of his irritability now ended up being directed at Elsie and Spud Murphy, for lack of any better target, Jack finally having grown out of that position. Although Jack and E.J. both moved into the flat shortly after the rest of the family was settled in, Jack was not home too often in the daytime, either working for the Pear Growers' Association or attending classes at Sacramento Junior College. He was not often available to divert Mac's attention away from Spud Murphy's teenage fallibilities, and Spud Murphy now found himself as the primary target of Mac's constant frustrations. Elsie continued to receive her share of his ill temper, sometimes giving as good as she got, but she invariably ended up crying out her frustrations. Many were the times Spud Murphy lay on his bed listening to his parents arguing, tormented by the cruelty and pointlessness of it and the intolerance and bitterness that seemed to be so deeply embedded in Mac's nature. Adding to that torment was the resentment Spud Murphy still carried in himself over the callous abandonment of Abdul.

Spud Murphy thought that he and Elsie should be kindred spirits, in the sense of their having similar difficulties occasioned by Mac's irascible temper. One day, after getting his ears pinned back by Mac, Spud Murphy made the mistake of appealing to Elsie for sympathy. Instead of sympathy, he received a stern reprimand for his lack of understanding..

"Don't disparage your father, Spud Murphy. Remember that he is my husband and I will always defend him. You should listen to him carefully and try to be the man he is. The food on your plate, the bed you sleep in, the clothes you wear— you have those things because of his love for you and his dedication to your welfare. Every day he forces himself to go to the shops and face the drudgery of a job he despises. You surely see that he has ability and genius far beyond the qualifications of any other person who is likely to set foot in this house. But remember this: talent without the means to express it is the cruelest of all burdens imaginable. Because of the times we live in, your father works for fools. Consider yourself privileged to have him for a father and cherish every moment God grants you to learn from him."

"None of that makes it right for him to get so sarcastic every time he talks to one of us."

"Just walk in his shoes, Spud Murphy, before you condemn him."

After his morning classes at Sacramento Junior College, Jack would often stop by the flat for lunch on the way to his job at the Pear Growers' Association. While he ate his sandwich, he would flop down in the only easy chair in the house, a green velour-upholstered monster that Mac had bought surplus from the Pullman car shop at the railroad. As he ate, Jack studied whatever of his subjects that he felt needed his attention. One that he studied regularly at the flat was a course in mineralogy, which deals with the classification and identification of mineral specimens. The universally accepted text for this subject, since it was first published in 1837, was *Dana's System of Mineralogy*, in its sixth edition in 1939.

When Mac came home from work, he was accustomed to eating his supper and then having a short nap in his easy chair before going down to the basement to carry on with whatever project he was currently involved with in his workshop. It became his habit to glance at a few pages of whatever book Jack might have left on the small table beside his chair. After discovering *Dana's System of Mineralogy*, Mac began spending an increasing amount of time with Jack's mineralogy texts, and proportionately less time in his workshop. When the following semester started at the junior college, he enrolled in Dr. J. B. Nichols's mineralogy class and in a class in crystallography, which was an allied subject that also drew his interest.

In the course of his studies, Mac decided he needed a refractometer of his own for determining the refractive index of mineral specimens in the field, which, along with *hardness*, is a principal determinant in the identification process. The college had a refractometer, but Mac considered it to be of poor quality and it was also always in demand. Mac turned to his basement workshop and designed and built a compact and accurate refractometer that found a generous market with other students and amateur 'rock hound' club members.

The success of the refractometer brought about the manufacture of other tools and instruments for mineral hobbyists, which kept the basement shop operating at a lively pace at the same time that Mac continued the more serious pursuit of an academic education, attending evening classes at Sacramento Junior College under the tutelage of Dr. Nichols. The basement workshop in which there was a lathe and drill press and other metal-working equipment became a developmental shop for the design and manufacture of lapidary equipment and the instruments necessary to the identification and cataloging of minerals.

Spud Murphy was assigned a minimal amount of lathe work, as detailed by Mac, and in addition was expected to clean the shop, sweeping up the metal lathe turnings and keeping the workbench neat and orderly. The tools were all stored neatly in drawers and bins that were made especially for that purpose. Larger tools had their place on the wall. A clean shop was Spud Murphy's contribution to the orderliness, if not the happiness, of Mac's existence.

It is hard to say exactly what event in their relationship ignited the first spark of rebellion in Spud Murphy, inspired generally by Mac's high opinion of himself and his low opinion for the efforts of anyone else. Once ignited, it didn't take much for the spark to become a conflagration. Certainly, by the time of the eighth grade oratorical contest, the embarrassment Spud Murphy felt as a result of Mac's overweening sense of

superiority over the rest of the world, but even more notably by
the presumption of superiority that Mac bestowed on Spud
Murphy, as a sort of sacred birthright, was a constant source of
irritation to Spud Murphy. As other similar incidents occurred,
his resentment of Mac's arrogance grew unabated.

Mac would occasionally give Spud Murphy a less demanding
lathe project to work on, along with the routine grinder work of
sharpening cutting tools and drill bits and performing other
common tasks that an apprentice would expect to do under the
watchful eye of his journeyman instructor. Unfortunately for
Spud Murphy's sense of self-worth, even the most trivial or
routine of such tasks could elicit Mac's criticism, no matter how
carefully Spud Murphy executed them. It took all the skill of a
master craftsman to pass inspection under Mac's critical eye.
Every task, however non-critical its actual purpose happened to
be, had almost unattainable requirements related only to the
manner of its execution.

Spud Murphy continued to do Mac's bidding with a growing
resentment that was engendered by what Spud Murphy
considered to be the unwarranted criticism of his work. Finally
there came a day when, indignant beyond his control— from the
sting of Mac's critical indictment of his efforts, and from the
hostile manner in which that indictment was delivered— Spud
Murphy backed away from the bench screaming, *"Why don't
you just go to hell, you old bastard!"* Spud Murphy saw Mac's
eyes narrow and his hand reach for the thing closest to hand on
the bench between them, which happened to be a three-foot
length of two-by-four. He decided his survival depended on
getting as much distance as possible between himself and that
two-by-four, and the man who held it. He evacuated the
basement in the most expeditious way possible, scrambling up
the stairs and through the yard and around the house onto the
sidewalk. When he was at the corner of the block by Dean's

house, he glanced back. Mac was coming fast and there were only about five steps separating them. Spud Murphy turned the corner with all the burners on, picking up speed with every step. When he had gone a block, he glanced back again and Mac was at the alley half a block behind him and losing ground, having dropped the two-by-four. Spud Murphy didn't look back again until he was at the railroad tracks that cut through town on "R" Street, behind the Diamond Match Company. Mac was nowhere in sight. Spud Murphy slumped down on the ground against a stack of lumber and started bawling.

That night he slept on the ground between two stacks of lumber along the railroad track. The next day, he was downtown by daylight, crossing the alley between "J" and "K" Streets, to where he had walked with the hazy notion of getting to the railroad yards and hopping a freight train out of the city. Not because he intended to go to some-place in particular, just that he thought getting out of town was about the only option he had left. He deemed it impossible to undo what he had so irrationally done and was therefore faced with its consequences through eternity: alone, sick at heart, without friend or purpose left in life. Getting out of town was the only thing he could think of doing. The problem with that course of action was that he somehow needed to get his few belongings from the flat.

In crossing the alley he noticed two bicycles leaning against the brick wall near a door that was the alley delivery entrance to an office building. The one closest to him was not locked. Suddenly reckless, he decided to appropriate it until he left town. "Who cares?" he thought. " I need it to go home and get my things. And what difference does it make now, anyway?" He walked up to the bike and didn't even look around to see if he was noticed. He swung his leg over the seat as though he owned it and was down the alley and into the next cross street in the blink of an eye. He glanced back as he turned the corner out of the alley and there was not a soul in sight.

He spent the day watching the house, waiting for Elsie to leave so he could go in and get his things. He didn't want to talk to her, knowing they would both cry if they had to say good-bye. He figured that Mac was at work, because the pickup was not sitting in its usual place by the curb in front of the house. The 1934 Ford Sedan that had replaced the Model A when they moved to town was there and it never moved all day, which is how he knew Elsie never left the house. He decided he would probably have to leave without his things, because it was too risky trying to get them. His pocketknife, which was the only really important thing he owned except for his rifle, which he couldn't take anyway, was in his pocket. It was a birthday present from Mac. He could find work and buy anything else he needed.

That night he found the hobo jungle under the Jibboom Street Bridge, where he shared a scant meal of thin soup and stale bread with two hobos who were traveling through. He fully intended to leave on the next freight with them, but that evening in front of a smoky fire on the riverbank, he told them his story and in return got some exceedingly wise counsel.

"So you did something stupid, and now you want to punish yourself by doing something even more stupid. Kid, listen to some good advice. Go home and face the music, before you end up in jail, or maybe worse. You don't belong out here."

The other said, "You've got a bed to sleep in, a father with a job who buys your grub, and a mother to cook it for you and so you want to play hobo. What do you think this is out here, the comic strips?" In the morning, when he woke up, his advisers had already gone.

Two days later, he was peddling the stolen bicycle on Thirty-third Street in back of Arata Brothers' store near Folsom

Boulevard and Jack pulled up along side him in the '34 Ford Sedan and said, "Hi."

He stopped the bike and said, "Hi."

Jack said, "Where'd you get the bike?" and Spud Murphy answered, "I bought it for five dollars."

Jack had not always been Spud Murphy's strongest supporter. Originally resentful for what he correctly considered to be the preferential treatment accorded to the clownish Spud Murphy by Mac and Elsie, Jack had of late assumed a more protective role in defense of his younger brother, owing in part to the natural processes involved in the aging of both of them, but intensified by the problems of Jack's previous relationship with Mac. More than anyone else, Jack realized what Spud Murphy was up against. Now he felt called upon to use the wisdom of his own experience in an effort to save his younger brother from similar heartbreak.

"Hungry?"

"Yeah."

"When did you eat last?"

"Yesterday."

"Mother misses you."

"Yeah. I know." He didn't really know, of course, but any other state of affairs would have been unlikely.

"Maybe you could drop by around dinner-time. She keeps putting your plate on the table like she was expecting you to drop by."

"I'm not going back there to have him kick the snot out of me like he did you."

"I don't think that would happen."

"Why not? What do you think he'd do? Give me a medal?"

"I don't think he'd do anything."

"I don't know…"

Thirteen

"Take the bike back. Put it back where you got it. Don't get caught, though. Then just walk into the house at dinnertime and sit down at the table and keep your mouth shut. Don't say anything smart or act scared. And don't walk in like you're lord and master of the place, the way you usually do."

"I don't know."

"Well, think about it. It's better than what you've got now. I've got to go. But no matter what else you do, take the bike back. I'm telling you. If that's the only thing you do, do that."

"Are you going to tell them you saw me?"

"No."

He didn't put it in exactly the same spot by the door where it had been, but it was close enough so someone would have to see it and the owner would forever wonder how it happened that it was brought back after almost a week, and left in the same place from where the thief had taken it. He coasted up, standing on one pedal and jumped off, leaning it against the wall and walking away from it all in one continuous motion so even if he had been seen one wouldn't know for sure that it was actually he that rode in on the bike.

He walked into Kress's five and dime and used the public rest-room to wash his face and pull the tangles out of his hair. At five minutes after six o'clock he walked in the front door of the flat and into the narrow dining room and sat down at the empty plate at his usual place as though he had never been gone, except that he avoided looking directly into his father's eyes. He did look into his mother's, though, and saw the tear that trickled down her cheek as she wordlessly passed him the platter of roast beef and carrots and potatoes. He dished himself and ate. His father stared at him intently for a while but said nothing.

Fourteen

Spud Murphy seemed destined to be forever starting out again in a new school, without the company of old friends whose presence would lend assurance in the new surroundings. In the fall of 1940 he found himself slated to attend C.K. McClatchy High School, rather than Sacramento High School, where he thought he was going to be, and where Bill was now a member of the junior class. McClatchy was actually the more distant of the two schools from the house on "S" Street. The dividing line was 29th Street and Spud Murphy lived two hundred feet west of that line. Bill's house was the same distance east.

As with junior high, Elsie gave Spud Murphy bus fare, but again, after the first day, he chose to walk, finding the crowded closeness of the bus uncomfortable and the frivolous horseplay of the older high school students intrusive upon his desire for solitude. There were a few students that he recognized as being from California Junior High, but they continued to leave him alone until they needed help with their homework, and he accorded them the same courtesy, as though they were of a different species, which in some respects they may well have been. He found himself once more, alone amongst a crowd of strangers. "Well," he thought, "there are worse fates."

Even the concertmistress was missing, which to Spud Murphy was a great relief, having either moved away or, in some other unremarkable manner, absented herself from the realm of his existence. He hoped that it was not that she had given up the violin, because she was, in Spud Murphy's honest opinion, truly talented.

McClatchy High School offered classes in military training that could be substituted for what Spud Murphy saw as the ego-deflating competition of physical education, which could correctly be construed as meaning that in spite of his two redeeming scoring efforts in the ninth grade basketball tournament, he was still coming in last in the hundred-yard dash, and striking out, more often than not, whenever he came up to bat. Electing for the military, he enrolled in the Reserve Officers Training Corps. His choice of R.O.T.C. had, in the beginning, more to do with maintaining anonymity and avoiding competition (he thought) than fulfilling any career ambitions. That perception changed two short weeks after the semester began, when President Roosevelt signed the Selective Service Bill into law on September 14 and the draft began a month later. There was some self-satisfaction on Spud Murphy's part at that time for having elected to take R.O.T.C. He could practically see himself on the sands of the Sahara in khaki tunic and white kepi, leading a company of draftees on temporary assignment to the French Foreign Legion.

The rest of his classes were the standard college preparatory courses of which he had few particular preferences but again willingly accepted Elsie's guidance. Of the standard courses, history and English were his favorites. They were courses he would have chosen even if they weren't required. He was indifferent about mathematics and science but he considered foreign language to be an absolute waste of time. Because a foreign language was a requirement for college admission, he didn't have much choice, other than to opt for French over either German or Spanish. Mac spoke a little French that he had picked up in the two years he spent in France during the war. Spud Murphy figured he might as well garner a few points by having something in common with his father. He took a course in mechanical drawing because the orderliness of geometric shapes and properties pleased him, much as the drawing of airplanes had in the sixth grade. To please Elsie, he signed up for orchestra, without her even having to suggest it to him.

By the end of the first week of classes, Spud Murphy despaired because none of his classmates was conspicuous for having any qualities that would coax him to extend himself to encourage their friendship. Immediately after that thought occurred to him at the end of Friday's sixth period history class, he caught sight of a student he hadn't noticed previously, as she made her way out of the classroom alone. In a room full of boisterous sophomores celebrating the successful completion of their first week of high school, this girl stood apart, distinguished by an air of self-confidence and an unassuming dignity. Spud Murphy was struck by the sense of peace and quiet that smoothed her features.

She remained on his mind over the weekend, and on Monday she was in none of his other classes, but at sixth period he watched her as she entered the classroom, taking a desk across the room from where he sat in the rear of the class. It was obvious she was a late enrollee, at least in the history class, and every bit as much a stranger to the other students as he was. She struck him as being resolute, someone who would probably stand by her own convictions, and would not be easily swayed by group pressure. Nor would she be found hiding in a cluster of students who looked to majority opinion for their decisions. By her reactions to those around her, it was plain to see that she was honest, not one to spend her time play-acting or pretending. He imagined her as someone who could look you straight in the eye and return your smile (if you had one) without a show of embarrassment. Beyond question of a doubt, she was a person he would like to have as a friend.

After class he followed her to her locker with the intent of introducing himself. The corridor was crowded around the lockers, with the students anxious to divest themselves of their excess books so they might catch their bus or whatever else they had come there looking for. When he came up to her, she was in the act of opening her locker door, and in so doing, she stepped back, and her bare forearm grazed his. Not a firm contact, only the lightest of touches, and maybe not even that; maybe just the nearness of her arm to his so he could feel the radiant warmth of a magnetic attraction that leaped the gap between them and spurred the tingling rush of blood from his suddenly beating heart.

It was an accidental touch, or a near-touch, and as their eyes met, he nodded to her, and said "Hi." Unable to do or say more because of the constriction in his throat, he moved on his way. But the emotions that suddenly twisted his gut, found their way to his chest, to form a knot around his heart and all but stop his breathing.

After many days spent working up his courage and practicing his smile in front of the bathroom mirror and trying out different little speeches, also in front of the mirror, he one day found himself face-to-face with her after school and he bluntly asked her permission to walk her home. To his great surprise and eternal gratification, she said she would be honored. He insisted on carrying her books and clarinet, although she said she was perfectly capable of carrying them herself, and then he insisted on stopping at the drug-store where Twenty-first Street and

Fourteen

Freeport Boulevard came together and buying her a strawberry ice cream sundae with his bus money which his mother continued to give him in part, knowing full well that he had discontinued using it for its intended purpose.

Her name was Bonnie, and she was exactly as Spud Murphy had imagined her to be: a country girl, honest, straight-forward, and uncomplicated. Her family, consisting of her father, mother, and younger sister, had lately migrated to Sacramento from Quincy, the county seat of Plumas County, in the northeastern part of the state. Their relocation to Sacramento had to do with finding a means of survival during the latter days of the Depression, complicated by the serious health concerns of her father. She was a class ahead of Spud Murphy, except for not having her necessary history credits, and she played the clarinet in the school's marching band. She was also intelligent and very pretty, managing somehow to be both at the same time. She quickly became, in all respects, and almost before the sundaes were half-gone, the sole proprietor and custodian of Spud Murphy's heart. It bothered him some that she didn't always seem to understand the importance of that trust and become properly inspired by it. But then, he never bothered to tell her how important it was, either, for fear that she might decline the honor and be frightened off forever.

Bonnie had a friend Noreen, and through Noreen, Spud Murphy was introduced to Noreen's friend Aaron, a boy with whom he instantly developed a strong friendship. It was unusual that those two should have taken such an immediate liking to each other because their home lives and personal natures were as different as night and day. Like Bill and Bonnie, Aaron was a year older than Spud Murphy. He also was a rarity among the acquaintances Spud Murphy had acquired up to that stage of his life: a stable and responsible boy from a financially secure family, whose members all seemed to be focused on worthwhile, long-term goals. The lives and aspirations of the family members, to external appearances at least, were all in harmony and demonstrated the stability and emotional maturity which Spud Murphy's life so sorely lacked.

Aaron's father was an engineering graduate of Stanford University and he held a position as a minor official in the state bureaucracy. He was a very controlled and stable person who enjoyed the orderliness of bureaucratic consistency and routinely took his family camping and fishing on the Rubicon River for two weeks each summer. He was a member of the prestigious Sutter Club, where Aaron and his brother Dick and occasionally one or two of their friends had access to the tennis courts. Of course, that was at those times when the courts were not in use by club members.

Aaron's mother was content to be just a mother and a wife, with no particular need for other sources of personal fulfillment beyond maintaining her social position and caring for her family and nourishing their ambitions. She was socially compatible with other women who were wives and mothers of similar ambition, having no compelling financial hardships to contend with.

The lives of Aaron's family members seemed to be neatly regimented, with little disruption of one by another. They always cared for each other, were rarely volatile, and were close to ideal in their intra-family relationships. They practiced accommodation of each other's wishes as a matter of respect and good breeding, as opposed to the homesteader method of rule by paternal fiat.

McClatchy High School existed to serve the more genteel populations of Sacramento, or at least the mothers of many of its students thought it did. Students that came from less affluent neighborhoods often bore the stamp of that circumstance, in one way or another, and in a class-conscious society such as a high school population, they often found themselves excluded from

the social rites that were intended to define the group. This
worked to create a different class of misfits that belonged to no
group at all, the individuals of which were mavericks. Such
would have been the case with Spud Murphy, were it not for his
newly asserted friendships with Bonnie and her friends.

In the beginning, Spud Murphy would not have thought a
thing about being left out of whatever social life there happened
to be, if the exclusion wasn't meant as an intended slight. And
even then, when he got over the bruised feelings from being
slighted, he still might not have cared— except that now,
exclusion would mean his opportunities for associating with
Bonnie would be limited, or even curtailed, and that friendship
had quickly become the most important part of his life.

Through those close, intimate friendships and through others,
less formal, that sprang from them, Spud Murphy found doors
open to him that he otherwise might never have entered, at least
not in high school. As a result of Noreen's mother's influence he
was invited to join an off-campus social club that limited its
membership to properly connected McClatchy High School
students. Aaron, Bonnie, and Noreen, of course, were members,
and after a proper evaluation of his dossier, Spud Murphy was
also invited to join. The TNT Club held its formal dances
monthly in the Clunie Clubhouse at McKinley Park, employing
the best of the local orchestras. On at least a couple of occasions
the nationally popular Dick Jurgens Orchestra was persuaded to
stop in Sacramento for a one-night stand when traveling between
engagements at Chicago's Aragon Ballroom and the Catalina
Casino on Santa Catalina Island off the coast of southern
California. Dick Jurgens had grown up in Sacramento and started
his band-leading career while attending Sacramento Junior
College. Knowing the orchestra business as he did, Spud
Murphy surmised that either Dick Jurgens felt he owed a lot of
favors for the start the town gave him before he hit the big time,

or that the rich daddies of the prissy little princesses who wanted their pictures on the social pages of the *Sacramento Bee* ponied up a lot of dough to get him to play a one-night stand at the Clunie Clubhouse.

The matronly dowagers who organized and chaperoned these formal balls (they could hardly be called 'dances') made sure that every boy's and every girl's dance card was completely filled, so there were never any wall-flowers, and no boy ever danced with the same girl more than three times in one evening. Spud Murphy spent his whole time, except for those three dances, looking over his partner's shoulder to see who Bonnie was dancing with, and how close together they did their dancing. The other important rules were: (one) that all attendees had to be chauffeured both to and from the ball by a parent; and (two), that no boy and girl ever went outside of the clubhouse to stroll hand in hand through the darkened paths and gardens of McKinley Park. To make sure of that, there were always matrons standing guard duty at the doors of the clubhouse that opened out into the park.

The boys had to furnish their own boutonniere and a corsage, which was indiscriminately placed on a table at the entry with other corsages for distribution to the girls, in random selection according to their arrival times. It took some creative sleight-of-hand on occasion, but Spud Murphy always made sure his corsage ended up on Bonnie.

Dancing With Tears In My Eyes

Al Dubin and Joe Burke

Those who dance, and romance, while they dance,
They seem so happy and gay.
Though they sing, while they swing and they sway,

Fourteen

Somehow, I can't feel that way.

I've been dancing with tears in my eyes,
For the girl in my arms isn't you.
Dancing with somebody new,
When it's you that my heart's calling to.

Trying to smile, once in a while,
But I've found that's so hard to do.
I've been dancing with tears in my eyes
'Cause the girl in my arms isn't you .

In his sophomore year, Spud Murphy extended his record of straight A's in all of his subjects. He was a favorite with all of his teachers, particularly Mrs. Farthingham, his English teacher, and Mrs. Edmunds, his history teacher. The teacher who most inspired him was Sergeant Meniatis, the regular army sergeant who was on assignment to the school as an R.O.T.C. instructor. The disciplinary training that Spud Murphy had internalized under Mac's thumb stood him in good stead in Sergeant Meniatis's classroom. At the time, he hadn't recognized the value of the habits that were being formed and only later, when he found himself at ease with military protocols, did it occur to him to acknowledge the value of Mac's rigid position on matters of discipline. Sergeant Meniatis was impressed with Spud Murphy's military aptitude and rewarded him liberally with promotions as the term progressed, all of which impressed Mac greatly, and in much the same way as had the 'Vision of War' speech. It kept Spud Murphy on good terms with his father for a considerable length of time.

Bonnie lived on Harkness Way, which was near the Tower Theater, toward the west end of Broadway. If Spud Murphy was driving the pickup on an errand for Mac, he would occasionally find himself on Harkness Way without quite knowing how he got there. Then, of course, in order to keep from looking like a complete idiot, he would have to stop and go up to her door and knock, in case she had already seen him. When her mother answered the door, he would say, "Oh! I was just wondering if Bonnie was at home?" Bonnie's mother would disappear without a word, and in a few moments Bonnie would be there and they would sit on the top step while he made up a big story about how he just happened to be going by and as he noticed her house he was inspired to think about asking her to a movie.

He used that line a couple of times and the third time he used it she started laughing.

"What are you laughing about?"

She laughed some more, and when she could stop laughing, she said "Because this street doesn't go anywhere. It's a dead-end," and then she sat there smiling at him. "It only goes to my house."

He felt his face burning, and for one of the few times in his life, he had to drop his eyes in embarrassment. When he lifted his gaze to meet hers, he said, "Well, I guess that's where I was going, then."

One day she said to him, "I know a place we could go, if you want to. Across the river, in West Sacramento, there is a man, a friend of my father's, who has a stable. He has a couple of horses he said I could ride, anytime I want to. Maybe if you could use your father's pickup we could drive over there and go riding some Saturday or Sunday. Would you like that? Maybe we could ride down along the river in the cottonwoods. We could take our lunch and have a picnic. Do you think we could?"

"I could ask my father for the pickup, or the car, maybe."

Spud Murphy made sure to catch Mac in his most affable mood before approaching him about using the pickup. Of course, he felt it necessary to explain the circumstances of his request.

Fourteen

"Why, sure, son. Why not? Glad to see you attentive to your girl's needs. It pays to keep the womenfolk happy— they mean a great deal to us." Spud Murphy was astounded. He couldn't imagine Mac acknowledging anything so sentimental as that. Not in a million years!

He didn't bother to tell Bonnie about his early years between six and nine as a night hawk on the Chisholm Trail, during the times when he was riding for the old Double-Bar B. He was moved to do so, but she was so excited and happy about her role as boss wrangler, it was a whole lot more fun to stand around and watch her saddle up Spud Murphy's gelding, which was her personal hand-picked choice for him to ride because of its having such a gentle nature. Just so he wouldn't be embarrassed, you know, in case he didn't know which end of the saddle went forward and which end back.

They rode down-river on the Yolo side toward Clarksburg, staying in the cottonwood groves that made a wilderness of the gentle slope that ran between the river and the base of the levee. Occasionally they came up and rode the lip of the levee to avoid an obstruction on the slope below. He followed behind her mostly, except where the trail was wide enough to let them ride abreast. After an hour's riding they were ready to stop and dig into the picnic lunch she had tucked into a saddlebag. He got the ground cloth and she laid the lunch out on it. They were quiet as they ate, only mentioning how good the lunch was, and how peaceful the day, and how pretty was the place they found for their picnic. The horses, dragging their reins, grazed nearby. When they finished their sandwiches, he moved closer to her and reached out to her, taking her hand in his. They sat there for some time, just holding hands, as they rested their backs against a cottonwood and quietly watched the slowly passing river traffic.

On another warm Saturday morning, Spud Murphy and Aaron sat at courtside at the Sutter Club waiting for a tennis court to be free. As they waited, they passed the time discussing the matter of intelligence.

"Aaron, I'll bet you never did bother to ask yourself how come your dad never calls you an idiot or a moron?"

"I never did. I never even thought about it. But now that you mention it, maybe it's because he's sorry for me."

"Aw, come on, now. You know better than that. It's because you're not a moron, and what's important is that he's willing to admit to you that you're not. You may not know as much as he does, but it's not because of a lack of brains— it's just because he recognizes that you're not old enough yet to have learned everything in your life that he has in his."

"It really bothers you when your dad puts you down, doesn't it?"

"Yeah. I hate for him to do that. It makes me think he feels cheated for having ended up bringing such a stupid kid as me home from the hospital." For a short time, they were silent, as their attention turned to the match that was being played, the players engaging in a long rally with the ball arcing hypnotically back and forth across the net. After the end of the set, the players exchanged courts. Spud Murphy took advantage of the break in the action to resume his conversation with Aaron.

"You know, there are times when I feel that way about the kids in school, that they're just plain stupid. Then I realize I'm being just like Mac, but I can't help it. The only difference between us is that I don't say out loud what's in my mind. He'd say it's because I haven't got the guts to speak up and say what I'm thinking. He'd say 'a spade's a spade and you might as well call it by its name.'" Spud Murphy paused as though gathering his thoughts and then went on. "Most of the time I feel that Bill's a complete idiot. You know, my friend that goes to Sac High. I hate it when he says or does something foolish. It's like he disappoints me by being stupid. But I don't say anything."

"You don't see me as being stupid, do you?" It was more a statement than a question.

"No. Of course not."

"Well, sometimes I am."

"That's for you to say, if that's what you think, not me. But I don't think it's true. You may do dumb things once in a while because you haven't figured them out yet, but you don't act like a total nitwit as a rule, any-more than I do."

"What's the difference, if I think I am?"

"Think what you want, it's just not so. You started out pretty smart, smarter than most, just like I did, and you're already smarter now than you were last week. Next week I suppose you'll be smarter yet, a regular quiz kid, practically. I don't see that happening much with the kids in school and my dad sure doesn't seem to see it happening with me. He acts like I was supposed to have been born with a college education, magna cum laude yet, so there's nothing left to learn."

The players finished their match and put their rackets away in racket presses. The boys took possession of the vacant court and their conversation came to an end. Spud Murphy won his match with Aaron in straight sets and therefore concluded that Aaron probably had much the higher intelligence quotient of the two of them.

Shortly after Aaron reached the age of sixteen, he passed his driver's test and got his license. His father never refused him the use of the family car on Friday or Saturday nights if there was no other need for it. The obliging Aaron always included Spud Murphy in his plans when considering a weekend agenda, and since Spud Murphy never missed an opportunity to take Bonnie to the movies, that option was always included in the considerations. Aaron would not likely have made movies his first choice, nor was he smitten by love for the somewhat snobbish Noreen, as Spud Murphy was for Bonnie. But Aaron was a friend, and that is just the kind of thing one friend does for another. After the movie they would always stop at Russ's Barbecue on Alhambra Boulevard for hamburgers and milk shakes and once they drove down Freeport Boulevard past the airport just to feel daring, but they never parked along the deserted back roads south of the airport that were so popular with many of their classmates.

At other times they went to Noreen's house because she had an automatic record player that would take a whole stack of 78 rpm records. They sat on the front porch in the semi-dark, sharing their feelings and experiences, or talking about their dreams of the future and listening to "Moonlight Serenade" and "Tonight We Love" from Tchaikovsky's "Piano Concerto" and recordings of Tommy Dorsey and Russ Morgan and Carmen Cavallaro and all the rest of their favorite song renderings and orchestras.

At the beginning of the second semester of his sophomore year Spud Murphy was elected to represent his homeroom on the student council, an office he neither sought nor wanted. He was conspired against by Mrs. Hullen, a very undemocratic homeroom teacher who was unduly influenced by the fact that he had made it through the first semester with perfect grades. On that basis alone she conscripted him to run for the position. It didn't take many weeks before he was convinced that the student council was silly and meaningless, but Mrs. Hullen wouldn't allow him to resign.

In R.O.T.C., he was promoted from corporal, a rank he had attained halfway through the first semester, to sergeant, which kept him in favor with Mac. Aside from the fact that desire to stay in Mac's good graces was a compelling factor that stirred his patriotic fervor, military topics on their own merit always evoked in Spud Murphy's mind the seductive and romantic images of heroic members of the 13th Hussars at Balaclava and the French Foreign Legion in North Africa, as well as other real and fictional heroes of the nineteenth century.

By the time school let out for vacation in the summer of 1941, Jack had gone to work for the U.S. Army Corps of Engineers. The corps was short handed, with many World War I bases being reactivated and new installations being built for the rapidly developing war effort. Jack used his good graces to arrange for Spud Murphy to be hired by the corps also, cautioning him to falsify his age by adding two years to his real age, so he would meet the age requirement for government employment. When Spud Murphy reported as instructed to make application, Jack's boss, being a helpful sort, filled out Spud Murphy's application himself. When he came to the part about age, the form didn't ask for "age," it asked for "date of birth." The boss said, "Hey, kid, what's your date of birth?"

Without thinking, Spud Murphy, all aglow about getting a real job, and prepared to say he was seventeen when asked, was temporarily stumped and blurted out his true birth date. "July 29, 1925, sir." The boss went on to finish the form and then sent Spud Murphy outside to the equipment yard to wait for an assignment to a crew. In about the time it took him to run his eye down the list of items on the application form, he exploded in a profusion of cuss words and came storming out through his office door hollering, "What do you think this is, kid! You can't work here. You ain't old enough!" Spud Murphy had about the same feeling in his gut as he did the day he won the footrace up the basement stairs with Mac five steps behind him.

He went down to the State Employment Office, where he had originally been headed when Jack tried to help him get on with the corps. He was told there that he couldn't be sent out for a job interview because there were too many men with families still looking for work. He told them he was homeless and hadn't eaten for two days, so they sent him out to apply for work with a landscaping company, which hired him to start the next morning. That evening while he was setting the table for dinner, Elsie asked him about his day.

"How did the new job go, dear?"

He poured out the whole story and she said, "Oh! I'm so sorry. But you're a good gardener. I know you'll make a wonderful landscaper. Maybe that's what God means for you to be."

"Well, that's not what I mean for me to be," to which Elsie just smiled. More like a grin, it was, but off to the side, where he could not see.

When Jack came home from work, he said to Spud Murphy, "You jerk! You just about got me fired. You made me look like a fool, sending a fifteen-year-old kid to apply for a job with the federal government!" He was still ranting when Mac came up from the basement, where he had been working since he got home earlier from the shops. The first thing out of his mouth when he heard the ruckus was "Now what?" as though he was at his wit's end from being waylaid by a continuing parade of people to rectify their screw-ups, when the fact was, no one had even mentioned asking him for an opinion. After Spud Murphy filled him in with all the details he snorted "HMPHH! indicating the absolute disdain he felt for anybody with such substandard mental capabilities.

Later that evening, after thoroughly humiliating Spud Murphy, Jack told him it was just as well he hadn't gotten the job with the Corps of Engineers anyway, because a better job had come along. It was on a survey crew run by Blackie Zimbicki, a crew chief well known in the local surveying community whose rear chainman had fallen victim to the temptation of John Barleycorn once too often. That night, in

Fourteen

preparation for Spud Murphy's first day's work under Blackie, Jack gave him a substantial cram course in surveying techniques, including how to give a back sight, how to do up a surveyor's tape (which is called a chain) in figure-eight loops of five feet and snap it into a circular roll, the fundamentals of measuring distances between points on the earth's surface with the aid of a plumb bob, the various terminology used by surveyors, and finally a strongly- worded admonition to not screw up this time. After the lesson, Spud Murphy ran across town to the landscape contractor's office and left a neatly lettered note on his door which read:

> I'M SORRY. MY FATHER WON'T LET ME
> WORK FOR YOU.

Blackie was one of the crew chiefs employed by an engineering firm whose owner was Joe Spink. As luck would have it, when he reported for work the next morning, Spud Murphy found himself in competition with a junior college student four years his senior, for the job Spud Murphy thought he already had nailed down. It developed that at the same time Blackie told Jack that Spud Murphy could have the job, Mr. Spink was hiring his nephew— whose course of study at the junior college was civil engineering—for the same position. Mr. Spink's nephew had already taken a semester of surveying, so it was a foregone conclusion in every body's mind, except Spud Murphy's, as to who was going to get the job.

On that fateful morning, when Blackie announced to no one in particular, "There is a plumb bob and a chain in the box behind the back seat," Spud Murphy scrambled in ahead of the nephew and sat on the box with the chain in it while he strapped the plum bob sheath on his own belt. Then he undid the tape in a long continuous ribbon and asked Blackie where the back sight was, all as though he'd been doing nothing but surveying for the last hundred years. When Blackie answered him, Spud Murphy took the line rod and lit out running. After lunch Blackie pulled out a pack of Phillip Morris cigarettes and offered one to the nephew, which was refused, and one to Spud Murphy, which wasn't refused, and Spud Murphy lit a kitchen match on the seat of his jeans to light his and Blackie's cigarettes. Then he listened with his mouth shut while Blackie and the head chainman traded ribald stories until the lunch half-hour was over. At the end of the day Blackie dropped Spud Murphy off at the flat on "S" Street and told him to be out on the street in front of the flat, ready to go to work, at 7:30 the next morning. Spud Murphy never asked how much he was getting paid, but on Friday when he collected his paycheck he figured it out from the number of hours worked and it came to fifty cents an hour which was the standard wage that an experienced rear chain-man would make anywhere in town. Spud Murphy never crossed paths with the nephew after that and he never asked what was said to him or anything about him. When Ariel heard about the situation and how it had worked out he said, "Well, it just goes to show that nephews sometimes aren't worth much in a Depression."

People weren't buying or selling much property or doing much development work in 1941 so surveying was usually not a very steady occupation, but Spud Murphy was a hard worker and fit in on the crews he worked with. Both his employers and fellow employees liked him and when work ran out with one firm he was passed on to another firm that had work, and so on through the summer. At no time was he unemployed. He worked successively for Joe Spink, Frank Reynolds, Frank Talbot, Joe Spink a second time and finally L. K. Jordan, who was the general manager and engineer for the North Fork Ditch Company. He never missed a day of work all summer. He brought his paycheck home each week, mostly intact, and gave it to Elsie, who put it in a savings account at the Bank of America. When summer was over, the account had more than two hundred and fifty dollars in it.

Blackie was the one who put Spud Murphy up to going to work for Mr. Jordan. Blackie knew Spud Murphy could use the part-time work while he was going to school. He also knew Spud Murphy could handle the extra work without hurting his scholastic standing. Spud Murphy had a natural talent for drafting and fifty per cent of the North Fork Ditch Company's need was for a draftsman.

Spud Murphy went to work for Mr. Jordan in midsummer of 1941 and was continuously employed by him until December. Mr. Jordan was an extraordinary man, ramrod stiff, the ultimate military engineer. He was West Point educated and his personal traits and manners evinced the starched stiffness of nineteenth-century Victorianism. His uniform consisted of polished brown high-top shoes and leather puttees, cavalry britches, a starched white shirt laundered daily, a black string tie and a campaign hat with U.S. Army Corps of Engineers' acorns. His demeanor was identical to Mac's in its degree of uncompromising sternness, but he rarely spoke other than to direct or explain and he did not censure at all. If censuring had been necessary, Spud Murphy figured somebody would be looking for a new job.

The field-work consisted of establishing profile elevations on the miles and miles of ditch line that was maintained as a water distribution system for the county areas northeast of Sacramento. The company's main office was located on the ninth floor of the Forum building in downtown Sacramento, where the ditch profiles were kept on vellum rolls, updated from time to time, to determine those sections of ditch that needed to be re-excavated or re-aligned. In addition to assisting Mr. Jordan in taking the field elevations and recording them on the vellum profile sheets, Spud Murphy acted as chauffeur for Mr. Jordan's local business travel and his trips from home to office, and to the railroad station for his frequent business trips to San Francisco.

The company provided Mr. Jordan with a shiny blue 1940 Plymouth business coupe for both his official and personal use, but he didn't normally drive himself because of a war-incurred back injury that bothered him most of the time. Spud Murphy took the Plymouth home evenings and weekends and cleaned and polished it more painstakingly than if it had been his own. He picked Mr. Jordan up punctually at whatever hour of the day or night that Mr. Jordan wished and delivered him to wherever he wanted to go.

Spud Murphy and Bonnie sat in the freshly waxed and polished Plymouth in front of Bonnie's house, the evocative trombone glissandos and muted violins and pulsing bass of Russ Morgan's orchestral arrangement of 'Alone' emanating from the radio in the dash. The setting was a symbolic focus of Spud Murphy's exalted state of happiness. Bonnie sat looking mostly straight ahead, occasionally turning her head toward him to lend emphasis to her words. He was turned more to face her. Her hand, clasped in his, rested on the seat between them, its softness against his palm creating a strange and wondrous magic that stirred his heart with an emotion for which he had no words.

"Do you wish sometimes that you still lived in Quincy?" he asked.

"Most of the time."

"I'm glad you don't. I wouldn't be sitting here with you if you did."

She countered the obvious implication of his last remark by saying, "Don't you ever wish that you still lived in Plymouth?"

"No. I wouldn't want to be there. I don't like it here either, but I wouldn't want to be back in Plymouth. I don't know where I'd want to be. Just traveling, I suppose."

"You still have to live somewhere. You can't just spend all your time traveling."

"If I was in the Marine Corps, I could. Most of the time, anyway."

"Why the Marine Corps? You're in Army R.O.T.C. and it seems that you would enlist in the army if you wanted to do something like that."

"No, I think the Marine Corps has more opportunity for travel. I could apply for sea duty. Did you know that there were marines aboard John Paul Jones's ship and that was before there even was a regular army or a navy? His ship, the *Bon Homme Richard*, was originally a privateer known as the *Duras*. And at other times the marines went to Tripoli to fight the Barbary Coast pirates and they fought in Nicaragua and in China during the Boxer Rebellion and lots of other places like that. The army doesn't go anywhere unless there's a regular war like in France and then they just sit there in trenches trying to wear each other out. The Spanish-American War was okay but that was because of Teddy Roosevelt and the *Rough Riders*. They don't even have cavalry anymore. At least not to do any fighting."

"You couldn't very well get married if you did something like that."

"You could if you wanted. There's always a base with housing somewhere and you'd have leave so you could go home once in a while."

She didn't offer a response to that and they sat there for several moments immersed in their own thoughts until Spud Murphy asked her, "Why do you like Quincy so much?"

"Well, because all my friends are there, I guess."

"I'm your friend, too."

"I know. But you could come there, too. It's more than that, though. We had horses and my dad delivered oil to all the big ranches and we could ride all over and it was prettier with the mountains and the rivers and lakes and meadows and deer all over. I just liked it and I didn't want to leave it because it was my home."

They were quiet for a long time, watching the late afternoon shadows move time past them, unaware of the magic of the moment they were caught in, but both of them feeling the bridge between their hearts through the touch of their clasped hands.

He broke the silence with an agonized and startled suddenness. "Good lord!"

"What?"

"I was supposed to pick L.K. up at five o'clock and drive him to the depot."

"What time is it?"

"Ten to five."

She was already getting out of the car and when the door latched behind her he had the transmission in gear and the clutch engaging, and he smoked the tires pulling away from the front of her house. He didn't even think to wonder what his precipitous departure might do to his standing with her mother and father.

It was almost all the way across town from Bonnie's house on Harkness Avenue to where Mr. Jordan lived on 38th Street and Folsom Boulevard. When Spud Murphy pulled into the curb, Mr. Jordan's tall, forbidding figure was pacing the porch in his impatience. He turned menacingly down the stairs, briefcase in hand, and came directly to the driver's door. Spud Murphy expected to be yelled at and peremptorily fired and he slid across the seat to the passenger's side because Mr. Jordan obviously intended to do the driving himself, bad back and all. Mr. Jordan got in and slammed the door shut, reaching to the dash to turn the radio off, which he did with such force that the knob broke off in his hand. No word was spoken until they arrived at the depot and found the train still waiting, delayed by some blessed circumstance not of their making, and then Mr. Jordan said, with dispassionate calm, "I do not tolerate lateness. Do not ever let it happen again." And it did not, not ever, and, for not having fired him, Mr. Jordan achieved preeminence in Spud Murphy's list of heroes, heretofore unmatched by man or god.

With the beginning of the fall semester of 1941, the TNT club scheduled an evening hayride at a ranch near Fair Oaks to take the place of the usual monthly dance at the Clunie Clubhouse. There were too many wagons and not enough chaperones or else the chaperones just didn't want to get hay in their coiffures. Spud Murphy and Bonnie sat alone, buried in hay in the back of a wagon minus its chaperone and he kissed her lips tenderly, with his arms around her holding her close against his beating heart. When they got to where the wagons were all pulled up in a circle around the bonfire, they chose to forego the hot dogs and roasted marshmallows and soda pop. They sat side by side on a log at the outer limits of the circle of light cast by the fire with their arms around each other's waist and her head on his shoulder.

On a Friday night later in the month, Mac let Spud Murphy use the pickup to take some of his and Aaron's classmates to the Woodland-McClatchy football game. There were numerous other students who had wheedled their parents out of the use of the family automobile on that particular evening, it being one of the more important games on the McClatchy schedule. The game was unusually well played with close scores and a lot of school rivalry coming from the cheering sections. McClatchy won the game and in the order in which they were able to maneuver their vehicles out of the parking lot, the celebrants drove in a caravan down the main street of Woodland in a mindless noisy madness of blaring horns and cheering students, celebrating their exuberance for life itself, more than just the victory of a single football game.

Spud Murphy was following the brand-new shiny black 1941 Packard limousine that Ellis Katz's father had generously provided for his son's use. Without warning the entire caravan came to a sudden stop, except for the pickup with four crammed into the cab and another half dozen in the back. After the crash, everybody jumped out and stood looking at the broken glass of the Packard's left rear tail-light and the demolished bumper, grill, head-light, fender and hood of the pickup. Ellis Katz said, "What the hell did you do that for? Can't you drive? My old man is going to raise hell, you jerk." He probably went on to say some more unflattering things, but Spud Murphy was not interested in hearing them and had stopped listening. After appraising the damage everyone got back in their various vehicles, except some who chose not to ride in the pickup anymore. Spud Murphy took the River Road back to Sacramento and there wasn't much cause for celebration on the way.

He got home at about one in the morning after dropping Aaron and Bonnie and Noreen and a couple of others off at their homes. Mac was waiting up for him, remaining seated in the massive parlor-car chair that Spud Murphy frequently referred to as the seat of judgment. His arms were folded severely across his chest and he had the baleful look of the Grand Inquisitor on his countenance.

"You're late. You had an accident, didn't you?"

"Yes, sir."

"Dammit. Why don't you ever use your head?" Mac was on his feet, heading out the door to look at the damage and Spud Murphy followed him, explaining.

"I hit the brakes but they just didn't stop fast enough. The car I ran into had hydraulic brakes and the mechanical brakes on the pickup just wouldn't stop it in time. I was probably too close behind him, anyway."

"Probably? What do you mean, probably? What you were doing was horsing around and not paying attention. There's no 'probably' about it. Now look at that mess. Well, you can damn well pay to have it fixed."

"I didn't figure on sending you the bill, sir. Mom's got my money in the bank. I earned it and I can pay for the repairs."

"You sure as hell can. It ought to come right out of your hide, and if you start acting like a smart-ass about it, it will."

Spud Murphy took the pickup to the Ford garage on Monday morning. In one week they made all the repairs— took the dents out, installed a new headlight, and painted it— and when the repairs were complete Elsie drew two hundred and fifty dollars out of his bank account for him to pay the bill. After the repairs were paid for, he had twenty dollars left which he used to pay for a new taillight lens and frame for the Katz family's Packard.

With the beginning of his junior year, Spud Murphy's academic standing began to plummet— the first reversal of any kind his grades had suffered since the embarrassment of Miss Joseph's fifth grade class. The downward spiral accelerated with his continuing disinterest in schoolwork until it virtually went into free fall. He completely lost interest in his classes, except R.O.T.C., considering the other subjects to be a waste of his time. He had a proven ability to hold a man's job, and that was all he felt obliged to do at this point of his life. Unfortunately, he had a high enough standing in most of his classes to maintain his grades, except for algebra and French. It was unfortunate because having leeway only prolonged the inevitable, making the truth more difficult to face when it did become known. In mid-October he received a six-week notice of failure in both of those subjects. Half a dozen girls from his algebra class whom he had helped in the previous semester did their best to prime him for the test, but he failed it anyway. The failure notices had to be returned, signed by one of his parents. He carefully forged Mac's signature on each of them.

Homestead

Sometime after wrecking Mac's pickup and after he got the failure notices, Spud Murphy walked downtown after school to the Marine Corps recruiting office in the Federal Building on "I" Street. He talked to the recruiting sergeant at length and found out much of what there was to know about the corps and the requirements for enlisting. He had turned sixteen in July. Adding a year to his actual age, he told the sergeant he was seventeen years old and he talked about his R.O.T.C. class and the high marks he was getting. The sergeant said, "Any time you're ready, come on down and we'll get the paper-work started on you."

Spud Murphy realized quite clearly that between the wall that was growing between himself and Mac and the closeness he felt for Aaron and Bonnie, he was rapidly growing apart from both Mac and Elsie. He worked intermittently after school through the week and on Saturdays, as Mr. Jordan needed him. If he had spare time beyond that during the week, he hung around the recruiting office. On Sundays and on those Saturdays when Mr. Jordan didn't need him, he was with either Aaron or Bonnie or sometimes both of them, often with a couple of Aaron's other friends who lived in Fair Oaks. Almost any escape was preferable to facing the growing estrangement he felt toward his mother and father, for which he held himself responsible and shouldered a great deal of guilt.

Every day there were reports in the newspaper or on the radio of Japan's war with China and its hostility toward other Asian countries. A lot of argument arose out of the Japanese claims for the establishment of a *Japanese Sphere of Influence* encompassing much of Southeast Asia, which didn't rest well with Great Britain, the major stakeholder in that part of the world. It also threatened developing American interests along the Pacific Rim. There was increasing speculation in the news that pointed toward the possibility of a U.S.-Japanese war.

Fourteen

At dinner one night, with all the family around the dining table and the discussion centered on the draftees, Spud Murphy waited for a pause in the conversation, which was focused on the likelihood of Val (E.J.'s boyfriend from Sacramento Junior College) and Jack being picked in the next draft. At the most auspicious moment, with a perfect sense of timing at a lull in the conversation, Spud Murphy startled them all by asking, "When the United States goes to war with Japan, will you sign for me so I can join the Marine Corps?" He asked it of his mother, although he never looked at her directly so it was left suspended in mid-air until she felt the absolute need to provide an answer. Recovering from the shock brought on by the audacity of the question, she replied, "Certainly not!" and everyone looked at her and then turned to look at him as if he was a little bit simple-minded. He let the subject drop and made a promise to himself never to bring it up again.

Armistice Day, November 11, 1941 fell on a Tuesday, and Spud Murphy spent several hours on the preceding Sunday working on his uniform in preparation for the parade through the downtown commercial area of the city. He borrowed Elsie's steam iron and with meticulous care he removed every vagrant wrinkle in tie and shirt and trousers and then sharpened the creases in his trousers and the pleats of his shirt and blouse with equally fastidious precision. For two hours he labored to apply a spit-shine to his dress belt and shoes that would have been the envy of a member of the king's own guard.

In addition to celebrating the signing of the armistice agreement that marked the end of the World War, the parade provided the major opportunity for the R.O.T.C. units and bands of Sacramento's two principal high schools to be judged in face-to-face competition. Spud Murphy made sure as he worked on his uniform that he would not be one to bring discredit on his school.

As he pressed and shined and polished Spud Murphy likened his uniform to the costumes he had worn in one or another of Mac's theatrical productions. It occurred to him that costumes and uniforms alike were all a ruse to fool an audience somewhere into believing something, which wasn't necessarily true. That fact itself was not particularly startling, he had just never before seen it in quite the same light, where the container and its wrappings do not necessarily describe what the container holds. Imagine, with a little bit of grease paint and a few yards of cloth you could outwit the whole of civilization, or at least a good part of it. The thought caused him to look deeper into the metaphor and extend the artifice of costume to that of attitude. "If people could only change their attitudes as easily as they switched their costumes," he mused, "you would have the answer to a whole lot of the world's misery."

Spud Murphy realized he had been successfully using that tactic through most of his childhood, at least up until the time Abdul was abandoned during the move back to Sacramento. He had learned the utility of it in the first place from observing the hopelessness of Jack's rebellion against Mac's disciplinary tactics. Deception fit right in with Spud Murphy's precocious, wisecracking style. He had used guile successfully to produce harmony because it didn't make sense to him to suffer the consequences of disharmony when there was an alternative. It was true that it was not Jack who was the one who should have had to modify his behavior, but who cares? If it pleases the tribal elders, why not? Under the circumstances, rebellion was pointless, in Spud Murphy's eyes. So he wondered, "Why am I so caught up in it now?" He had no answer.

Mac and Elsie and Billy watched the parade with thousands of other spectators and cheered loudly when Spud Murphy's unit marched by. They waited for the whole parade to pass so they could also clap for Aaron as his company went by and for Bonnie playing her clarinet in the McClatchy band.

On Friday, December 5, Mac and Elsie left Sacramento after work to spend the weekend at the homestead, taking Billy with them. Spud Murphy spent Saturday morning playing tennis with Aaron at the Sutter Club. In the afternoon he stayed at home, reading *The Four Feathers*, by A. E. W. Mason. Saturday evening he and Aaron took Bonnie and Noreen to a movie at the Alhambra. Afterward they stopped at Russ's for hamburgers and milk shakes. On Sunday morning he slept in until ten o'clock. When he got up he toasted two slices of bread and poured a glass of milk and was sitting at the kitchen table finishing the last of the milk when E.J. came out of her bedroom where she had been ironing and listening to the radio. She had a startled look on her face and she said, "The Japanese have just attacked Pearl Harbor."

Fifteen

On the Monday morning following the bombing, Spud Murphy's first period class was R.O.T.C. He went to the registration office after first period and asked about the procedure for transferring to a school in another state. The registrar, who was a very helpful lady, told him it was just a matter of returning his books and uniform and any other property that belonged to the school and of letting her know the city he was moving to and the name of the new school, so she could send his records on. She said if neither of his parents could come to the administration office they should send a signed note explaining the circumstances of his leaving.

He spent the afternoon carefully crafting a note in his father's handwriting, at which he was quite adept, explaining that the family would be moving to Omaha, a division point on the Union Pacific Railroad. That railroad, he explained, together with the SP and the C&NW, shared maintenance responsibilities for the transcontinental rail route from San Francisco to Chicago. The note also said that both he and Spud Murphy's mother were so busy getting prepared for this unexpected move he didn't see any way that it would be possible for either of them to get to the school's administrative office before their very imminent departure.

On Tuesday morning Spud Murphy carefully folded his uniform and put it in a paper bag with his R.O.T.C. manual. He went to school as usual and when the bell rang for first period he went to the R.O.T.C. classroom and turned in his uniform and manual. When he was done there, having had to explain in detail to Sergeant Meniatis that his family was moving to Omaha because his father's job had been transferred there, and promising to enroll in R.O.T.C. at the new school, he went to his locker and cleaned it out, taking his books to the registrar's counter. He gave the registrar his father's note and turned in the rest of his books. The registrar asked him if he had found out the name of the school in Omaha he would be attending so they could forward his transcript and Spud Murphy said he had not. The registrar gave him a post card with some blanks to be filled in at the new school and the McClatchy address on it and said, "As soon as you know what school you'll be in, have the registrar there fill this card out and drop it in the mail, so we can send them your records." It took less than a half hour to check his books in and finish the small amount of paper work. He was amazed at the ease with which people could terminate their high school careers if they were disposed to do so.

It was ten o'clock by the time he arrived at the Marine Corps recruiting office. There were ten or twelve others ahead of him, all of them waiting to enlist. The sergeant put an enlistment form in his typewriter and began typing the information that was called for on the form. Spud Murphy furnished the information as the sergeant typed, being extremely careful to give the year of his birth as 1924 so no one could escape the fact that he was seventeen years old. Shortly before noon a navy doctor in uniform entered, followed by a hospital corpsman. After silently scrutinizing the assemblage with evident distaste, the doctor said, "All right, sergeant, we may as well begin," after which the doctor disappeared into the adjacent examining room with the corpsman. One by one as the sergeant called their names, the new recruits went into the examining room where the doctor asked them questions about their medical history, checked their tonsils, had them read an eye chart, and examined them briefly for hernia and prostate problems and indications of venereal disease. Each one had to turn in a urine sample, for which they were handed a small sterile bottle by the corpsman, as the doctor finished his examination.

After Spud Murphy's medical exam had been completed, Sergeant Knott called him up to his desk. Shuffling through the papers there, he said, "Son, you need a release from one of your parents. This is the form for it. Take it home with you and have one of them fill in the blanks and sign on the bottom line where the 'X' is. You can bring it back to me tomorrow."

"My father's leaving town, sir. The company he works for is sending him to Omaha."

"Well, then have your mother sign it."

"She's not alive, sir. She was taken by tuberculosis some years ago."

"I can't enlist you, son, without a release from one of your parents, or if you don't have any parents, your guardian. That's the rule. I'm going to write out here on this Western Union form what I need my father to say in a telegram so I can legally sign you up. If you pass the physical okay and I get this telegram delivered here by Western Union, you're in. If not, I can't help you. If I were you, I'd get on the phone to Omaha right away." One could tell that the sergeant was obviously feeling harassed, resenting the sudden invasion of his office by hordes of eager young civilians intent on defending their country's honor, or, as in Spud Murphy's case, escaping the monotony of their depression-stagnated lives. Spud Murphy guessed that Sergeant Knott had probably never before in his life seen such a demand for his enlistment services.

The Western Union telegraph office was between "J" and "K" Streets, about two blocks from the Federal Building. Spud Murphy went there and asked the telegrapher what the best time was to send a local telegraph so that it wouldn't be delivered until the following morning. The telegrapher said to write it out anytime and put the instructions on the form as to when it was to be delivered. Spud Murphy didn't want to let the telegrapher see him writing it out himself. He asked him for a couple of forms that he could take over to the S.P. shops where his father worked, because his father was the one who needed to send the telegram. Spud Murphy took the forms with him over to Kress's and ordered an egg salad sandwich and a cherry coke which he consumed while he wrote out the telegram, giving the required authorization for his enlistment. He wrote exactly as the sergeant had specified, signing it with Mac's name, which he considered to be no mortal sin, because Mac's name happened to be exactly the same as Spud Murphy's name, with the slight difference of not having a 'Jr.' on the end of it.

After he sent the telegram, Spud Murphy walked across "K" Street to DeVon's Jewelers. He told the salesman, an older man who looked like he was someone's grandfather that he wanted a gold locket that a girl could wear on a chain around her neck. The salesman brought out several inexpensive lockets that he chose on the basis of their being what he assumed would fit within Spud Murphy's means. After Spud Murphy rejected all of them, the salesman asked him what price range he had in mind. Spud Murphy then told the salesman that he had just joined the Marine Corps and he wanted to give his girl something special for his leaving, that she could keep his picture in, and so she would have cause to remember him. "I want it to be nice," he said. "I don't care how much it costs."

The salesman knew better than to put too much stock in that, but the next piece he brought out was an elegantly crafted, solid-looking, fourteen-karat gold heart with a beautiful little five- or six-point diamond set in the hinged front leaf of the locket. Spud Murphy instantly said, without even an inquiry as to its price, "I'll take that one."

The salesman examined the small tag on the locket's chain and said, "You have a good eye for quality, son. That will be one hundred and seven dollars. Do you wish for it to be engraved?"

"Can I put it on lay-away? I can give you thirty dollars now."

"I don't see a problem with that. Will you be making regular weekly payments?"

"I have the money in my bank account right now. I just need for my mother to get it out. And about the engraving. Is there room to put on the back of it, 'Bonnie, I love you. George'?"

The salesman said, "I think there is room for that. And perhaps the year, 1941, on the inside, as well?"

Spud Murphy watched him make out the sales invoice for the locket. Without saying anything about it, the salesman discounted the sales price by twenty dollars and made no charge for the engraving. After paying thirty dollars from the money in his wallet, the amount left owing was fifty-seven dollars. He folded the invoice copy and put it in his wallet. The salesman put the original of the invoice and the locket, in its gift box, in a brown envelope with Spud Murphy's name on it and put it in the safe. When Spud Murphy saw the locket securely put away, he felt safe in leaving it in the store and turned to leave. The salesman straightened up, closing the door of the safe, and put out his hand to Spud Murphy. "God bless you, son," he said.

He was in a quandary as to whether to go home or not, worried about getting caught in the deception he was creating.

He was nervous about someone from the school calling or coming by to check up on his story about moving. He was also worried about Aaron or Bonnie calling to ask Elsie why he hadn't been in school, or someone else finding him out in some unforeseen way. He decided that spending another night at home was the safest and wisest thing to do, even though he was desperate to have his departure over and done with in the shortest possible time.

After dinner he put the invoice from DeVon's in his top dresser door where he knew his mother would find it, and then he helped her with the dishes and later got his violin out and practiced exercises from the thick green Schirmer exercise book for violin. Elsie came into the living room and sat down with her knitting and listened to him practice. When his playing changed to Robert Schumann's "Traumerei," Elsie left her knitting and sat down at the piano and they played "Traumerei" as a piano-violin duet. When they finished, he put his violin away and went down to the basement where Mac was working, which was something he hadn't done at all since they had their altercation. He swept the floor and cleaned the bench and put away some of the tools that Mac wasn't using, and neither of them spoke in any deeply meaningful way other than to try to maintain the illusion that there was not a bottomless, unbridgeable chasm separating them

The next morning he waited until he heard the pickup start and Mac leave for work before coming out to the kitchen for his breakfast. After he had eaten, he put his arm around his mother's shoulders and gave her a peck on the cheek. He said, "See you," to E.J. and Billy, who were both eating breakfast at the dining room table, and went out the front door exactly as he had done every day for the last two and a half years since moving from the homestead. When he was out of sight of the house he started trotting and he trotted all twenty-eight blocks across town to the Federal Building, making it in record time.

There were more recruits there and the sergeant didn't have the results of the physicals yet, but the telegram had been delivered. Sergeant Knott told him it was all in order and said, "Just take a seat on the bench, son, because the doctor will be back about ten." He didn't even question the authenticity of Mac's typed-out signature appearing fifteen hundred miles away from the supposed location of Mac's corporate self, except that once when he passed in front of Spud Murphy and their eyes met directly, Spud Murphy heard him mutter, "Omaha, huh?" When the doctor came in he handed the sergeant a stack of medical forms. After watching the sergeant pour over them for so long a time that Spud Murphy became convinced he had failed the physical for certain, he heard his name called. When he went up to the desk the sergeant said to him, "Okay, son. You're all set. Sign your name at the bottom of this sheet. Be back here at three-thirty sharp, ready to go. Don't take anything with you but the clothes you're wearing. You'll stay in San Francisco tonight and be sworn in tomorrow. Good luck to you, son. You'll make a fine marine."

Spud Murphy had four hours to kill. He wandered around the streets but he didn't see much of what he looked at. He could have hung out with the other enlistees but he purposely chose not to do so. He could have gone to a matinee in the time he had but he didn't have any interest in sitting through a movie. He settled for buying a pack of Wings, which cost twelve cents at the tobacco shop at the corner of 9th and "I" Streets and crossed the street into the plaza to sit on a bench and smoke a cigarette. A couple of bums saw him light up and approached him to ask for a smoke and he gave each of them a cigarette. He wasn't hungry but he went to Kress's and sat at the lunch counter. He ordered a sandwich and a Coke and smoked another cigarette. He talked to the counter girl for a while and told her he had just joined the Marine Corps. She said her boy friend was in the Navy but his ship was home-ported at San Francisco so he was safe when the 'Japs' bombed Pearl Harbor.

He kept watching the clock on the wall behind the counter and asked the counter girl several times if she was sure it was right. When the clock said two-thirty, he walked the five blocks back to the Federal Building in as many minutes. The others kept coming back in groups of twos and threes, having already begun the process of forming friendships. At three-thirty the sergeant began calling the names of the men who were to board the train. Spud Murphy stood at parade rest with his back to the wall by the doorway, his expression deadpan, but an anxious knot in the pit of his stomach until he heard his name called. Then with a feeling of relief he lined up with the others in the corridor outside the recruiting office door. The sergeant picked out the most mature-looking individual, one who appeared to be in his early twenties, to put in charge and to whom he gave a thick, official-looking envelope containing their enlistment and travel documents. When they were all somewhat in line they straggled off in the direction of the railroad depot, following the sergeant in a group that looked more like a flock of turkeys than a military formation.

The train pulled into the Oakland terminal at about six-fifteen in the evening. Another sergeant on duty there took the envelope, calling off their names. As he called the names the recruits boarded a blue U.S. Navy bus. When all were accounted for and loaded, the bus took them across the new San Francisco-Oakland Bay Bridge to San Francisco where they were deposited in groups at a number of different hotels. As they got off the bus, the sergeant, who had accompanied them on the drive across the bay, gave each one a chit for his hotel room and another for breakfast in the morning. He also instructed them to be 'on deck' in front of their hotel the following morning at 'oh-eight-hundred-hours' for transportation to the Federal Court House, where Spud Murphy and at least forty other recruits were simultaneously sworn in as members of the United States Marine Corps at around ten o'clock on the morning of December 11, 1941.

It was late afternoon before Spud Murphy and his fellow recruits boarded the Southern Pacific passenger train *LARK*, with its deluxe Pullman accommodations, bound for Los Angeles, and Spud Murphy felt he could safely sit back and take a deep breath, satisfied that the possibilities of his being intercepted along the way were rapidly decreasing. He couldn't believe the ease with which everything had all fallen into place.

The *LARK* was an all-first-class overnight passenger service that ran nightly between San Francisco and Los Angeles, which meant that it had sleeping berths for all the passengers. It also had dining car service for dinner and breakfast, due to the time of its departure and its morning arrival in Los Angeles. After dinner in the luxurious dining car, with its spotless, starched tablecloths and napkins and gleaming crystal and silver, Spud Murphy found the Pullman porter and asked him to make up his berth so he could get to bed early. Not that he was the least bit sleepy or tired. He just had it in his mind to avoid the ritualistic celebration that usually accompanies an escape from reality, such as is provided by enlisting in the military in defense of one's country. He lay awake until long after midnight, listening to the rhythmic click of the wheels on the rail splices. For a time he savored the thrill of victory. He was free! He was a marine! He had escaped!

Feelings of victory were soon followed by other feelings marked with uncertainty. He could see Abdul, looking back at him from halfway down the flat, urging him with joyous tail wagging to hurry on to explore the world. But with that thought he also recalled the ominous mist and shadows of the grove of live oaks at Cascara, embracing all sorts of unseen and unknown terrors. He thought of Bonnie and Aaron and longed to celebrate his freedom with them, but he had never hinted to them of the plans he had been harboring in recent weeks, which now had suddenly become reality. Although he had thought of telling them, he never could, because for one thing, there was always the chance of failure, and for another, he didn't want to make them part of a conspiracy. The possibility of getting Aaron and Bonnie involved could only serve to weaken his own resolve. Because they had never been a part of it, he couldn't expect them now to celebrate his victory. He thought of Mac, wondering how he could be so insensitive to other people's feelings. Finally, he thought of his mother, but there was only confused heartbreak in those thoughts, and so he shut them out of his mind.

In Los Angeles they debarked from the train and boarded a Marine Corps bus. The bus took them south along the coast to San Diego and the Marine Corps base, which housed the Recruit Depot, otherwise infamously known as Boot Camp. As they debarked from the bus a marine corporal gave them their assignments from a roster that contained the names of all the incoming recruits for that day. Spud Murphy's assignment was to Platoon 202. Strangely enough, so far as Spud Murphy could recall, none of the other recruits that had come from Sacramento were assigned to that same platoon. He thought, wryly, that some things never change. The drill instructors for Platoon 202 were Sergeant Z. W. Wood and Corporal J. O. Spiller. Spud Murphy was appointed as squad leader for the first squad of Platoon 202. How the decision to name him squad leader came about was a mystery Spud Murphy was unable to solve, but after observing the unmilitary conduct and appearance of his fellow recruits, he didn't for a moment dispute the legitimacy of it, irrespective of his youthfulness.

It took Mac only two days to locate Spud Murphy, once he started looking. He didn't even bother to ask Bonnie or Aaron where Spud Murphy might have taken himself off to. He knew Spud Murphy wouldn't confide to his trusted friends the kind of information that would expose them to censure or that would prove embarrassing. Much to Elsie's distress, he didn't even start looking until Spud Murphy had been gone for five days. When Mac did get around to looking, the first person he talked to was Sergeant Meniatis. Without knowing it for sure, he told Meniatis he suspected Spud Murphy had enlisted.

Sergeant Meniatis was beside himself with anger and frustration. "That kid is officer material!" he exploded. "What the hell is the matter with him? All he had to do was be a little patient and finish high school. They would have paid for his college or even sent him to West Point. He's the best student I ever had."

"If he did enlist, and if they should find out, what action do you think they would take?"

"Probably just send him home. But it would become a part of his record and any chance he ever had for a military career would be out the window. But that's the army, and I don't think that's where he's at."

"Marine Corps?"

"That would be my guess. I've seen kids like him before. The kind with stars in their eyes. Do you want me to call downtown to the marine recruiter?"

"No. I'll go down myself."

Sergeant Herbert Knott, U.S.M.C., saw Mac sitting on his waiting bench and thought, "Oh, damn! another old geezer from 1918 who wants to tell me how he kicked hell out of the 'krauts' twenty years ago, and kid himself into thinking he's still in shape to do the same today. Where in hell do they all come from?" Mac was attentively eying the half dozen or so recruits waiting their turn in the examination room, but Sergeant Knott waited, and when Mac looked up at him, he pointed at the straight-backed chair beside his desk.

"Can I help you, sir?"

"I don't know. Maybe. Did you sign up a youngster, last name MacClanahan, on Thursday or Friday of last week?"

"Yes, sir. I did. A mighty fine young man, too. He'll make a real marine. The corps can use men like that."

"He's a minor and he didn't have permission to enlist."

"Oh, hell! Excuse me, sir. I got a telegram— you're saying it was a forgery? Well, in that case, we'll have to bring him back. He may have charges brought against him. I don't know. But we'll bring him back, you can be sure. It's too bad. He seemed like such a fine young man."

Even after he knew where Spud Murphy was, it still took Mac some time to figure out what it was he wanted to do about it. To Sergeant Knott he said, "Don't let's do anything in a hurry. Give me a little time to think about this, now that I know the story. Let it ride for a day or two."

"Are you saying you might give your permission?"

"I don't know. I need time to think about it."

"I certainly hope so, sir. If we have to bring him back now all hell will break loose."

"I understand, Sergeant. I'll get back in touch as soon as possible."

Over the years, Mac had occasion from time to time to turn to Ed Weida, his friend and supervisor at the S.P., and Spud Murphy's violin teacher, for advice of a personal nature. He intended to do so now, but since it was a workday and still early in the day, he had several hours to wait before Ed would get off work. Not ready to face Elsie until he had talked to Ed, Mac found himself driving to the homestead.

Fifteen

Out of habit he ran the pump to fill the storage tank, although in mid-winter there was hardly any evaporation loss to replace. He climbed to the top of the lookout rock and sat there for a long time remembering what the homestead had looked like the first time he and Elsie and Spud Murphy walked over from Leighton's cabin to look at the property they had in mind to acquire. After an all-encompassing survey from the vantage of the rock, he walked across the draw to the empty granary and corrals. Returning once more to the house, his eyes lingered over the thousand details of the construction itself, the garden plot, the landscaping, the yard fence and gates, the shop with its forge, the woodshed still half full of cord-wood, and all of the host of small things that had turned the forty acres into a *home.*

That evening Ed Weida heard Mac's story through without interruption. When Mac had concluded his tale of Spud Murphy's defection, Ed said, "I can scarcely expect you to believe what I am about to tell you, my friend, but it is true, none-the-less. Before I came to America, I was confronted with the identical situation that you find yourself in, except that I was the son who ran away. From the time I was a child, my mind was set on becoming a sailor in the German Navy. My father wouldn't give me his permission to enlist and when I did so against his will at the age of fifteen, he had me returned home under close surveillance. That in itself was sure to attract the attention of my friends and acquaintances, and subjected me to much public humiliation. In my determination to assert my independence and accomplish my goals, I ran away again at the first opportunity and signed on with the crew of a German merchant vessel. That angered him so much he would never consent to see me again, even when I was older and more in sympathy with his reasoning. Mac, I hope your relationship with Spud Murphy does not end in that way."

Homestead

On 20 December 1941 at 16.30 hours, Platoon 202 was dismissed from close order drill to its assigned area at the edge of the Parade Deck, except for Private MacClanahan, who was required to remain standing at attention after the formation while being addressed by Corporal Spiller. "Private MacClanahan, marines in basic training are not allowed to have visitors. It interferes with their education. Are you aware of that?"

"Yes, sir!"

"Private MacClanahan, you have a visitor. You may stand at ease." With that Corporal Spiller turned toward the Training Battalion offices at the end of the Parade Deck and signaled with his raised arm to the offices. A solitary figure detached itself from the building and came toward them. Spud Murphy would have recognized that purposeful stride anywhere. "Aw, damn it all to hell!" he said, under his breath.

Corporal Spiller, addressing Mac in a respectful tone of voice that Spud Murphy didn't know he was capable of, said, "You have fifteen minutes, sir," and moved out of sight and hearing behind the nearby reviewing stand that fronted on the Parade Deck.

Mac wasn't smiling— it would have been too much out of character to wish for that— but his voice and face were less harsh than Spud Murphy could remember them being for some time. "I didn't get a chance to say good-bye, son, and wish you well when you left, so I hope you'll forgive me for coming down and interrupting what must be a pretty exciting time in your life. Your mother and I both want you to know we care for you more than we sometimes remember to say, and we're going to miss you greatly. We're very proud of you and when it's all over we'll be waiting to welcome you home."

Spud Murphy said "Thank you, sir." He felt the stinging in his eyes and hoped he could keep from crying.

Fifteen

Mac was silent for a moment, and then he added "Your Mother found the invoice from De Von's in your dresser and wanted me to tell you she would draw the money to pay it from your account, and that she would make sure that Bonnie gets the locket."

"Yes, sir. Thank you, sir."

After Mac left, Spud Murphy handed Corporal Spiller the twenty-one-jewel Bulova wrist watch Mac had brought with him as a Christmas gift to Spud Murphy from him and Elsie. Corporal Spiller said, "It will be in an envelope in the safe at Battalion Headquarters with your name on it. You can reclaim it when you graduate from basic training."

Spud Murphy said, "Thank you, sir" and ran to his tent to get his rifle. He needed his rifle to perform the calisthenics exercise that was referred to in the Marine Corps as "up and on shoulders." It was Corporal Spiller's opinion that one hundred repetitions of that exercise was an appropriate penalty for his having had a visitor and for thereby interrupting the educational process.

Acknowledgments

I am deeply grateful to a number of people without whose efforts and encouragement this book would not have been possible. First and foremost among them is my wife, Mary, chief custodian of the family archives and research assistant par excellence whose persistence and focus uncovered a wealth of historical data and background material from the microfilm files of the Sacramento Bee. In that effort the staffs of both the Sacramento County Library and the California State Library at the state capitol also deserve recognition.

For the magnificent job he did of restoring a number of priceless photos from the family album, as well as providing generally wise counsel and encouragement through out, I am indebted to Renaissance man Earl Hajic.

Special acknowledgment is made of the contributions of Julius Albiani, Bud and Eunice Wolin, and Goula Wait, who stirred my memory and brought back recollections of school days and other days, music lessons, gold dredging, and the Crinolines and Cutaways

And to Joe Fortine, of American Book Publishing, for the thought-provoking commentary that accompanied his editing, and always went directly to the heart of the matter.

G.R.M.

About The Author

George MacClanahan brings with him the wit and wisdom of seventy years of dedicated observation, extending through six generations of his own lineage and reinforced by graduate studies in social anthropology, the purpose of which was to establish a benchmark against which to examine the capacity of a child to assimilate the essentials of social integration, as well as its ability to shoulder responsibilities far beyond the stultifying limitations usually imposed by modern, over-protective societies.

George has a degree in civil engineering from the University of Alaska; until retirement at age sixty-two he was a registered professional engineer engaged in construction management in Alaska and, more lately, in his birth state of California. His interests in the fifteen years succeeding his retirement have centered on exploring the nature and cause of intergenerational conflict as it is evidenced by patterns of behavior and communication that have unrelentingly survived from generation to generation.

Preferring the role of "story-teller" to that of author, MacClanahan chooses to cloak his writing as much as possible in the warm and personal phraseology mindful of spoken communication. "Homestead" is a splendid reminder to humanity of its own small and uncomplicated beginnings.